CRITICAL HITS

CRITICAL HITS

WRITERS PLAYING VIDEO GAMES

EDITED BY

J. Robert Lennon and Carmen Maria Machado

Graywolf Press

"Ruined Ground" by J. Robert Lennon. First published as "How I Spent My Plague Year Inside a Video Game" in *Literary Hub*, April 20, 2021. Reprinted by permission of the author.

"I Was a Teenage Transgender Supersoldier" by nat steele. First published in *Polygon*, December 19, 2021. Reprinted by permission of nat steele, *Polygon*, and Vox Media, LLC.

"Clash Rules Everything around Me" by Tony Tulathimutte. First published in *Real Life*, June 27, 2016. Reprinted by permission of the author.

This publication is made possible, in part, by the voters of Minnesota through a Minnesota State Arts Board Operating Support grant, thanks to a legislative appropriation from the arts and cultural heritage fund. Significant support has also been provided by the McKnight Foundation, the Amazon Literary Partnership, and other generous contributions from foundations, corporations, and individuals. To these organizations and individuals we offer our heartfelt thanks.

Published by Graywolf Press
212 Third Avenue North, Suite 485
Minneapolis, Minnesota 55401

www.graywolfpress.org

Published in the United States of America

ISBN 978-1-64445-261-5 (paperback)
ISBN 978-1-64445-262-2 (ebook)

2 4 6 8 9 7 5 3 1
First Graywolf Printing, 2023

Library of Congress Control Number: 2022952326

Cover design: Adam B. Bohannon

CONTENTS

In my first memory of the medium, I am standing behind Eric and he has black hair. His mother couldn't have watched me more than a handful of times in my childhood, but I can visualize the living room vestibule where we are standing as clearly as if it's my own house. I'm probably seven? It must be around 1993. I remember that Eric is playing *Super Mario Bros.*, but only because my little brother's name is Mario and I make the connection with confusion. Eric offers to let me play, once, and I hold the controller like the alien object it is. I try to move Mario and somehow die immediately. Eric takes the controller back and keeps going. I watch. I am always watching.

I was not allowed to play video games as a kid. My mother was scornful of them, talked about them the way she talked about all television that wasn't PBS. (Only bad parents, she said, allowed their kids' brains to rot that way.) It would never be allowed in our house. In *her* house, she clarified.

By the time my brother came along—and got old enough to want, and ask for, such things—she had relaxed on this point, for reasons unknown. For him, anyway. My bad parents gifted him a Game Boy for some holiday; later, a PS2. Sometimes I borrowed the Game Boy and took it to the bathroom and played *Pokémon* all night. And sometimes he let me play alongside him. But it never lasted very long. I wasn't any good. I didn't feel a rhythm when I played; I had no intuitive sense of the process. It did not feel like reading or writing. It felt like being asked to perform a dance I'd never heard of.

But I still enjoyed it. I enjoyed the sense of being lost; the clarity of solving a puzzle; the pleasure of turning a corner into some new wonder.[1] I enjoyed it so much that when we eventually got a computer—I was twelve, almost thirteen—I took my babysitting and birthday money to Electronics Boutique in the Lehigh Valley Mall.[2] Drunk with power—my parents didn't quite understand that computer games were simply video games on the computer, and had not had the foresight to dissuade it—I bought *3-D Dinosaur Adventure* (came with its own 3D glasses!); *Myst* and its ilk (iconic); *Theme Park* (when you went bankrupt, a cutscene showed your businessman protagonist jumping off a ledge in the reflection of a family photo on his desk); a series called *Eagle Eye Mysteries* (Encyclopedia Brown by way of the Boxcar Children); a historical mystery called *Titanic: Adventure Out of Time*; *Oregon Trail* and its many sequels (needs no introduction; I always started the game as a doctor and packed a harmonica and was notorious for misfiring my gun and injuring someone in my wagon party).

In the college dorms, I lived next to a room of seasoned gamers, who played so much *Halo 2* that I am certain the sound of its gunfire would put me to sleep at this very moment. The gamers, who became dear friends, patiently tried to help me play several times, but I found myself utterly unable to aim or shoot and would stand in a corner and fire maniacally at the walls until the scrimmage mercifully ended. Later, when a few of us moved into a house together, I got hooked on the Elder Scrolls game *Oblivion* and played as a fistfighting cat-person; I spent so much time on it I began to dream that I was my Khajiit self, running around the Cyrodiil landscape coldcocking every random character who crossed my path.

---

1. It also cannot be denied that the fact that it was being discouraged—at all, and along gendered lines—made it that much more appealing.
2. Or, to be more precise, me and my babysitting and birthday money *were taken to* the Lehigh Valley Mall, where I said I intended to go somewhere far more in-character, like Waldenbooks for the newest *Animorphs* installment or Natural Wonders for a velveteen satchel of tumbled semi-precious stones. I did that, too—of course—but first Electronics Boutique, with its floor-to-ceiling racks of shimmering jewel cases.

When I dated my first and worst boyfriend, I was completely en-amored with his copy of *Fable II*, an open-world fantasy RPG with a series of charming features I adored, including a companion dog and the ability—as a buff female melee fighter—to have sex with and father children with other women. I liked the game so much I put off a necessary breakup until I'd finished the main plot.

Another boyfriend—the second and best—could not believe I'd never played *Portal*. In his bedroom, he sat me at his elaborate PC setup, slipped huge headphones over my ears. "What are you going to do while I play this?" I asked, and he smiled. "Just watch," he said. I shrugged and started playing, and shrieking with delight, and mar-veling over the physics of the thing. Every so often I'd turn around and he'd be watching me; he seemed genuinely pleased.

Years later, in grad school and on the heels of the end of a horrific re-lationship, I returned to Elder Scrolls—this time, *Skyrim*—and played on my friend EJ's couch. He gently ribbed me about my obsessive col-lecting of in-game foodstuffs; I explained that it felt insane to walk past anything and not pick it. "See?" I said as I raided a garden full of cabbages,[3] feeling serotonin cascade through my brain. Eventually EJ sweetly fell asleep on the futon next to me; I played until the sun came up and walked home through the streets of Iowa City feeling calmer than I had in a year. When I eventually slept, I dreamt of the collect-ing by Ralston Creek: the banks littered with plates and bowls, books and armor, herbs and dried goods, all to be added to an inventory with infinite space.

After school, when I moved to Philadelphia, I would often take a bus into New York and stay with my friend Tony, who had a PS4. It was next to Tony—who, like my old boyfriend, seemed content to

---

3. Recently, on a trip to Krakow, I was touring a basilica with two Polish dykes and talk-ing with them about—what else?—topping and bottoming. How you know what you *are*. When the conversation meandered toward video games, one of them said, "Oh, that's another way you can tell. Are you a killer, or a collector? Tops prefer to kill; bottoms col-lect." I though back to *Skyrim* and my cabbages. Then to my love of melee combat; the way it felt to run swinging into a crowd of enemies. "I like . . . both?" I said, taking a photo of the vaulted ceiling crowded with stars. "Aha," she laughed. "A switch."

watch me play, and genuinely happy to be sharing something that also gave him pleasure—that I played *The Last of Us*, *P.T.*, *Until Dawn*, and the beginning of what has become one of my favorite franchises, *Life Is Strange*. On his couch, I decided to buy a Playstation of my own, and after that played video games the way a hungry woman sits at a table full of food—hardly knowing where to start; grinning wildly at the satisfaction of her voracious appetite. I played RPGs, puzzle games, first-person shooters. Indie games that played like ergodic novels; games with obscure and impossible-to-parse lore. Horror games that made me scream and throw the controller in terror. Games that made me sob. Games I played without really understanding them. Games hard enough that I had to watch play-throughs on YouTube and cheese specific bosses to advance. Games so buggy I had to delete them. Games I didn't finish. Games I got stupidly good at. Games I've replayed many times since. There was *Horizon Zero Dawn* and its sequel. *Hollow Knight*. *Resident Evil: Biohazard*; *Resident Evil: Village*. *Hellblade: Senua's Sacrifice* and *Assassin's Creed* (*Odyssey* and *Valhalla*). *Ghost of Tsushima*, *Death Stranding*, *The Last of Us* (again), *The Last of Us Part II*. *Control*, *Far Cry*, *Fallout*. *Alien: Isolation*. *Red Dead Redemption 2*. *We Happy Few*, *Vampyr*, *Prey*, *The Last Guardian*. All of the *BioShock* games. *Life Is Strange*, *Life Is Strange: Before the Storm*, *Life Is Strange 2*, *Life Is Strange: True Colors*. *Everyone's Gone to the Rapture*. *Stardew Valley*. *Witcher 3*. Needing more—and wanting to be able to play at a residency or traveling, if the mood struck me—I downloaded Steam on my computer and played *Amnesia: The Dark Descent*, *The Beginner's Guide*, *Broken Age*, *Dear Esther*, *Don't Starve*, *Firewatch*, *Gone Home*, *Her Story*, *Inside*, *Kentucky Route Zero*, *Limbo*, *The Long Dark*, *The Novelist*, *Oxenfree*, *Return of the Obra Dinn*, *SOMA*, *The Stanley Parable*, *Tacoma*, *That Dragon Cancer*, *Undertale*, *The Walking Dead*, *The Witness*, *The Wolf Among Us*. I began to play games with friends so inexperienced they could not use the controllers on their own; unused to the mechanics, the camera on the screen would vacillate dizzyingly, wildly, exactly the way I used to shoot—read: not shoot—in *Halo 2*. So we started to play together. They told me where to go and I took them there and they told me what to click and I did it and in that way we moved through the story together; inch by inch.

In an early draft of this essay, I focused a lot on the gendered nature of these experiences; how often I was receiving (literacy of, access to, skills for, experience with) games from men. I mentioned my anxieties about identifying as a gamer. I talked about Gamergate.

But as I keep writing I am struck far more forcefully by the intimacy of the form; the way the experience of it is specific, even erotic. What did it mean to receive someone's tutelage? To let yourself be watched? To open yourself up to new ways of understanding? To die over and over again? To experience pleasure vicariously, a kind of compersion. Knowing only what you do not know, being in awe of the form's avenues of pleasure.[4] Letting yourself want, play for days, cheat, give up. Letting yourself try again. Sharing games that aren't even really designed to be shared.

In 2018, when I was touring my first book, I mentioned during a Q&A after a reading that I'd tried to start playing *Bloodborne*—the newest entry in a famously punishing franchise made by From Software—but given up because I found the game too annoyingly, relentlessly difficult. I'd hardly been able to make any progress at all.

In my signing line, a very nervous-looking guy came up to me. After pre-apologizing—clearly aware of the optics of a man explaining how a video game works to a woman—he began to stammer out a defense of the game. Not as a way of shaming, but explaining that yes, it had a steep learning curve, but once you figure out the mechanics, it was like magic. As he talked, he got more animated; his hands swooping around describing how it becomes like a dance, like a

---

4. Once, while playing some open-world game while extremely high, I sat crouched outside a bandit camp I was meant to clear out and listened to the mindless chatter of the NPCs (non-player characters) patrolling inside. *They have their own lives*, I thought, moved beyond reason. Their own absurd patterns and habits and relationships and existences. After the dialogue circled itself several times, my partner came into the room and asked me what I was doing. I tried to explain that I was basically playing *Waiting for Godot*, except I was Godot. *I was God.* Then I started crying at the beauty of it all. The patience with which she looked at me, reader! The tenderness.

perfect dance. "You will love it," he kept saying. "You will love it." He was so impassioned that I went home, redownloaded the game, and began to play. And he was right. Once I found the rhythm, I found myself able to slaughter my way through the blighted and horrifying landscape; lean into the insanity of the lore; appreciate the game's commitment to its bit.

After that, I played the next game in the franchise, *Sekiro*; now, I continue to pour much of my free time into the high fantasy horror open world of *Elden Ring*. Recently, after giving a talk at a fundraiser, I was encircled by several beautiful high femmes who gave me advice about how to access a particularly rune-lucrative level. We talked loudly, excitedly, far too long. There was such joy in the conversation; a peculiar investment in a stranger's success at some obscure shared task. I wrote their advice down on my hand. (As of the time of writing this, I cannot defeat Commander Niall to save my life and I need the left half of the Haligtree Secret Medallion; please send help.)

Here is an anthology that holds every way in which video games are dear to me: How they permit us vicarious pleasures (Ander Monson, "The Cocoon") and pains (Jamil Jan Kochai, "Cathartic Warfare"). How they reach out to us from our childhoods (Octavia Bright, "Staying with the Trouble") and connect us to other people (Stephen Sexton, "No Traces"). How they ask us—require us, beg us—to interrogate our relationship with our homes (J. Robert Lennon, "Ruined Ground"), our ideas about free will (Charlie Jane Anders, "Narnia Made of Pixels"), and how our fantasies become our myths, which in turn become our history (Vanessa Villarreal, "In the Shadow of the Wolf"). How they witness, speak to, alleviate, and bear metaphors for illness (Elissa Washuta, "I Struggled a Long Time with Surviving"), depression (Larissa Pham, "Status Effect"), gender dysphoria (nat steele, "I Was a Teenage Transgender Supersoldier") and euphoria (Max Delsohn, "Thinking Like the Knight"), grief (Nana Kwame Adjei-Brenyah, "This Kind of Animal"), the complex landscape of our identities (Keith S. Wilson, "Mule Milk"), redemption (Hanif Abdurraqib, "We're More Ghosts Than People"). It is an anthology that holds space for writers who are compulsive gamers (Tony Tulathimutte, "Clash Rules Everything Around Me"), former gamers (Alexander Chee, "Ninjas and Foxes"), parents of gamers (Eleanor Henderson, "The Great Indoorsmen"), and game writers (MariNaomi, "Video Game Boss"). Reluctant gamers and avid gamers and people who wouldn't call themselves gamers at all. This book—the first of its kind, as far as I and my coeditor can tell—has more room inside it than you'd expect. What a pleasure and a gift to be at its helm.

Covid haunts these pages, of course. We got stuck inside for years and remain kind of stuck, and video games are a way of filling the vessel of that stuckness. But the pandemic even haunts the reprinted essays that predate its existence—call it the dread of knowing what's coming. You are reading this book sometime after my writing its introduction, and you almost certainly have that same dread. Who knows what horrors will arise between my typing this and your taking it in? I can hardly imagine it. The levels I haven't reached. The chapters I haven't unlocked.

But joy haunts these pages, too. Play. We imprint on the medium and the medium imprints on us. Even when we get locked inside, art gives us a window. A door. An escape hatch. A crack, at the very least, to breathe.

Before the book tour for my (sad, difficult, hard-to-talk-about) memoir, I bought a Nintendo Switch. At the end of almost every event, I went back to my hotel room and played *The Legend of Zelda: Breath of the Wild*. One of the only ways I knew how to come back into my body—because I was always gone after those readings and Q&As, always completely dissociated and vacated and empty empty empty—was that stupid little tune that played when you cooked a meal. The crackle of fire, a grunt and then a humming, the clatter of metal striking metal, the rhythmic sizzle and bubble of ingredients. The flourish of horns at completion. Link's delighted laugh. Sometimes I didn't even do side quests or paraglide over the landscape or fight monsters; I just cooked digital food until I fell asleep. It always got me to the next morning. And then I'd get on a plane and do it all over again. In the sky, the actual sky, on my way to the next sad place. Cooking this thing and that. That little song at the end! The ascending chime.

In that memory, I am good at something, and it is a bridge. I can hold it in my hands, move myself through space. It is real and not real. It carries me away, for a little while. It will carry me into a pandemic. (The pandemic has not happened yet, but it is coming.) The memory of the game bears me through the memory of the time. But most importantly: I play. That's the best part. In the memory, I am always playing.

Carmen Maria Machado
Brooklyn, NY
December 2022

CRITICAL HITS

I Struggled a Long Time with Surviving

ELISSA WASHUTA

Prologue

Summer is here again and I miss my friends. I don't mean the real ones I've forgotten how to talk to because I have no news to share but symptoms. I do miss them. But I'm referring to my imaginary video game friends, my good influences who never produce anything but spiked bats and health kits and other things they carry to keep them alive.

We're so close to the solstice I can nearly taste its rot. After the world ends and starts over, I imagine this smell will come back first, the bacterial exhalation of nature digesting itself. My yard smells like a bog and looks like it wants to be a meadow. The black flies that will outlast us all are getting strong from my blood. The wet heat out there is too much for my busted exocrine system. I wait until evening to pull the thistles that defy death in my garden and lay teeth into my arms. I'm afraid of this land and all the living things I'd rather not fight. I intervene in the honeyvine milkweed's strangling of lamb's ear and choking out of mint. Its menacing spirals around the stems feel like nearly human bad intentions. Fighting my land is neither tedious nor gratifying. It's just that I have to go outside from time to time.

When I see the season's first twinkle of fireflies rising from the grass, I remember that time is real and the future has to come.

My world is a brick house that has spent a century refusing to sink into the soggy earth. Inside, there is a place I want to go. A year ago, I visited a virtual world that looked like the summertime Ohio that was killing me. That first pandemic summer, my long mystery sickness began to make itself unmistakably known, and I spent all my evenings inside video games at the end of the world, playing as a survivor who cannot let their emotions get the best of them. In *The Last of Us*, we don't talk about Joel's dead daughter, killed on outbreak day as he carried her away from the apocalypse.

The game asks me to begin by playing as Sarah on the last night of her life. "ADMITTANCE SPIKES AT AREA HOSPITALS! INCREASE DUE TO MYSTERIOUS INFECTION," the day's newspaper says. A neighbor, infected and ravenous, shatters the patio door, and Joel shoots him dead.

While watching the world change from a car window, Sarah asks her dad, "Are we sick?"

"No. Of course not," he says.

"How do you know?"

When the car crashes and Sarah's leg breaks, the game asks me to become Joel. It puts the little girl in my arms and tells me to run.

The Quarantine Zone

Twenty years pass and Joel remains uninfected. He's now a grizzled smuggler, corralled with other survivors into a walled-off section of Boston where the military keeps everyone safe by denying them things that make life worth living. The government is long gone, most people dead or turned. Outside, in bombed city neighborhoods, the *Cordyceps* fungus rages through what's left of the population, starting in the brain, killing whatever spirit of a person enlivens a body, then taking over the rest of the host until they're more fungus than person. It blooms outward through the skull, taking the eyes, leaving the mouth that clicks to echolocate. The infection spreads through bites and through spores that concentrate in closed areas and dissipate in the air.

Joel has become a sullen man who does survival crimes. He's going to escort a fourteen-year-old girl across the United States for apocalypse reasons. The trip with Ellie begins as a transaction: guns for services. She needs to be delivered to the Fireflies, an antiauthoritarian group that kills soldiers and tags walls: LOOK FOR THE LIGHT and REMEMBER WHO WE WERE! They believe they can create a vaccine and restore the world. They need Ellie because she's the only person on earth known to be immune, bitten but never turned.

I first played this game last June, early in my year inside with a sickness nobody could explain to me. I'd shown up at the ER straining to breathe and afraid to die, but the doctor in hazmat gear found me to be COVID-negative. Still, she wanted to admit me overnight: even after I calmed down, my heart did not. Nurses taped electrodes to my chest and came in the middle of the night for my blood. In the morning, doctors discharged me without having figured out the cause of my seated near-fainting spells, doom panic, labored breathing, tachycardia, burning red feet, stabbing organ pain, spreading rash, low body temperature, excruciating headaches, elevated liver enzymes, or numb limbs. They said it was stress.

By the time I began playing the game, the sickness had eased, but it had changed my body. My primary doctor said it seemed like mono, but I'd already had that in college. Bloodwork and Google led me to suspect that this latent virus I'd had for almost half my life had been reactivated. Viruses lying dormant in our cells don't necessarily cause problems, but catalysts like intense stress, immunosuppression, and other infections can allow the virus to resume replication and bring back symptoms. The Epstein-Barr virus, which causes mononucleosis, can attack the brain, spinal cord, eye nerves, lungs, heart, pancreas, lymphatic system, skull bones, and blood. It can make the body attack itself: there are rare cases of the now-infamous cytokine storm, but more commonly, the body mistakes some healthy part of itself for something it's supposed to kill.

The possibility of reactivation is controversial. The medical community agrees that EBV can reactivate, but how often it does is another issue. Three of my doctors believe it could have happened in my case, based on symptoms and bloodwork that can suggest but not conclude. They might be humoring me.

"Don't tell anyone about your condition," Joel tells Ellie once they've made it out of the city alive. "They'll either think you're crazy or they'll try to kill you."

Bill's Town

I'm a week away from pausing my world and entering the little coma of general anesthesia. The surgery doesn't really have anything to do with my sickness, at least as far as the doctors are concerned. I am unfixable. After the summer of 2020 finally released us, I was diagnosed with Sjögren's syndrome. It's a surprisingly common but poorly understood autoimmune disease, affecting the entire body, capable of progressing to debilitation or remaining mild for life, nonadherent to any one definable progression. The cause is unknown, but the Epstein-Barr virus is thought to have a role in triggering onset.

For those months between hospitalization and diagnosis, I pushed for answers about the state of my immune system so that I could know just how unsafe I was outside my house with a deadly virus circulating. Everyone else had that virus to worry about; my own sickness mystery was a project for only PubMed and me. I hardly went anywhere but the medical center's many outposts, where technicians executed doctors' orders for long lists of blood tests, ultrasounds of my shallow tissues, magnetic brain pictures, the CT scan's cross sections of my torso, and a little piece of my slick inner lip. I never get to see what the doctors see, but for years, they've told me about the mess: ovarian cysts, esophageal acid burns, a piece of mystery metal, a dead gallbladder, and then, after its removal, an absence.

Radiology reports unremarkable organ lesions nobody is willing to explain. The doctors tell me I shouldn't worry about it. Everything is normal. Two of them have told me to read *The Body Keeps the Score: Brain, Mind, and Body in the Healing of Trauma*. My surgeon doesn't need to open me up to know she'll find scar tissue inside me next week, but that must not be a metaphor, because she says it doesn't mean anything.

Joel and Ellie have escaped the QZ but still have a long way to go. Joel needs to see a man about a car. In a small town outside Boston,

Bill, the sole survivor, has surrounded his safehouse with trip-wired bombs, barricades, rope traps, and barbed fences. This is the place I've thought about most. We reach it by way of the woods, where there are no patrols, so we don't have to run for a while. The trees enclose a cluster of flat-roofed buildings ringed by chain-link fence.

When I was a child, I drew plans for lava moats and spikes to surround my fortress-house. I dreamed about running toward safety inside shuttered buildings, escaping some threat outside. The nightmare recurred until last summer: one afternoon, I went outside for a walk and recognized the feeling of the bright sky looming over my naked head. I was inside my nightmare. In my dreams, I never went back. Bill's town exists in miniature in my head because I need an enclosure to retreat into when my own walls aren't enough.

Bill's town is full of infected. Buses parked by the high school never made the intended round of evacuations. In the houses, furniture barricades block stairways and windows. The stacked dressers and chairs could have been dropped in from my dreams, and I feel the way I did three years ago, the day I bought the brick house, ascended the attic stairs, and locked the door behind me, just to know how it felt. The lock can be turned by a screwdriver; the town is full of infected who were once people who lived somewhere.

Pittsburgh

The Pittsburgh QZ, like all QZs but Boston, has been overtaken. A group of rebels known as Hunters took the tank and the Humvee once used to control them; now they're up for torturing and killing anyone who passes through. They ambush us and we survive. They search for us and we kill them one by one. The difference between us and them is that they're non-player characters and that they pile up dead bodies in a garage.

In Pittsburgh, Ellie becomes a killer. I don't mean to say she hardens. I mean she grabs a gun and kills a man. He had Joel pinned underwater, and so one of them was going to die. Bafflingly, Joel is mad about it. It's been a long time since he had a feeling, I'm guessing, and as his heart opens to the girl who is not his daughter, his brain recognizes the feeling as a threat. Feelings are bad for survival, and lingering on them long enough to say them out loud is even worse. Hunters wait on the other side of the wall. From Joel, I'm learning the pleasures of having some things I don't want to talk about. Why I can't meet up next week, why I'm having surgery this time. At some point, the hero has to let emotion break through and words come out, and I can't stop holding down the feeling yet, but I guess I have to say this part: I asked the surgeon to sterilize me.

We keep making it out alive. The body keeps making more blood. Last year, the lab took dozens of vials of mine. An article titled "How Much Blood Is in Your Body and How Much You Can Lose" says I have at least a gallon—hundreds and hundreds of vials. My body can regenerate its cells while it fights an endless war against itself. It's no place for a child. In Pittsburgh, we kill the men, but more will come. NO HOPE, says a tagged wall beneath a mantle of kudzu.

Joel's backpack is filling with artifacts, like maps amended with circles and Xs, military pamphlets concerning stages of infection and evacuation orders, and handwritten scraps with warnings between people long gone from here. Stories from the decades since Outbreak Day live in the notes. Collecting is the only way to piece together the complete picture of devastation. Outside of games, I'm drawn to forms, and I hoard abandoned sheets of census questions and symptom scales.

When I saw the word *sterilized* on the form, I understood why I had to keep affirming that I really wanted this. I had asked for a tubal ligation; I didn't think of the word *sterilize*. Forced sterilizations of Native American women were widespread in the 1960s and 1970s. It's estimated that the Indian Health Service sterilized at least a quarter of Native women from 1970 to 1976, maybe more. IHS lied to them and told them the procedure was reversible, or told them nothing and just completed hysterectomies and tubal ligations during tonsillectomies, appendectomies, or C-sections. Or IHS threatened to withhold welfare benefits or take their children away if they didn't consent. Or the patients didn't understand the consent forms.

■ CONSENT TO STERILIZATION ■

I have asked for and received information about sterilization from

_____ . When I first asked
Doctor or Clinic
for the information, I was told that the decision to be sterilized is completely up to me. I was told that I could decide not to be sterilized. If I decide not to be sterilized, my decision will not affect my right to future care or treatment. I will not lose any help or benefits from programs receiving Federal funds, such as Temporary Assistance for Needy Families (TANF) or Medicaid that I am now getting or for which I may become eligible.

I UNDERSTAND THAT THE STERILIZATION MUST BE CONSIDERED PERMANENT AND NOT REVERSIBLE. I HAVE DECIDED THAT I DO NOT WANT TO BECOME PREGNANT, BEAR CHILDREN OR FATHER CHILDREN.

I was told about those temporary methods of birth control that are available and could be provided to me which will allow me to bear or father a child in the future. I have rejected these alternatives and chosen to be sterilized.

I understand that I will be sterilized by an operation known as a

_____ . The discomforts, risks
Specify Type of Operation
and benefits associated with the operation have been explained to me. All my questions have been answered to my satisfaction.

I understand that the operation will not be done until at least 30 days after I sign this form. I understand that I can change my mind at any time and that my decision at any time not to be sterilized will not result in the withholding of any benefits or medical services provided by federally funded programs.

I am at least 21 years of age and was born on: _____
Date

I,_____ , hereby consent of my own

free will to be sterilized by _____
Doctor or Clinic

by a method called _____ . My
Specify Type of Operation
consent expires 180 days from the date of my signature below.

I also consent to the release of this form and other medical records about the operation to:

    Representatives of the Department of Health and Human Services,
    or Employees of programs or projects funded by the
    Department but only for determining if Federal laws were observed.

I have received a copy of this form.

_____   _____
       Signature   *Date*

You are requested to supply the following information, but it is not re- quired: *(Ethnicity and Race Designation) (please check)*

Ethnicity
☐ Hispanic or Latino
☐ Not Hispanic or Latino

Race *(mark one or more)*.
☐ American Indian or Alaska
☐ Native Asian
☐ Black or African American
☐ Native Hawaiian or Other Pacific
☐ Islander White

I wanted the surgery for years. I never wanted children. There's no room in me for anyone to grow. I waited for the desire to show up once I got my life together. But a loving partner, good job, and house changed nothing. And when I realized I could decide not to have children, and nobody could make me do it, the future turned from a black screen to an expanse of grass and trees and houses all the way to the horizon.

A government pamphlet illustration from that time depicts two tipis and two couples with long hair and single-feather headbands. With one slouching, frowning couple stand ten little Indian children holding hands and one horse. The other couple stands up straight and holds hands; with them are one child and ten horses.

My mother wasn't sterilized in the seventies and so I was born in the eighties. I told the surgeon to take my fallopian tubes, which will make me the end of a maternal line that has been here as long as language. I keep a promise to them in my heart: I'll do everything I can to keep being happy they brought me to life.

The Suburbs

We go underground. Down in the sewers, we find a settlement. Some-one set up a room full of blue water kegs like the one that still sits empty in my basement, unready for doomsday. With the basics in place, the survivors built a reenactment of the dead world they must have loved. In the dark, we find a schoolroom with an alphabet puzzle mat and kindergarten chairs. Bookcases and bulletin boards make bedrooms with temporary walls. Nobody lives there now, un-less you count the infected. "I got infected pounding at the door," reads a note dotted with blood, between an adult's skeleton and a group of small bodies under a blanket. "If it comes down to it I'll make it quick."

We find our way out into sunlight and into a neighborhood like mine, with two-and-a-half-story houses spaced feet apart. On the front of a house with three attic windows, like mine, someone has painted, "I'M ARMED / NO TRESPASSING / WILL SHOOT ON SIGHT."

I search every room in every open house. There are no survivors, only notes: "You're the adult while I'm gone. . . . Don't open the door to anyone but me. Save your bullets." I've missed these rooms nobody's been in for years and the weedy lawns nobody needs tamed.

There's no open world in this game, no map, no time, no wrong decisions to be made. After a while, lingering is pointless; I have to move forward.

Tommy's Dam

Months pass. I meet our characters in Jackson County, Wyoming, where Joel's brother, Tommy, lives in a settlement run by his wife and her father. Tommy is a former Firefly, so Joel thinks he'll know where to find them. He doesn't tell Ellie that he intends to leave her and get Tommy to bring her there himself. When she learns, she gets on a horse and takes off.

We find her in a house, reading someone's abandoned diary, astounded by the triviality of their worries about outfits and boys. She doesn't want to go with Tommy.

Joel wants to know, "What do you want from me?"

Ellie wants to know, "What are you so afraid of?"

What Ellie wants: "Everyone I have cared for has either died or left me. Everyone except for you."

What Joel wants: "You're not my daughter, and I sure as hell ain't your dad. And we are going our separate ways."

What I want: the feeling of being in a house I know is safe until an enemy hears me coming. I want what Bill in his safe house wants, the protection of trip wire and the warning signs marking it. What people wanted from the furniture barricading doors and the boards nailed over windows: another day alive. Ellie wouldn't understand, but the little worries are taking me down. I need to retreat from the obligations that are slowly killing me, or, even better, I need the extinction of tasks and accountability. I want to reset the world before it summons me back. I don't want the game's world of death—I want us all to live. If someone were to peel off the inboxes and calendar alerts layered onto me, they would not find a person who's whole. I would still be trying to survive, but in the open air, I might have a chance to do it.

On the way back to town, Joel asks Tommy where to find the Fireflies, then tells Ellie to get on his horse. He doesn't come out and say he's changed his mind, and he definitely doesn't say why.

The University

As far as Tommy knows, the Fireflies have set up shop in an abandoned university lab. The campus is emptier than mine. The horse picks through tall grasses as I steer him toward brutalist slabs and Colonial Revival brickwork. The only living beings we meet are golden trees, a troop of uncaged monkeys, the fungal people roaming the dorms, and the smog of spores waiting for somebody to open the door. IN LOVING MEMORY has been painted in red over a makeshift memorial. Next to a lava lamp and boom box, I find a newspaper clipping reporting that the U.S. military will be suspending their search for survivors waiting for evacuation. A handwritten addendum reads, "Found this in town. WTF? No one's coming!!!"

My own university, the third largest in the country, is an incubator of ideas but also infections. I get a sickness every winter that I can't clear until spring. In my previous job at another institution, I swear I got swine flu while teaching a class of 120. Far worse was the sickness I came down with as an undergrad: it stayed with me all through senior year, not recognized as viral for months because the symptoms were indistinguishable from the listed side effects of newly prescribed psych meds. I had a high fever and rash my psychiatrist identified as a drug reaction, but I wonder whether that was the onset of what was eventually found to be mono. I smoked cigarettes to stay awake on long drives that year; I've been tired ever since.

When summer ends, my university says we will begin again. I'm not ready. I'm content here, collecting artifacts: journal entries from a student who's been waiting nine months to be saved, skull X-rays with a dark smear in the deconstructed face, a Firefly's audio recorder that tells whoever's listening that the group relocated to a hospital in Salt Lake City.

"There have been years that felt like we were onto something," the recorded voice said. "Like we might eradicate this thing. Those were usually followed by years of utter despair. Like this entire fucking thing was a goddamn waste of time. It feels like the past few years were more of the latter."

The future has been carved down to a sliver. I don't know when I'll be forced out of shelter or what I'll find outside. I don't know what I'm working toward, just that I'm far from being done. I sleep less and less, unable to relax because the email doesn't want me to. The insomnia feels like a hole in my head, like in that X-ray—a central nervous system hollowed out. I refuse to think past tomorrow. The anesthesiologist is going to delete time, like the parts of autumn and winter that will disappear after this chapter ends.

But first, we have to make it out of the science building, where Hunters have found us. In a cutscene melee on a balcony, Joel falls, and a piece of sharp rebar goes right through his abdomen. Ellie pulls him off the wet red spike. We make it out. I stop here.

Lakeside Resort

I sleep for a day. After crossing the dreamless expanse of hours, I become Ellie, armed with a bow. I waste arrows on a deer that bleeds a path I track across the white floor of the forest. I meet a gentle-voiced man who says he won't hurt me. We trade, carcass for medicine. Joel is too sick to move, hidden in a basement so cold I can see Ellie's breath. When she pulls the blanket down and injects the antibiotics, I can nearly feel the heat from his wound, sewn up and inflamed.

The gentle-voiced man finds us. Until he captures me, chokes me, and knocks me out, I'm Ellie; once I'm healed enough to stand, I'm Joel, not so wounded I can't kill my way toward her.

A man with a cleaver chops a body to pieces, tosses pieces of arm to the floor. I'm Ellie again and I'm in a cage; I'm Elissa and I'm on the couch, cut four times in the abdomen, stitched and sealed with surgical glue. Parts of me are gone.

Beneath the cleaver, Ellie shouts that she's infected, and when the men flinch, she escapes. The game's winter is a blank of white sky, blizzard haze, and snowy ground. This is an obliteration place—a treeless town, nothing living but men with guns. Fires burn in barrels. A bell rings and rings and rings. Ellie and her switchblade kill and kill and kill.

In the boss battle, the gentle-voiced man has caught up with me. He's ready to fight. "I know you're not infected," he says. "No one who's infected fights this hard to stay alive."

He's wrong. It doesn't take long for the infection to consume the part of a person that equivocates about wanting to live. Everything has a mandate to survive. The fungus takes over the brain and supplants the human's dreams and fears. Is the person still in there? There is no answer to this because the game doesn't care to give one. Anyway, Ellie is immune, and she's fourteen, and headed to Salt Lake City to give herself to a cure to save humanity. When she escapes from the soft-spoken soul who plans to either keep her as a pet or eat her, what should she do once she grabs his machete but use it?

Bus Depot

Winter is long since passed and we're nearly at our destination, approaching the city on foot by way of a highway packed with useless cars. Joel talks about the future, how he's going to teach Ellie to play guitar. She's preoccupied and isn't listening. Inside one more building we have no choice but to enter if we want to proceed, Joel says he's noticed she's quiet today, but she says she's fine.

She's yanked back from oblivion when a herd of giraffes passes by the depot's broken windows. She runs through the building after them, and we find one eating the kudzu that covers the walls. Ellie is smiling again as she brings a little hand to its massive jaw. We take to the roof to watch the herd cross the savanna surrounded by a wrecked city. The game lets the player stay awhile to watch—how long, I don't know. The moment is unbearable, and I can't stand to hold it, because soon I'll be leaving this whole world. This time should be for resting, but I can't tell anyone why, and in the world I'm returning to, there is no rest without a reason. It feels like there's something to process, but it's easier just to get back to work.

Here, with Ellie and Joel, the story won't advance until I decide to move on. The giraffes turn their faces to the treetops. I'll never be ready to leave. But I'd rather keep moving than stand here and think about what I'm about to lose.

Joel pauses at the exit door. "We don't have to do this. You know that, right?"

"What's the other option?" Ellie says. The other option, Joel says, is to just be done.

Ellie's head shakes and shakes. "After all we've been through. After everything that *I've* done. It can't be for nothing."

When they're walking through medical tents, he can finally talk about losing his daughter at the world's end. When we head into the tunnels that will get us to where we're going, I'm still waiting for my feelings to return.

The Firefly Lab

At the hospital, Joel learns that the *Cordyceps* is part of Ellie now, and the surgeon can't extract the mutated variant from her brain without killing her. She's unconscious and doesn't get to decide. Joel kills his way through the Firefly patrol to the top floor. An eye chart spells out, RUNYOURNEARLYTHEREDONTQUIT!!

No. I am taking my time. I'm listening to the surgeon's recorded notes about the high concentration of fungus in Ellie's blood and spinal fluid, but normal counts of white blood cells and pro-inflammatory cytokines, and no signs of spread to the limbic system, the part of the brain that mediates emotions, the first to be hit in normal cases of Cordyceps brain infection. I'm reading the journal of the Fireflies' leader, which says, "When you're lost in the darkness, look for the light." Both artifacts are dated April 28—that day last year, my hand was still bandaged from a blown vein in the ER, and my inside elbow still stung from the blood that didn't want to come out in the night on the heart floor. I can hardly remember a lonelier night than that one when my arms were in so many strangers' hands. My boyfriend had driven me to the ER, and what I remember most from that time is that he turned onto the hospital's street and I finally understood, after everything that's happened, all my moments of peril, that I am going to die. No one can be with me in that. I had to get out of the car and he had to drive it away.

This time, for the surgery, they let him come with me. In the instant before I went dormant, I was touching his hand and I knew I was going to live.

The surgery was easy and I was not hard to wake. But my body, having hurt itself a little for a long time, took the anesthesia hard. In the recovery room, it hurt to breathe on my own, and my blood pressure wouldn't rise for hours. My airways are still hurting from the vapor. The largest incision crosses an old surgical scar, and a knot is forming under a numb patch of skin an inch below the X. My mother is a retired wound care nurse, and I could ask her whether the incision sounds normal, but I don't.

A surgeon holds out a scalpel between Joel and the small anesthetized girl on the table. The story can't continue until I make Joel lunge for the scalpel and sink it into the surgeon's neck.

Ellie is unconscious in Joel's arms when we run from the place where nobody is saving the world. We pass another eye chart—
RUNYOURNEARLYTHEREDONTQUIT!!

Every moment of my life, since before I fell sick, it's been like this. *Run, you're nearly there, don't quit!* I never listen when the doctors tell me the problem is stress. I want to talk about the virus and the killer cells that no longer recognize me. But I've lived with the virus for a long time, like nearly everyone else on earth. It is fixed in me for as long as I live.

In MRI images, my brain isn't visibly fucked, but every doctor tries to tell me my brain is the problem: it has been distressed for so long it broke the rest of me. Sure, there's a virus inside me, whether asleep or awake. But it lives in a system of dysfunction that can't be diagrammed. Surgeons could take me apart and they still wouldn't make sense of what's sapping my energy and rushing my heart.

If the virus has been living inside me for this long, in so many cells, is it really the problem? Or is it really stress? When I think of stress as a feeling, something I can control, it seems powerless against the physical substance of my body's systems that require no attention. But I have tried to control myself to the breaking point. I've chosen the removal of my fallopian tubes because I cannot take on the thing that's supposed to be my most basic purpose for living. The stress remains relentless, because it's not a feeling. It's a force to resist, the final boss I throw myself at again and again without a strategy guide to walk me through to the other side.

After Ellie wakes up in the back seat of a vehicle Joel's driving, he tells her the Fireflies don't need her, have stopped looking for a cure. Humanity will not be saved. He doesn't tell her it's because he made it so.

Jackson

The evergreens coating the hills near Jackson have no interest in the end of the world or the beginning of a new one. We're nearly there, but the car quit on us, so we pass through the lupines on foot. Joel leads the way up rock shelves. The town's huddling roofs come into view, and when we reach the peak, Ellie asks him to wait. She works up the nerve for a second, then says the thing she's been holding on to.

"Back in Boston, back when I was bitten, I wasn't alone. My best friend was there. And she got bit too. We didn't know what to do. So she says, 'Let's just wait it out. Y'know, we can be all poetic and just lose our minds together.' I'm still waiting for my turn. Her name was Riley and she was the first to die. And then it was Tess. And then Sam." People who were with us along the way but got bitten and died by gunshot. Two characters I haven't mentioned because it was easier to do this without them.

Joel's face is tough love, his gunmetal arms crossed. "I struggled a

long time with surviving. And you—no matter what, you keep finding something to fight for."

Ellie isn't hearing it. "Swear to me. Swear to me that everything
you said about the Fireflies is true."

Her eyes are so open, ready to catch what he throws. His are dark,
sheathed under a tense brow. When he looks her in the eyes and swears
to her, nothing slips out.

Feelings walk back and forth over her face as she considers. Maybe
she knows he's lying. Maybe she believes that there was never going to
be a cure. Either way, the future is gone, and she has to make a new
one in which humanity is not saved.

After a few eternal seconds, she says, "Okay." The screen goes black,
and we're done. There is no final boss but this devastation.

I signed my name under promises, so many I lost count, that I
understood there would be no turning back once I went under. The
forms felt like an affront. "You may experience regret," the surgeon
said before I signed the first of them. I resent the implication that I
don't know what's in my own heart.

I can't linger in the game once the story ends, but I'm not ready to
leave. I could play again and make different decisions—blazing guns
instead of stealth, health kits assembled instead of Molotovs—but
I know the future, that every time I'll end up in the evergreens and
lupines with my friend who wanted to turn over her body to the dying
world and my friend who wouldn't let it take her.

Deep inside me, a skyscraper leans so far it rests on another.
Houses dissolve into their foundations. Floral growth dismantles brick
walls and shatters pavement. A city center becomes a savanna. A dorm
is eaten from the inside out by intestinal bulges of putrid fungus
spreading up walls through stale air fogged by suspended spores. The
X under the place I connected to my mother is forming what she tells
me is a *healing ridge*, evidence my body knows how to rebuild, not just
tear itself down. The best thing I can do is rest, so I go back to the beginning of the end of the world, pick up my baby girl, and run.

This Kind of Animal

NANA KWAME ADJEI-BRENYAH

The first dead body I ever saw was a friend of my father's. A man I called Uncle. We drove from New York to Boston to pay respects. My father and I. Just the two of us. It was one of the few times we'd ever taken a trip out of state, or anywhere specific, together. We both wore traditional clothing. My father wore a full red and black cloth that wrapped around his body and left his shoulder exposed. I wore a kente shirt, also red with gold accents. I felt like a Charmeleon to his Charizard. In the hotel elevator a white family stepped in as we made our way to the funeral. I remember a little white boy looking up at my father in awe. His mouth literally agape, his hazel eyes trying to make sense of what my father was. When we got out of the elevator, the image of the boy and the parents' apologies still hanging in the air around us, I took a leap. I said, "He thought you were the king of Zamunda." My father laughed hard at this and I remember feeling a violent gratitude, a deep happiness as we walked toward his dead friend.

Disco Elysium[1] starts with primordial darkness. From an oblivion, the earliest voices in the game emerge. "I don't want to be this kind of animal anymore," you, before you become you, scream just prior to falling into an alcoholic, coma-like sleep. A slumber so deep that when you arise, hunched over on the floor of a trashed hotel room in

---

1. **Encyclopedia:** A 2019 role-playing game developed by ZA/UM.

your underwear, you don't remember anything about the world, not even your own name. *Disco Elysium* starts with a resurrection.

At that funeral in Boston, my father was welcomed with wide arms. Ghanaians are very good at dying. They do it with flair and panache.[2] With an incredible **Savoir Faire**. In Ghana there are billboards with the faces of the recently passed, and their dying ages. Funerals become massive celebrations of life. And still, this funeral for a Ghanaian man was bleak, deep, somber. My father's friend had died far too soon. I think he was barely fifty. People I didn't remember asked me if I remembered them. They noted how tall I'd gotten. My father laughed and joked with family and friends. They said I was handsome and without fail my father would chime in to say, "Well, of course, he looks like me."[3] People would laugh and I'd feel proud to see my father in this way, this person who made people laugh. This person everyone loved. This person people could turn to in grief to feel something other than sorrow. Again I was proud, even as I was terrified to be there in a room electric with death. The man who was not a man anymore was in a coffin, there but also long gone.

Many years later I was in a room with a dead body again. This time the one in the casket, the one adorned in lifeless glory, was my father's. Or rather, the body had once belonged to my father. Looking into it. Seeing the body, its closed eyes, makeup, gloved because the embalming on his hands hadn't gone great, I saw very clearly that our bodies are a vessel but not us. An echo of an echo of an echo. I forgot, briefly, that there were so many things he'd given me that felt like chains my whole life. Or no, I didn't forget. What happened was that as I looked at his former home, the truth that he was in so many ways the first antagonist in my life became less sharp with pain and more plentiful with nuance. It took my father's dying to see him, truly, fully, as a human. One who was as responsible as any for who I am today.

Playing *Disco Elysium*, I've been thinking more and more about

---

2. As Lady Lazarus said, it's an art, like everything else.
3. **Rhetoric:** He'd say the same things to the nurses who governed his last days when I was around.

who I am, or the pieces and parts that combine into what I and others think of as me. The protagonist screams, "I DON'T WANT TO BE THIS KIND OF ANIMAL!" which begs the question of the player: What kind of animal are you? Playing, I thought, well, I'm the child of Ghanaian immigrants. Born in Queens, New York, and raised in Spring Valley, New York. But those are broad labels. I'm the kid that heard stories of a wrathful God at bedtime. I'm the son of Jane who said I was the best thing that ever happened to her, and who sometimes spoke in tongues among thralls of others touched by the Holy Spirit, their bodies shaking and swaying, the room charged, overflowing with gospel and life as I stood, still, wondering, Why aren't I holy? I'm the young man who's had hands laid on him to dispel spirits that made him too talkative in class. I'm the one who thinks words on pages can save the world, who thinks the world is worth saving.

I'm the one who at age five or six makes a "joke" as the family returns from a church service. A Family Meal from KFC (including the chocolate cake) in hand. The same kid who, as we return to our twelfth-floor housing project apartment, is just as happy as he's ever been. The one who, happy and hungry, says something casually in the elevator as we float toward home, trying to be a part of the family's fun. I'm the kind of animal that at five or six makes a "joke," actually just a response to something his father says: "What are you, crazy?" in a tone parroting David Letterman, and the same animal who feels immediately that he's done something wrong. Who shrinks at the family's sudden silence. Who is almost already crying when the elevator dings open and we are released onto our floor. I'm the one who listens to his dad scream at him for disrespecting him, although even at five or six knows he is not being disrespectful, and the same one who cries as he is beaten with a yellow Wiffle ball bat for his "disrespect."[4]

My father was known for being funny, and yet one of the things he taught me first and most completely was how to be afraid. That's all to say I am very precise about being liked and doing the "right" thing. I

---

4. **Pain Threshold**: What doesn't kill you, amirite?

say, "I'm sorry" a lot.[5] As a kind of safety mechanism. And somehow, I still like to be considered funny.[6]

In *Disco Elysium*, it's your job to figure out what happened. How did this body hanging from the trees get there? In some ways it's a familiar affair, the hard-boiled thing. Strange murder, protagonist who, with the help of a partner, literally discovers himself. And yes, this game does feature an impossible-not-to-love teammate, Kim Kitsuragi, another officer who is by your side as you wander Martinaise, a district of a city called Revachol, where vestiges of battles won and revolutions toppled are everywhere.

What makes this game incredible, what makes it one of the most impressive artistic experiences I've ever had, is the way it represents the mind and how it asks you, the player, to discover just what kind of beast you are.

While I would never doubt that games are a cerebral experience, I would posit[7] that many of the games loved best by consumers are "of the body." That is, the primary mode of experience is assuming control of an abled figure that is or becomes pristinely equipped to move through the world and physically get shit done. *Disco Elysium* exists less in the body and more in the consciousness.

The game is literally a text to be read. In an interview Robert Kurvitz, lead designer/lead writer on *Disco Elysium*, says, "Text tumbles up. . . . We wanted to build a dialogue engine that's as addictive and as snappy as Twitter." As you play, you run through the beautifully hand-painted district and you speak to people. Each and every line of text[8] is accompanied by masterful voice acting. There is a personal quality to the conversation, which you read and listen to, and make choices that dictate their outcomes. Kurvitz continues: "Everyone says

---

5. **Empathy:** There are worse things than being sorry in the world.

6. **Suggestion:** You ARE funny. It's in your blood.

7. **Drama:** Performing the academic thing, are you? "Posit," sure, for sure in your wheelhouse. Keep it going, if you use words like furthermore and juxtapose they'll definitely think you know what you're talking about.

8. **Encyclopedia:** The script for the game is over a million words long. (**Composure:** Damn.)

they don't wanna read, but at the same time read is almost all they do all day long, messages, social media." If you've ever beefed with a random person on Twitter or Facebook, the team's attention-grabbing technique is familiar. *Disco Elysium* employs the base instinct to defend oneself, constantly. "The game needs to be very aggressive and confrontational to keep you there, and to keep your attention," but unlike the soul-sucking void that social media can often be, the writers here are intentional and precise with the energy they've gleaned from the player.

What kind of animal is this dude? The question finds answers in the form of the skills you choose to allot points to at the outset. There are twenty-four skills, paradigms of existence that together make up your person. **Encyclopedia** influences the characters' ability to pull raw facts about the world and what they encounter. **Drama** is your ability to act, lie, and to tell when someone is lying. **Inland Empire**, one of my favorite skills, is a kind of imaginative and para-sensitive quality described in-game as: "Hunches and gut feelings. Dreams in waking life." There are also two health bars, one tied to your physical **Endurance**, and one tied to your mental health, **Morale**.

Composure, **Electrochemistry**, **Empathy**, **Volition**, and **Suggestion** determine your ability to move through Martinaise toward your goals of discovery within and without. The more points you give to a particular skill, the more that particular skill will present itself in conversations and decisions. If you invest a lot into **Inland Empire**, for example, the part of you that understands the life beyond life will speak more frequently. An inanimate object might tell you their story.

In playing the game you discover a new animal, a new being, personal and derived from your own heart. New ways of thinking, about conversations you've had and will have, emerge. Often the game called me out. Most times when it sensed I was doing the safe or "right" thing. More than once, I chose the option to apologize and the game said in different ways, *You know what, you are sorry, sorry in the "sorry ass excuse for a man," kind of way*. I felt the game telling me, Nana, the writer, the boy in the elevator, the young man proud at a funeral, the son,[9] *You depend too much on sorry and charm and here those will not save you.*

Charm is not a named skill in the game because charm is nebulous and specific to each of us. We each Charm in different ways. What I consider my version of Charm in *Disco Elysium*'s paradigm would be a mix of the skills **Suggestion**, **Rhetoric**, **Savoir Faire**, **Composure**, **Reaction Speed**, and **Empathy**. The game forced me to consider myself on its terms and then once I did that I started to question how and why I came to be who I am. How often, if ever, do I pull **Authority** from my psychic toolbox? What is the nature of my **Volition**?

What kind of animal are you? Not who you hope to be. Not the mask you wear best. Who are you when that Charm shit doesn't work? What kind of animal are you, actually?

By stonewalling (and sometimes outright insulting) some of my more Charm/nice guy associated styles, the game invited me to take risks. To be the kind of bold I so often avoid being for fear of repercussion. It asked me to go to the hard places and discover what might be there. It asked me to flex aspects of my person that are used so infrequently I'd forgotten they were there. And they were there.

Make no mistake, the world of the game is brutal, but it also elicits empathy and stunning tenderness, which always feels like an oasis when it arrives on the screen. Charm is a shield, and it can also be a mask. Your character is perhaps the least Charming person in the world, but that's okay. You can't Charm death away, in the end. It asks us to be many things, to try and see outside of our comfort and find something out in the trying.

We are each a symphony of impulses, fears, desires, hopes, and thoughts. There are often harsh clashes among these different parts of ourselves. And many times in the game different skills will say to do exact opposite things. **Physical Instrument** might beg violence while **Empathy** might ask you to inquire about the pain a person is already feeling.

While living in *Disco* I found a new framework to consider my

---

9. **Suggestion**: Are you less a son post parent dead?

thoughts. And it was a reminder of just how much each of us contends with all the time, and having been reminded of that it was much easier to be gracious to myself and others. How many skill checks are the people around me failing at any moment? How do I respond when they do?

There is a moment, early in the game, where you are staring at a body, the dead and bloated and glorious body hanging from a tree. When you look close enough at that body, it tells you a story. It has a voice and you speak to it. That was the moment I fell in love with the game. Because it was then that I knew I'd be able to look back with clearer eyes at conversations I've had with the living and the dead and say what is hard to say.

Before the funeral, they ask you to say your last goodbye. This is at the actual funeral home. Miraculously you've produced over $20,000 to pay for this, and a limousine, and a box that will hold your father forever.

Your mother and sisters have had their own conversations. Now it's your turn. You, the son who spoke to him most as he disappeared from the earth.

You step to the body.

Morale: -1 Endurance: -1

It hurts to look at him, but you must. It hurts like the actual burning you felt in your chest at three in the morning when they called you. It hurts like that switchblade of relief you felt ashamed of soon after. *Finally*, your own body seemed to say.

Crying, because this is it, this is the last time you'll see the man you've looked at most.

Morale: -1 (*This is really hard.*)

"*It's going to be okay. I got it, Dad. Mom and sister A and sister B will all be okay.*"

Drama: Hopefully . . .

You look at him. He lived so much in a suit and there he is again. It seems wrong to wear a tie forever, but he would have liked the look.

Visual Calculus: *This is hardly the same person, and of course it is. Same cheekbones, though less hidden, same lips. Same but different.*

You're crying like you've just discovered tears and they are your new favorite thing.

Inland Empire: *You've done well.*

The **Inland Empire** speaks your father's voice. The body is a message box. It receives and begs to be received.

You wonder, if he thought that, would he tell you?

Inland Empire: *Except for the gloves, I am pleased.*

"I'm scared, I'm sorry. I wish you'd been different. But I'm glad you weren't too. I don't know."

It's true. He wouldn't like the gloves.

Drama: This all checks out.

Empathy: Seems legit. But don't forget it's not just you that is here for this person who hurt them.

You look at your sisters weeping, your mother dry-eyed.

Empathy: *"You couldn't have been different. You are all you knew."*

Suggestion: *"You could have been anything. There's so many ways to be."*

Logic: *"What you are is what you are."*

Inland Empire: *"Everything is nothing and nothing is everything."*

To his body, as a way to speak to him, you say, "I love you and I wish you were here."

Inland Empire: *I love you and where I am now, love is all that's left.*

And then the man you gave $20,000 to says it's time, and you go to put him in the earth.

After the funeral, still drenched in grief, I remember feeling that I was able to see and speak with those who had faced similar losses in a way I had not before. It was as though the loss of my father had added to my **Empathy** skill. It allowed me to **Conceptualize** differently. I thought so much of ghosts and how the dead inhabited my **Inland Empire**. I'm not the same animal I was before, and in many ways, I'm better now.[10]

Prose, my medium of choice, is particularly well equipped to handle

---

10. **Volition:** We here, still.

the interiority that we swim through as conscious beings. As you read these words, you are allowing me to occupy a sacred space that is normally just for you. Allowing me to let my mind take a front seat in your mind and drive the thing for a few moments. It's a gracious miracle. Thank you for it by the way. I played *Disco Elysium* while working on my first novel and I'm writing about it now because, in its representation of interiority, in its hyperpersonalized play experience, I think I witnessed a piece of art that far transcended what I thought the video game medium's inherent strength was.

I'm not here to tell you to play the game.[11] I'm here to say that *Disco Elysium* is a magnificent literary experience. *Literary* is a slippery and sometimes problematic word, but in this context I mean: via the precise use of language, it changes the reader. It makes you grow, gives you a new way of looking at the world, which is a mirror of all of us together, and it asks you really, truly, honestly, Who are you? Who are your dead? And gives you the space to try to answer.

---

11. **Suggestion:** Play the game.

Thinking like the Knight

MAX DELSOHN

I used to want through stories. My desire was refracted through made-up loves that were perfect, in that they didn't involve me at all. Here's an example: the story of nerdy scientist-monster Alphys and macho warrior-monster Undyne. It's a silly will-they-or-won't-they lesbian side plot of an indie RPG named *Undertale*. There are love letters, miscommunications, gushing confessions; then, a scene in the credits of the game in which Alphys and Undyne get their happily ever after. The two monsters sit together on a beach. Undyne inches closer and closer to Alphys, then kisses her cheek. Alphys's eyes saucer; her entire body flushes red. Then she passes out. Undyne laughs maniacally with pleasure and triumph, slapping her hands on the ground as sand flies into the air.

For twenty-two years of ambivalent lesbianism, stories like this were enough. I replayed Alphys and Undyne scenes from the game over and over on YouTube; I read Alphyne fan fiction, then started writing it myself, not to mention my daily scouring of Tumblr for rebloggable Alphyne fan art, especially of that beach scene. I'd done this sort of thing before, first with Marceline and Princess Bubblegum from *Adventure Time*, then with Pearl and Rose Quartz from *Steven Universe*. Then I'd log off and treat my girlfriends more like characters than people, love less like a partner and more like an audience.

Oh, who am I kidding? Less like love, more like worship. I proffered promise rings early, ate them out nightly, devoutly: girls were my gods, and I forgot myself in prayer. Mainly, I tried to forget my own body, my absurd softness, my fragile, awful wrists. I wanted to fuck girls, sans the "I." *Is it cool if I close my eyes*, I'd ask, or *only look at you?*

But that's the problem with audiences: at the end of the fun, they leave. So after six months or a year, I'd leave, fleeing stale feeling or whatever came next. No relationship could measure up to my cartoonish standards. I wanted to faint from a kiss on the beach and stay in that blissed-out dream, never wake up.

I assumed playing video games would only ever reinforce my dissociated way of life, that video games had no role in teaching me the potential of my own body. Then I found *Hollow Knight*.

It was Seattle, 2015. Everybody was asking each other which pronouns they preferred. I've since come to miss that question; in the context of pronouns, the language of preference has fallen out of favor, but it was this very situating of gender as an expression of desire, as *preference*, that unlocked the concept's potential for me back then. First, the question stunned me. What *did* I prefer? Not from women's bodies, but from my own? I knew, instantly, that I did not prefer *she*, had never preferred *she*, had worked around *she* as a creative constraint without much creativity. *She* was a slog, a fate I'd accepted, because girlhood was just that: fate. Preference was a matter of colors or ice cream flavors. Preference had nothing to do with it.

But somebody asked me. Pretty girl outside English class. I panicked, shrugged strangely, ran back to my apartment, tried to think of a better answer. To solve this question of *preference*, I decided, I'd have to devise a narrative, use my past to fill in the blanks. What had come before: cis, butchy lesbian, out at fifteen in an all-girls Catholic school. Immediately gets a Goth girlfriend, buys knee-high rainbow socks, makes an It Gets Better video, quietly hates her body, pretends she's not there during sex. This would serve as my beginning. The pronoun question thrust me into some vague middle period— what some might call gender transition. Beyond that was a mystery.

Lesbian to transition to what? I saw three distinct options: man, woman, or neither. For the next two years, I trudged through that harrowing middle and set out to test each ending: new pronouns, new name, new haircut, new clothes, new antidepressants, new, new, new. Still, the right ending did not occur to me.

I began to withdraw from stories. I stopped keeping up with my favorite TV shows, wouldn't watch any new movies. I deleted *Undertale* from my laptop. I grew nauseated at the thought of Alphys and Undyne's easy, lesbian love in a whimsical, faraway world. I missed work and stayed in bed so I could stare for hours at my ceiling. I wanted to stop thinking in beginnings, middles, ends.

The game trailer for *Hollow Knight* clarified nothing about its story or why I should care: it featured a swelling, mournful soundtrack and scenes from the game spliced with vague imperatives like "MASTER NEW POWERS" and "FORGE YOUR OWN PATH." But there were people in the YouTube comments saying the game was a masterpiece and likening it to a Picasso. More than that, it was part of a sale: just ten dollars on Steam. Amid my depressive episode, I decided to try it.

I spent a good chunk of that year and every year after that playing the game, a 2D action-adventure platformer created by Team Cherry, an Australian developer consisting of only three men. *Hollow Knight* is more than my favorite video game; it buoyed me through gender transition until I arrived at its elusive end, if the end of a gender transition can be defined as the moment you stop the constant adjusting because you've built yourself a body in which you want to live. Learning this beautiful, brutally hard game was what finally pushed me there.

To be clear: *Hollow Knight* does not lack in story. Its rich, even frustratingly complex lore inspires hourlong YouTube analyses and dozens of Reddit forums devoted to the mystical origins of the ancient bug-kingdom Hallownest. Yes, I can summarize the major plot points of the game, but I'm not going to. As a diehard fan, I feel comfortable saying that the lore's accessibility is not one of its strengths; in fact, it's a testament to the game's success that I went into my first run with deep-seated reluctance to invest in its story. Instead, what I loved about *Hollow Knight* right away was its inscrutableness, its indifference, its downright narrative unfriendliness.

But first let's talk more about *Undertale*. In *Undertale*, you play as Frisk, a human child who falls into the Underground, where monsters (like Alphys and Undyne) were banished after losing a war with the humans. The *Undertale* "battle" system combines turn-based combat and mini "bullet hell" in which you navigate a small heart, which represents your soul, through enemy-specific attacks within a small, square battlefield—frog monster Froggit attacks with jumping frog bullets, cyclops monster Loox attacks with tiny bouncing circles, and so on. Avoid the bullets long enough and you can spare a given monster instead of killing it. Depending on how you treat each monster you encounter, the plot unfolds in radically different directions, and the rest of the creatures will respect or fear you accordingly.

What draws so many players to *Undertale*—if you're not there for the lesbian-monster love story—is the emotional roller coaster of playing a video game that implicates your values. The first time I played, I assumed I had to kill monsters to progress. So I killed the first Froggit I met. I killed Undyne too. Only later, as other monsters inquired after and mourned their fellow Underground residents, did I process the consequences of my actions. As soon as I beat the game, I started over again, this time vowing to play a violence-free run.

The world of the game seduces easily; the characters, the dialogue, and the plot twists are singularly heartfelt. But during my second, violence-free, run, when I had a basic understanding of the Underground but still had multiple endings to unlock, I grew bored. Without the narrative intrigue combined with the slow, disembodied nature of the combat, I lost focus. Though Alphys and Undyne's long-awaited love affair would continue to play out on my Tumblr, I rushed through the game as if I'd been assigned to. I was suffering through a major feature of the game that I hated—in this case, dragging a pixelated heart around a tiny black box—to access the cutscene on the other side.

For a ghost-bug, the knight's movements are remarkably intuitive. You use your nail (read: tiny bug sword) to strike in four directions: up, down, left, right. On contact, your nail recoils. This recoil increases when you attack in the air, and you'll often attack in the air. Enemies brandish shields and approach from all angles to stab, swerve, plummet, and charge. The only way to heal in battle is to focus your Soul. The only way to get Soul is to strike enemies with your nail—no health flasks, no running out the clock. Hit to kill, hit to heal.

Hollow Knight is a button masher's worst nightmare. Push the knight a hair too far to the right or time a jump a fraction of a second late and you're clobbered by the swarm of spiders you were barely keeping at bay. With combat this demanding, controls have to be tight. As Team Cherry cofounder William Pellen told *Game Informer*, the developers wanted *Hollow Knight* players to feel like "any hit they take or mistake they make could have been avoided right up until the last second." You have ultimate responsibility for the knight's body and how it moves. You run and hit and dash over and over and over again, each move executed in minute detail. Once you suffer the growing pains of learning the fundamentals of the controls, platforming challenges and boss battles take on a rhythm so intoxicatingly consistent you might call it a trance. By the time you've climbed your way out of the Ancient Basin or dealt the final blow to massive praying mantis Traitor Lord, you're weaving through the air with sublime, falcon-like efficiency.

The problem with button mashing is that, for a lot of games, it works. As a kid I button mashed my way through *Super Smash Bros. Melee* on the GameCube. Fast, directionless pressing will get you through most battles in *Melee*, just as fast, directionless living can get you through your own miserable, dysphoric life. Button mashing as a practice resists the nuances of a combat system in favor of beating the game as fast as possible. Battles become obstacles to surmount, rather than their own joy. But *Hollow Knight* demands you learn the potential of the knight's body. Platforming levels subtly prompt moves you'll need in combat; early enemies are small-scale models of the bosses to come. To some degree, all great games do this, but never this naturally, and never with this measured a learning curve or extraordinary attention to pace. No need to spam attacks or stack power-ups. I could beat the game on my own if only I stayed present and responsive to my enemy's movements, got creative with my strategies, learned from my mistakes. *Hollow Knight* respected me.

During that initial, honeymooning *Hollow Knight* run, I kept starting and stopping testosterone. Potential futures rapid-cycled before my eyes. Leg hair grew in fast. My period vanished and came back. Customers at my shitty desk job called me *ma'am*, then *sir*, then some nervous combination of the two. I had been stuck on transition as a problem of narrative: *Do I want to remain a woman? Do I want to end up a man? How do you end up nonbinary, anyway?* But as I got better at *Hollow Knight*, my imagination stretched further and my framework for assessing my transition evolved. My questions evolved too: *Do I like having more leg hair? Do I miss my period? Do I like being called* sir *at work?* Hormone therapy wrought concrete changes. It changed how people treated me, which spaces I had access to, what my body could do. I stopped caring about the deeper meaning behind moving from man to woman, from lesbian to not. I sought only to create a body that brought me the most pleasure, a body that felt good to use. I saw it now: preference was only the beginning.

So I kept playing. I stayed on testosterone and got hungrier, hornier, more energized, less weepy—welcome alternatives to my usual lack of appetite and chronic depression. I battled the Crystal Guardian and lost. I battled the Crystal Guardian and lost. I started lifting weights. I liked how my body looked with more muscle, but more than that I liked the way my body felt as I lifted, the sweet, greedy ache in my biceps as I curled dumbbells toward my chest. I battled the Crystal Guardian and lost. I battled the Crystal Guardian and lost. I battled the Crystal Guardian three more times, lost, lost, lost. My leg hair grew in thicker, blacker. It extended up my thighs, then my stomach, then my chest. I undid the top button of my shirt so hair could peek through. I battled the Crystal Guardian and lost, but this time, I noticed something: it was easier to avoid his crystal beams if I retreated to the right corner of the room. How had I not realized this before? I battled the Crystal Guardian and lost. I battled the Crystal Guardian and lost, but this time, I got closer to winning, closer than I ever had before. How had I never realized such an obvious weak spot?

I lost five or six more times. Then I beat the Crystal Guardian. These days I can beat him within a few minutes; the Crystal Guardian has plenty of weak spots to exploit beyond my camping in the far corner of the room. The reason he took me so long to beat is that I was still unlearning the limits of my old imagination. I didn't think to fight the Crystal Guardian differently than I had in the past, so I couldn't win.

But I could fight differently. I could win.

I said I wouldn't summarize the plot of *Hollow Knight*, and I won't. Play the game enough times and, sooner or later, you'll get the gist. There are wise mantises. There are vengeful moths. There are try-hard dung beetles. There are "wyrms," which are, I guess, worms. There are fiery gobs of pus called the Infection and glowing, sentient black shit called Void. The Hollow Knight has daddy issues, and the White Lady likes to fuck. You are the knight, but you're not the Hollow Knight. None of this is overtly explained.

I have often wondered if the lore of *Hollow Knight* is meant to be *so* opaque. To an extent, this is a feature of the Metroidvania genre, in which players are meant to feel that the world of the game continues to exist without them, whether they're traveling through it or not. So why do I enjoy playing it so much, despite my lack of investment in its story? Because a good story can't substitute for an embodied sense of wonder. Stories can point to what's possible, but they can't get inside your hands and show you how to move.

A couple of years into playing *Hollow Knight*, I scurry through the tunnels beneath the Resting Grounds and notice a crumbling section of the ceiling I've never seen before. I strike it with my nail and the ceiling gives way; I scale the black dirt walls until I arrive at the secluded home of the Grey Mourner, an elegant, flowery white moth. Outside her home is a simple bench; inside, her walls are covered with empty picture frames. She explains that she hides away so she can properly grieve her dead lover, a daughter of the Traitor Lord, who refused to acknowledge their relationship due to its "outside-ness." The Grey Mourner then asks if I will go to her lover's grave on the other side of Hallownest and leave a flower there.

I accept the quest. The Grey Mourner hands me a Delicate Flower. She tells me the flower is so delicate, in fact, that it will break if I fast travel with it or take damage of any kind.

Enduring, thwarted lesbian love: the kind of story I used to live in. Live through. Another, older version of myself would take this opportunity to learn every bit of lore surrounding the Grey Mourner. I would write Grey Mourner fan fiction, retreat further and further into their moment of union, their moment of loss. Spend hours crafting the unwritten details in my mind. Forget myself for days on end.

But that's not what I'm thinking when I meet the Grey Mourner. I'm not thinking in stories. I'm thinking like the knight. I'm thinking about how to move across this strange, vast world on my own, without taking a hit.

Mule Milk

KEITH S. WILSON

Do mules exist in the wild? I don't know what I'm doing when the idea occurs to me—probably washing the dishes, folding clothes. My favorite chores are those done in solitude and that elicit the daydreams of minor labor. But I feel, for some reason, briefly haunted by the question. Haunted because wondering this, if mules exist in nature, feels so familiar. The way a bar can be a haunt. The kind of place that, in theory, you can exit easily but in practice you only ever find yourself entering.

The earliest character from a work of fiction I can remember identifying with, *really* identifying with, is Terra from the video game *Final Fantasy VI*. Garfield is a jerk. Optimus Prime is cool but he is also a fire truck. And possibly reminds me of my dad. Michelangelo (the ninja turtle) is a party dude, but I am no party dude.

Instead, I see myself in Terra. I'll go on to name a cat after her. After Terra the cat is taken by an ex, I'll name a computer Terra. A camera. After that first computer breaks, I'll name the next one Terra. This one.

In the game, Terra is caring, and I aspire to be caring. She is beset with self-doubt. And though, unlike me, she is powerful, it is not her hit points that keep her on my team every moment I am given the choice.

She is an outsider, born in a place she cannot return to, and you can never tell if people look at her and know she is different, or if that is only something Terra feels in herself. One character, describing Terra, says of her, "She is afraid of what she is, and that is a painful thing."

Terra is a monster. Or more accurately, she is half-monster.

Repetition, or the feeling of it, isn't what makes a question a haunt. Other variations of questions repeat themselves. What happens when we die? What is justice in a world where the police answer to no one?

And recently: What is nature? I've been wondering, because Black poets, even those who write explicitly about nature using the word *nature*, are seldom considered nature poets. But also: Is a rock nature? If it is, is a rock wall? How long before a rock wall becomes nature if it isn't?

What if I am unsustainable? The meaning of this question changes as I get older.

In the illustration (it appears throughout the internet on hundreds of websites) the differences are made clear.

A horse has a curved back. A donkey's is straight. A mule's back is slightly curved.

In Kentucky, horses are a big business. The state's equine industry in 2012 was worth $3 billion and accounted for 40,665 jobs.

That, and coal, and bourbon, and tobacco, and the KFC empire, is Kentucky. My Kentucky, the Kentucky where I'm from, is so close to Cincinnati, Ohio, that you are always breathing its air. It's a little Appalachian and a little Midwest. Where I lived, there is a horse track. There are horses. But there's also the White Castle that wouldn't promote me to manager. There's the German-rooted Goettafest. There's being called every slur for someone with brown skin anyone can think of.

Toni Morrison wrote about my Kentucky in *Beloved*. I read the novel in school but didn't recognize where it took place, though I recognize it now.

Beloved is based on the real story of Margaret Garner, a former slave who escaped from Kentucky to Ohio. Who escaped from a slave-holding state but who was apprehended and forced, under the Fugitive Slave Act of 1850, to return to the South. Garner killed her child rather than turn her back over to Kentucky.

I say she was a former slave because this version of the story demands a slave. But telling it to myself, I draw out the ways she is like me. She was mulatto. That is, she was also half-Black. If you know the source of the word *mulatto* is "mule," you know the source of the haunt. All that is left is the answer.

Final Fantasy VI (Super Nintendo, 1994) was a watershed video game for its time. Bigger than that for me. It was foundational. I had never played anything like it.

Featuring a cast of fourteen characters (including Terra), *FF6* is a story of rebellion against an empire that uses chemical weapons, slavery, torture, and genocide to expand its reach. There are wild capers (posing and performing as an opera singer to thwart a gambler), political intrigue (convincing leaders across the world that centrism supports empire), and pathos (sending love letters via carrier pigeon on the behalf of a dying soldier). The cities are filled with pixelated hissing pipes, the 16-bit sound of wind hollowing out what industrialism hasn't already taken. The land is ripe with still images of beautiful yet wretched monsters—imps, dragons, giant squirrels. You are asked, in this era of role-playing game, to *imagine* their movement— that they are more than digital sprites.

The game had themes of spiritualism and nature's fragility (or vulnerability) and man's cruelty and an ongoing existentialist question that might be boiled down to: "How do we find a way to live through a world that doesn't just take away our belongings, our loved ones, and our humanity, but which becomes so wrapped up in the destructive nature of industrialism and capitalism that it begins enacting that violence even when there is no chance for profit?"

Or put another way: "What if there is no such thing as justice?" Put another: "What is the human spirit?" Or: "What is human nature?" Or: "Is this . . . is this our nature?"

I was eleven.

Ramuh: She is afraid of what she is, and that is a painful thing.

A fulcrum is a part of an animal that supports. A beast of burden is a working animal that carries.

Traditionally: farm equipment, food, military supplies. Also known as sumpter animals, or pack animals, they are in contrast to draft animals that pull loads but don't bear the weight directly upon their backs.

A mule, therefore, is all fulcrum.

Nature (from Latin: *natura*, "birth, initial character") is a recent concept, if what we mean by nature is the outside world. The place where, as Mary Oliver describes, "wild geese, high in the clean blue air, / are heading home again." The reason for its existence is practical. Or, if not practical, legal.

We need an agreed-upon definition of what nature is in order to conserve it. In order to rally. Interestingly, modern biologists often avoid defining nature in concrete terms. From an article linked on nature. com: "Hundreds of studies focus on the best ways to protect or to value nature, but none of them deign providing a definition of it."

Part of the reason for avoiding a definition is a preemptive conflict resolution. It all gets very philosophical very quickly. If I ask whether a mule exists if labor does not exist, my question has no effect on well-meaning biologists except to trouble them.

I find myself, too, troubled trying to imagine an American nature outside of aggression. Maybe it is the fault of the English lit classes, which present the themes of a book as binary conflict: Man vs. Man. Man vs. Himself. Man vs. Nature.

What kind of boxing matchup could exist with nature other than against man?

My favorite fact about mules: "Forty acres and a mule" was not a promise made to freed slaves. It was a delimiting promise made *against* the well-being of freed slaves. It was made to white southerners. The promise was that freed slaves would not be allowed to take *more* than forty acres and a mule from the land they were freed from.

It is my favorite because it marries a kind of hope for the future (forty acres) with the darkness of the word, the world, itself. Mule. And when said aloud, it is only a sound. *Mewl.* The sound a baby makes.

Some information about Terra:

- Terra isn't half-monster. Not quite. She's half-esper. Typically, nothing physically distinguishes espers from the monsters you fight, and most of the characters don't differentiate either. As a child, I didn't make any distinction. But the distinction is important to Terra.
- Terra, on the other hand, appears human. Mostly she looks the same as the other characters of *Final Fantasy VI*, though her hair color is the chlorinated green-blond of white summers.
- Terra has abilities granted to her from her esper ancestry. Unlike humans, Terra is naturally able to use magic.
- Terra can transform between human and esper—she is fully both, but never, it seems, at once. When she is in esper form, she glows. She is, in every sense of the word, awesome.
- Because she is valuable, because of her genetic heritage, Terra starts the game literally enslaved. You control her, because it is a game, but even in the narrative of the game, she is not under her own control. She is wearing a "slave crown," a mind-control device. What makes Terra valuable is her genetics: Terra was raised in human culture and that culture

interprets her body as a commodity and her difference as a right of colonial ownership.

- Terra finds that she doesn't seem to feel love. As an adult, I now wonder if Terra is asexual. Or aromantic. Or if she is experiencing the trauma of enslavement—of witnessing mass murder. Maybe she hasn't yet found it in her to date. Regardless of what she really is, she wonders. Each of her parents, her singularly human mother and her singularly esper father, fell in love. Espers love. Humans love. Is Terra incapable of love because she is *half*-esper?

When I talk about how much I love pigeons (something I manage, somehow, to do a lot), how I love the range and the luster of their colors, how I like that they are bold and come out in their regalia to see if you have bread, how I love the sound they make when they choose to make sound, people will sometimes ask what the big deal is. Why pigeons?

Maybe you are different from me. That is why.

Maybe you are like a bird other than a pigeon. But when a lot of people ask a question, it is like something that rubs the heel of your foot until it hardens and shines. But it isn't a foot, not even the weird feet of a pigeon, but an emotion, so a reverse rock-tumbler effect is given instead to a natural feeling that begins as round and is polished to an edge. Over and over. For me, it becomes shame.

I have explained: I live in the city. In the city, pigeons are nature.

Some facts about mules from SPANA (Society for the Protection of Animals Abroad, a global charity devoted to veterinary care of working animals such as horses, mules, elephants, and camels):

- The skin of a mule is less sensitive than that of a horse and more resistant to sun and rain.
- Militaries have depended on mules for millennia.
- Some mules have been known to make whimpering noises.

But is it true? In one sense pigeons seem to have adapted to the city. But they live in cities, not because they were bred for them, but because cities happen to be shaped the way the pigeon prefers. Pigeons want to live on cliffs. We want to build them.

But really: Can mules exist in the wild? The answer is simple. It's hardly worth talking about. I google it.

Because I wonder: *How* can mules exist in the wild? They are bred, and therefore exist, to labor.

If you say someone is a mule, you are saying they are a smuggler. They carry. If you wolf something down, you eat it. It's a natural gift of wolves. If someone is catty, they are fighting, metaphorically, for territory. If you outfox someone, you are clever, the way a fox seems to evade capture (and what is more natural than to run from man?).

But a mule labors. Or, one is stubborn as a mule—one refuses to labor. (And historically, people forced to labor are always accused of an inborn proclivity to laziness.) But the etymology, if I were to go into it, if I were to identify with it as I do, would mean nothing to the actual nature of a mule, if mules exist in nature. If a tree falls in a forest, but with mules.

The practical problem is that mules are sterile: 99.9 percent cannot impregnate or become pregnant. They receive thirty-two chromosomes

from their horse parent (statistically, the mother) and thirty-one
from their donkey parent. Lining those chromosomes up is like taking two different-sized halves of a zipper and trying to make do.
And so while there *have* been mules that could conceive, since 1527
there have only been a little more than sixty cases on record. In the
whole world.

You could, if you wanted, memorize the name of every baby born
from a mule since the beginning of recorded history. You could do it
in a day.

That's the practical problem with imagining a mule in the wild. The
philosophical problem is: Are mules a technology? Can a technology
exist without us?

The spiritual problem is personal, as all spiritual problems are. *Mule* is
the root of *mulatto*, the slur and racial categorization for descendants
of Black and white ancestry in the Americas. It shouldn't mean anything. Truly, it doesn't mean anything. And yet, if you have ever been
hurt by someone, hurt deeply, and then met another person whose re-
semblance to the first made you incapable of full detachment from a
phantom hurt—you understand that what you think and what you
feel can knowingly, even comfortably, be at odds.

I want them to exist in nature. I don't fully know why. There is certainly a kind of satisfaction that passes, itself, for love when you know
you were born because someone chose to have you. My parents chose
to have me. But the romance of capitalism is in the way that, whether
or not it's true, you are convinced that all labor you remember is labor
you opted into.

I want a mule to exist in nature and I know that they cannot. So I
hold off. It is like the way I will sometimes see how long I can go without looking in the mirror. Games that I never question until I realize
nobody is playing them but me. But here:

According to an article titled "Did Humans Create Mules?," by Madeline Masters, "Where the two animal types coexist in the same habitat, it's possible for horses and donkeys to breed in the wild to produce mules. This happens rarely, however, and nearly all the mules humans use they bred themselves."

The answer is maybe. In theory. Probably, but hardly any.

Is that an answer? It is. It has to be.

When we choose to mitigate our damage to nature, it's rarely the policy to walk away from a place entirely. To let it be. Great effort is made and much research conducted to determine what was "originally" in a place, what "ought" to be there, or what "naturally" might occur. There is an overlap between conservation efforts and nationalism, which is, so often, also a looking-back at an idealized past.

It brings to my mind:

The extinct auroch is the ancestor of all modern cattle. It has been described as pitch-black, with a stripe along its back, with slender legs and a much larger skull than a cow. It has a body for fighting and living in the wild, which justified its small udder. It was an animal born to nature, which meant the auroch was made less of meat than of muscle. In 1627, the last auroch died in Poland. Since then, humans have been determined to bring aurochs back.

The idea seems like science fiction, but it is more bumbling than that. One famous attempt, through "back breeding," is as low tech as it gets, since it is essentially the rough process of domestication (though pretending to be its opposite). A 10,000-year-old technology that produced dogs from wolves and mules, one generation at a time, from donkeys and horses. The theory goes that through selective breeding, the fundamental traits of an animal, like the auroch, can be brought out of its descendants. Michelangelo (the artist) said that "every block of stone has a statue inside it and it is the task of the sculptor to discover it." What if every child is a block of stone containing the ideal statues of its forebears?

It might be no surprise that the project was Nazi-affiliated. In the early half of the twentieth century, two German zoo directors, Lutz and Heinz Heck (brothers) spent twelve years mixing breeds of domestic cattle with Spanish fighting bulls. These Heck cattle now graze parts of Europe. They are creatures that absolutely do not have auroch DNA. Not any more than the cattle that preceded them, anyway. They superficially appear—in ways—like the auroch. They are around the same size, yes. But their heads are like that of an auroch's if that head was pulled like taffy.

When they graze, are they natural? Can they ever be? I doubt that it matters to the Heck, so long as there is grass. They were made for one reason and they live for another.

Another mystery. After a writing conference, I sat down in my seat on the airplane and found myself next to a fellow writer and friend. During the flight we talked about all kinds of things but at one point we got on the subject of horses: being from Kentucky, I had my opinions. And she had worked with them throughout her life. She told me that she had been told by an employer that mules could not drink the milk of their mother because of something in her colostrum colloquially called anti-donkey. That their donkey blood was rejected by a poison in the horse mother's milk.

At the start of *Final Fantasy VI*, Terra is being escorted by two soldiers of the Empire to investigate an esper sighting. Tritoch, an esper who is, essentially, a giant bird, sits frozen in ice deep within the caves of the mountains above Narshe, a colliery town. Though Terra is wearing a slave crown and is incapable of doing anything but kill for her masters, and though Tritoch is frozen and cannot speak, Terra sees herself in that ice, in Tritoch, and everything changes. This was what it was: to believe you held an awareness of yourself and yet to still be startled to see, for the first time, your own reflection.

After an explosion caused by some sort of magical-electrical interaction between the two, Terra blacks out, awakening in a bed in Narshe without her crown and with little memory of anything surrounding her life or the actions on the mountain.

In the world of *Final Fantasy VI*, espers are something like spirits of the earth—what a dryad or a nymph or a river god is in Greek mythology. They are individual instantiations of Gaia, of nature, and when they die, their bodies transform to magicite, a crystalline material that the Empire has discovered works as fuel. Their corpses are the fuel for the war machines of the Empire. To the humans of the world, espers with free will are monsters and dead ones are coal. The Empire invades the spirit realm and in less than the lifetime of its first emperor, they commit a total genocide of every living esper.

Terra is the only half esper in existence. She may be the only one that has ever lived.

In one scene, you find a "research facility" (a factory). And in that factory, bathed in heavy grays, hooks and chains dangling from the ceiling, you watch espers thrown onto conveyer belts to be slaughtered. If espers are the earth itself, this is the dynamite in mountaintop removal and the laws supporting blood diamonds. If espers are animals, it is killing a humpback whale for lantern fuel. It is cutting down an elephant to make piano keys. But since espers have language and culture, they are not only metaphor. They are alive. They are spiritual or monstrous in exactly the ways humans are.

I didn't view the espers as a people because I was too young. And yet I did. I didn't view Terra as being half-Black, and yet I did. I saw that she was between worlds. And that what made her valuable to the Empire was also what would kill her.

The anti-donkey question elicits less obsession from me. I google it, and find nothing. Whether mules can exist in nature—Maybe? All we can do is look out our windows and see—feels personal. Something I practice every time I play a game and choose to be a monster. There is something metaphorical there, to be sure: anti-donkey, a poison in mare milk that kills mules, makes of the mule a Beloved. A horse's most precious thing that she cannot keep.

It is too specific to move me in a personal way, since what, really, is the metaphor of a baby dying from its mother to me, who is lucky enough to have a loving mother?

Instead, it feels mythological. It is the origin myth of a racialized, mixed people.

But I do check. Having found nothing on the internet, I message a doctor on Twitter. She studies mammals and milk drinking, and is an associate professor of evolutionary biology. I ask her about anti-donkey. Her answer boils down to this:

> *I have not heard of this and it is total garbage*
> *(sorry that was really blunt)*
> *but NONE of it passes the sniff test*
> *horses can nurse mule offspring*

To paraphrase, poison is a trait that is exceptionally rare in mammals (and much more common in insects and reptiles). And traits that would immediately kill children are unlikely to remain in the gene pool.

Around 50 percent of mules grow wolf teeth. Wolf teeth are not what you might imagine: they are small and cylindrical and vestigial, the remains of teeth the ancestors of horses and donkeys once used to eat twigs on trees when they roamed the wild.

It is probably the case that wolf teeth are called this, not because they resemble the teeth of wolves, but because they are bad.

What makes a wolf tooth bad? If an animal lives the way an animal lives in the wild, the answer is often nothing. The arguments for pulling them are like those of pulling wisdom teeth in humans: problems may or may not arise if they are not taken out. Just as problems can arise *from* taking them out (see: infection).

But the true issue with wolf teeth is human in nature: for instance, they can upset the alignment of any bit placed in a mule's mouth. If the bit sits crooked, when the farmer pulls the reins, the mule may not turn.

I have been accused by strangers on the internet of inserting politics, of inserting race, in places where it does not exist. Of course I do. If I do not, I am not there. And that is someone else's fantasy.

A primary reason mules are bred is that they are less stubborn than donkeys. No mule is stubborn as a mule.

There are no Black people in *Final Fantasy VI*. Not in the whole World of Balance, or later, in the world where nature has been killed, the World of Ruin. Or if there are, I did not recognize them. It would be another ten years before I saw a Black character in a video game.

Terra (whose name you may have noticed means *Earth*) was not Black, but she was also, to me, never white. And if hers was our world, she would not be white either. If her world is anything at all like ours, the process of enslaving her would require the apparatus of her society to metamorphose her into something, anything, that deserves debasement. She could be anything. Esper, auroch, mule. So long as she was neither free nor capable of hoping to be.

When I identify with the mule, with the monster, in part it is because I have been forced away from identifying with the man. I imbue myself in a creature and lend it my humanity so I can see my humanity, but I also identify what I am with biological difference, with racial essentialism. Or do I turn away from the game and choose not to play? Or do I play, but play as not myself, in a world that would not imagine me?

In middle school, during the time I first played *FF6*, one of my best friends called me an oreo. We were chasing each other in the cafeteria at recess—some invented game—and he said it unprompted. I laughed. I didn't know *oreo* was a slur for a Black person who acts white. I thought he was calling me the cookie, and the absurdity of it, or the awkwardness, made me laugh. It hardly seems possible that there was nobody in that cafeteria but just us two. But perhaps because I still don't know why he said it, that is how I remember it. Being alone.

In the days before the internet was so accessible, it was much harder to know how long a game was, and *FF6* was much longer than most (around thirty-five hours). The halfway point of the game could have been the end of any other game, and so facing off with Emperor

Gestahl atop a floating island at the source of all magic feels climactic. When Kefka, the Emperor's scheming Iago-like general, murders the Emperor and takes the power for himself, *that* is what feels like the plot twist. But then what is actually surprising is that when you heroically face Kefka, you lose.

The Emperor's aims were as elementary as they were capitalistic: Take over the world. Have it. But when Kefka takes control, he makes himself a god. And he destroys everything. The continents are undone and rearranged. He kills all the grass and trees. After waking up from the disaster, you get in a standard fight, but your enemy, a monster, takes damage without your doing anything. You don't have to lift your weapon at all and everything will die.

Unlike more contemporary portrayals of evil as "plausibly" logical (the Marvel Comic Universe's Thanos, whose famous snap kills half of Earth's population in order to create "balance" in the world, and is a villain whose villainy is half-jokingly defended by people on the internet), nobody knows why Kefka kills everything. That is the nature of actual cruelty. We can theorize but we might never know.

There is a category of paintings called casta (Spanish for "caste") that I find intimate and familiar, despite its having originated three hundred years ago, thousands of miles away. I hate the paintings, but cannot deny a monstrous part of me loves being seen in something so old. Casta paintings portrayed mixed-race families—white Spaniards, indigenous people, and Black Africans in various "fractional" combinations—with the aim of demonstrating that through intermarriage, through selective breeding, pure whiteness could emerge from the corruption of genetic Blackness.

"The genre's premise . . . purported that successive combinations of Spaniards and Indians resulted in a vigorous race of 'pure' or white

Spaniards, while the mixing of Spaniards and Indians with Africans led to racial degeneration," wrote Los Angeles County Museum of Art curator Ilona Katzew in the wall text of her exhibition *Painted in Mexico, 1700–1790: Pinxit Mexici.*

Mulattos (mulatos/mulatas) abound in these paintings. They look just like me. And they communicate: we have imagined this world, and we can imagine a better one, in which I exist not in flesh but only here, as a warning.

In the last moments of the game, the magic of the world is finally dying out, and consequently, Terra is losing the half of herself that made her Black to me—her esper half. In the last moments of her living in that hybrid body, before she becomes only human, Terra races beside the zeppelin that carries the rest of your party. She is flying. To think that this is a thing she could have done at any moment and chose not to. That to protect herself, she hid her true nature. That this choice, too, is labor.

Sometime much after my talk with the doctor about anti-donkey, I stumble across an article about neonatal isoerythrolysis (NI), also known as jaundice foal. The story is about a newborn foal named Hannibal, who, from a blood test, was determined to have NI. This phenomenon occurs when two conditions are met: (A) the mother mare happens to have antibodies that are directed against the specific blood type that is (B) inherited by the foal from the father. These antibodies are passed on through the colostrum—the mother's first milk—to the child, killing it.

Hannibal's name is a reference to the mask he was forced to wear for the first twenty-four hours of his life. During this time, his mother was milked and that milk was thrown out to save him. It is a death caused not by poison or toxins but by antibodies. By the blood attacking the blood.

And it is not a condition born from the existence of mules. Hannibal, his mother, and his father are all horses.

I read this story that contains not one mention of a mule, and I invent one. I invent one and feel for him, more, somehow, even than Hannibal.

And sometime even after this I learn that though mules cannot have children, they can nurse them. There may be no such thing as anti-donkey, but there is such a thing as mule milk.

Staying with the Trouble

OCTAVIA BRIGHT

A ten-year-old girl sits at an overflowing desk in the basement study of an old farmhouse, surrounded by bundles of papers tied with red string. The stone floor is cold; the walls are a deep burgundy. A beam of gold autumnal light falls across her shoulders from double doors that open to a wild garden outside. The adults are out—gone to pick apples or for a walk or to do some other dull grown-up thing—so the house is empty save for an excitable old Labrador called Persephone, and the girl. She's fixated on the screen of a laptop computer, her face lit blue by its glow. To her, the dog and the piles of paperwork and the farmhouse don't exist. All that matters are the pixelated letters floating in front of her:

Lingerie is
a. sexy.
b. a kind of car.
c. a French food.
d. edible.

She chooses *a. sexy* because it has the word *sex* in it and she's done this enough times by now to know that if there is an answer with *sex* in it then it's the right one.

Correct.

She likes the encouraging shape made by the letters, but quickly presses Enter for the next question—two down, three to go.

> **The world is**
> a. flat.
> b. spherical.
> c. a big place.
> d. near Fresno.

She types *b.* and then, impatient, presses Enter. She does not enjoy being patronized.

> **The term "Working Girl" refers to**
> a. a secretary.
> b. a lady of negotiable virtue.
> c. an industrious woman.
> d. an employed female.

If there's a word for woman in the answer it's almost as safe a bet as *sex*, but looking at this she doesn't know which one to choose—there are too many other words she doesn't understand. She picks *c.* and immediately regrets it.

> **Oops. You blew that one!**
> **If you miss another, you can't possibly be 36.**

Knowing it's her last chance, she hits *Enter* again and her heart sinks at the question that flashes on-screen: American history. At least the sex ones are usually pretty obvious.

> **Who was not Vice President of the United States in 1973–74?**
> a. Gerald Ford
> b. Nelson Rockefeller
> c. Thomas Hayden
> d. Spiro Agnew

With a heavy sense of futility the girl guesses *d.*, and with its maddening, familiar message, the game chastises her:

You're a kid!!
Shame on you for trying to deceive a friendly game like this!
Please play again when you're older.

Until I came to write this essay I did not, in fact, play again when I was older, but the ritual of trying to answer some version of these five questions was a regular one in my life from the ages of ten to twelve. Something that happened in furtive, unsupervised moments at my uncle's fruit farm in the English countryside. It had a vegetable garden and apple orchards, and sometimes there were pigs or cows in the surrounding fields. My long-dead grandmother's coats still hung in one of the wardrobes. In an attic bedroom there was a large trunk full of my uncle's old comic books, a mixture of *Beano*, *Viz*, and stories about American teenagers and American superheroes. It was a special treat when I was allowed to read them. He was one of my favorite adults because he never really spoke to me like I was a child.

It was the nineties, and America appeared to me a land of total permissiveness: on TV I watched *Saved by the Bell* and fell a little in love with Zack and a little in love with Lisa, but most of all I fell in love with the idea of being an American teen. It seemed like you could do anything in California. I couldn't wait to grow up.

By contrast, the farm felt like a world facing backward, and the best portal out of it was my uncle's laptop computer. A black, boxy rectangle that got hot when it was on for too long, it had the standard games on it—*Minesweeper* and *Solitaire*—which I was allowed to play on my own as long as I sat properly at his desk (feet on the floor!) and promised not to touch anything else. I lost many hours to the world of tiny bombs and little gray squares, but eventually would get bored and start idly clicking around the other icons on the desktop. It's amazing how quickly children can find the things that are explicitly not for them.

For years all I could remember of the game was this: if you could get past those five questions and prove you weren't a kid you entered a gaudy world with a jaunty soundtrack that sounded as if a drunk person was hammering it out with one finger on an old electric keyboard. You played as a tiny white man with dark sideburns in a black shirt and a white suit. Even with no context you could tell he was a buffoon. The game started with you, the piteous fool, standing outside a bar that had a flashing neon sign saying something that for years I couldn't recall—Donny's or Jerry's maybe—beside a giant, tipsy martini glass. You had to use the keyboard to type instructions and then the little man would do what you told him: e.g., *go in bar, sit on stool, talk to bartender, order drink*. Inside, rendered in bright clashing colors, there was a pixelated jukebox and a pixelated moose's head and, behind the bar, a pixelated image of a nude reclining woman. (I had never been in a bar that had either of these things on the wall, and often wondered where you might find one.) There were other characters you could talk to sitting on high stools, and an open doorway through which you would find the bathroom, where you would discover a drunk man slumped on the floor. You could pick up a rose from the table opposite and give it to the buxom woman who sat on one of the barstools, which would piss off her boyfriend. Next door to the bar there was an alleyway where you could rummage in a bin, and where if you were unlucky you could get beaten up. I vaguely remembered a pixelated black cat.

It was an escape from the tedium of a childhood that I was starting to leave behind, enticed instead by the adult world of lust and drama and action. A world I was impatient to see for myself. Ultimately, though, the game was a puzzle I could never crack. There had to be more to it than just roaming around the seedy bar, but I never got far enough to discover what. My desire to know more about all the things I'd been told I'd understand when I grew up kept me trying, until eventually I was old enough for the information to find its way to me without my having to exert any effort at all, through friends' big brothers and the arrival in my life of internet chat rooms. As I got older, I'd sometimes reminisce about my frustrated adventures with

Larry the Lounge Lizard, but no one ever knew what I was talking about. I came to think of it as a sleazy fever dream, something I might have invented or embellished over time. It crystallized in my memory as my first illicit quest into the underworld of adulthood, a secret thing I did alone, knowing I wasn't supposed to.

Many years later, when I actually was thirty-six, I came across the game's real title in a novel. The book—which is great—is called *Tomorrow and Tomorrow and Tomorrow*, and I was preparing to interview its author, Gabrielle Zevin. It tells the story of a long creative partnership between Sam and Sadie, two video game designers, that begins in the late eighties and spans thirty years. Quite early on, Sadie mentions playing *Leisure Suit Larry*, and I squealed out loud to discover I had not dreamed up the strange little man in the white suit after all. He was real, not Lounge Lizard Larry but Leisure Suit Larry in the Land of the Lounge Lizards.

When I spoke to Gabrielle I learned that she too had played *Leisure Suit Larry* alone as a kid. "I also experienced it as a weirdly creepy thing that no one else did except me," she told me, and went on to explain that the game was made by a company founded in the late seventies called Sierra Entertainment (later renamed Sierra On-Line). The collaborative relationship between the husband-and-wife team who founded it inspired the dynamic between Gabrielle's protagonists— like Sam, Ken Williams was a programmer, while Roberta Williams's interests lay more in storytelling, like Sadie. Together, the Williamses pushed the text-based adventure game beyond its previous limits to include graphics as well. Curious to know more, after the interview I looked them up online, and learned that their groundbreaking work was so popular that within a couple of years, what began as a lo-fi operation run out of their home became a company of one hundred employees making $10 million in revenue. The first *Leisure Suit Larry* game, written by their coworker Al Lowe, was published in 1987 and billed primarily as a comedy. Even without an advertising campaign, it was a critical and commercial success, and over the decades it has spawned three remakes and nine sequels made by three different studios, the last of which—*Leisure Suit Larry: Wet Dreams Dry Twice*—was released in 2020.

Now that I had the right name, I found a version of the original game online and decided to play. I failed the first round of questions (it turns out I still do not know how to recognize a good pickup line, and my knowledge of American presidents remains patchy as ever), but when I did get in, I was hit by the thrill of recognition at the sight of the game's neon pixels. There was the bar! Lefty's, of course. Next came an immense wave of loneliness. I thought it was simply the effects of being transported back to those long, solitary hours of late childhood, days of complicated awakenings. But as I played on I realized, no, this is a profoundly lonely game.

When I first played I had no idea that the setting was a Las Vegas parody called Lost Wages, and that Larry's—and therefore the player's—singular goal was to have sex with a woman before the clock hit midnight (seven hours, in real time). If he doesn't, he shoots himself. Larry's backstory is that he's a thirty-eight-year-old computer programmer, a nerdy guy who lives in his mother's basement and who has never had sex. It is very important that he has sex. But because he is a lonely, nerdy, basement-dwelling guy Larry has no idea how to dress for this vital quest, so even though it's 1987 he reaches for the white leisure suit/gold chain combo made hip in the seventies by John Travolta, not understanding that fashion has moved on. Because above all Larry Laffer is meant to be, as his name suggests, a person you are supposed to laugh at.

This time I had the entire internet at my elbow with hints and playthroughs to consult, so I soon uncovered the mysteries that lay beyond the bar. They included a disco, a convenience store, and a casino hotel complete with kitsch wedding chapel next door. There was a payphone and a taxi that were vital to getting around, and you could win money to pay for both by playing black jack in the casino. I quickly learned there were various ways to die if you did things in the wrong order. Go against the design of the game and you get run over or beaten up, or find yourself in some other terminal trouble.

The whole thing is essentially a string of innuendos—an extended riff on the double entendre of "to score." At first, Larry is mostly the butt of the joke. He's always on the wrong side of every door, and, together with the game's often sarcastic narratorial voice, I rolled my eyes at this pathetic pawn caught in the libidinal thrust of normative masculinity. Fuck women or die! Ha ha ha! But the longer I played the worse I felt about all of it. The only two people of color in Larry's universe are racial stereotypes: a pimp and the convenience store owner whose unintelligible English is a punch line. Larry's quest to get laid is mapped via four potential conquests: a sex worker described within the game as "a mess," from whom he can catch an STD that will kill him if you don't figure out how to make him buy a condom from the convenience store first, and with whom sex doesn't appear to count because he paid for it; a woman named Fawn whom he picks up in the disco and who lets him believe she will fuck him if he buys her things, but ends up tying him to a bed and running off with his cash; Faith, a flirty receptionist who teases Larry but won't put out; and finally (notwithstanding a brief cameo from an inflatable doll), Eve, sex with whom presents the opportunity to win the game. Men are either obstacles to or potential facilitators of Larry's sexual goals: the pimp, the convenience store clerk, a bouncer, a taxi driver, plus the random threat of a drunk guy who roams the streets and who may or may not beat Larry up, or even to death. Women are either diseased, mercurial, prick-teases, or, well, responsible for the fall of man: so far, so incel.

Some of the game's regressive politics and puerile jokes were acceptable in the nineties and some of them were never acceptable at all, but its sleeper success seems to be down to the fact that people thought of it as risqué rather than sinister. Just a harmless joke. Of course, the only way to insist that this kind of humor is harmless is to maintain a smothering naivete about the very real harms caused by willful ignorance, sexism, and racism.

Which brings me back to the ten-year-old girl playing on the computer at the farm—what she knew and didn't know, what she learned, and what she remembered. When I think about what I got from *Leisure Suit Larry* then, it had very little to do with the game itself. I never found it funny. For me, the fun bit wasn't telling Larry Laffer what to do, but the thrill of knowing that *none* of it was allowed. This was then heightened by the unpredictability of whether I'd manage to answer enough questions correctly even to cross the threshold before someone came to get me for tea and I had to return instead to innocently searching a tiny grid for tinier bombs, like the good girl I was expected to be. My pleasure was found not in the transgressions offered within the game itself but those found in the context in which I played it. As an only child, at ten years old I was, like Larry, often on the wrong side of every door, surrounded by people who knew more about life than I did, and full of the sense that I was missing out. I wanted access to this other, illicit kingdom, and with every attempt to enter it, the adventure game I was really playing was that of my approaching adolescence.

So, it was never really about Larry. If anything, now I feel sorry for the little man in the white suit, who himself has no idea how to play The Game. He's written as a loser because he doesn't understand the rules of how to be a "real man," and this ignorance renders him at once pathetic and potentially dangerous. But the adventure Larry's on is rigged, hitched as it is to gender norms that offer no room for exploration, only a binary set of goals at which you either succeed or fail. It's ironic that the same game that led me to explore transgression and boundary crossing managed to do so while simultaneously reinforcing an intensely depressing and rule-bound "reality" about sex. The same "reality" being endorsed by the mainstream media as I came of age in the 1990s and early 2000s—one that's narrow and small, and full of dead ends.

Maybe that's why, now the underworld of adulthood is where I live full-time and I can go to a bar with a moose's head or a naked woman on its wall anytime I like, I look for games that tell bigger stories than this. These days the portals I seek are ones that take me beyond the limitations of the known into something more expansive. Lately, I've been playing a game called *Stray* where I get to be a cat whose best friend is a drone. Together we explore a postapocalyptic landscape looking for clues about what happened. There are ledges to jump off and baskets to ride in, carpets to scratch at, and a community of sentient robots whose faces display hearts when I rub up against their metallic legs. There are controls that let me meow and purr and curl up for naps in the middle of abandoned rooms, all actions that serve no narrative purpose at all, but encourage me to find in them the same pleasure as my feline counterpart, and for our desires to become ever more aligned.

Like *Leisure Suit Larry*, *Stray* is an adventure game, but the adventure it presents is big enough for all the nuance that *Larry* lacks. It manages not only to offer up the chance to live vicariously—delightfully—as a small and uncommonly cute ginger cat, but also to reveal ugly yet important to recognize truths about, for example, the catastrophic potential of humanity's harmful effect on the planet, or the ethical conundrums presented by the invention of AI. It's gently subversive: in the familiar neon-lit dereliction of a disaster zone, instead of giving me a gun to shoot, *Stray* suggests the solution, and in some ways the real adventure, is to adopt an animal point of view.

There's plenty to be said for interspecies collaboration, in both the virtual and the real world: as the feminist scholar Donna Haraway argues, we can learn a lot by becoming kin with other creatures. In her book *Staying with the Trouble*, she writes compellingly about the ways in which the human and nonhuman are entangled, and the need for them to work together in the face of systemic and climate collapse. In this, her perspective is aligned with the message at the heart of *Stray*, but I also found myself thinking about her writing when I went back to the land of the lounge lizards. Central to Haraway's thesis is the idea that "it matters what matters we use to think other matters with; it matters what stories we tell to tell other stories with. . . . It matters what stories make worlds, what worlds make stories."

We know the world that made the story of *Leisure Suit Larry* all too well, but how do we stay with the trouble it presents? By not letting it slip into the soothing fog of nostalgia, or under cover of the so-called harmless joke? By facing the fact that the trouble at the heart of the story it tells, and the world that story then goes on to make, is that masculinity is something a person can win or lose at? If, as Haraway argues, "it matters what knots knot knots, what thoughts think thoughts," then it also matters what games game games.

The longer I play *Stray*, the more catlike it coaches me to become. As befits its feline protagonist, the game it games is curiosity; I settle further into this new animal perspective, and even when I'm not playing I find myself looking for new places to explore, new heights to climb. *Leisure Suit Larry*, on the other hand, games the old, misogynist game of sexual conquest. If, to borrow from the story of Persephone (the Greek goddess my uncle's sweet Labrador was named for), I were granted permission to return from the underworld of adulthood to visit that younger version of myself, I'd tell her that the world she'll find unlocked by those multiple-choice questions will be seedy and disappointing. But it won't take long for her to discover there are more exciting boundaries to push. All she needs to do is stay curious.

Narnia Made of Pixels

CHARLIE JANE ANDERS

At some point during the second wave of the pandemic-o-rama, when we were still cooped up, all my friends started playing video games like *Elden Ring* or *Breath of the Wild*. I decided to do something a bit weirder: I set out to watch, or rewatch, movies in which someone leaves the real world and enters a video game. I couldn't travel in real life, so I thought I might as well go on a host of imaginary journeys into fantastical realms.

I've always loved portal fantasies, such as *The Chronicles of Narnia* and *The Wizard of Oz*. I strongly identify with any hero who's thrown out of their element and forced to learn the rules of a world they've never seen outside of dreams and half-forgotten stories—maybe because that's how I experience "real" life a lot of the time. And as soon as video games became a thing, I wanted to live inside them. I remember becoming deeply immersed in marathon gaming sessions and the bitter disappointment of returning to the physical world, which contained just as many repetitive motions but without the same thrills and sense of satisfaction. Even the earliest, most stylized 8-bit games allowed me to project myself into their narratives; far from being a barrier to entry, the blocky shapes of a run-and-jump game created a bigger space for me to insert myself into. So I was excited to discover the pretty big canon of movies that combined mystical doorways and video games.

What did I learn from watching a ton of video-game portal fantasies?

We've been telling the same basic story about a flesh-and-blood person going to live inside a video game for forty years. CG effects have become vastly better, but the visual language established by *TRON* in 1982 and in other early films remains in use: Steven Spielberg's 2018 *Ready Player One*, for example, still features a blue saturated video game world, and there's still an abrupt shift in pacing and tone whenever a gameplay sequence starts. But also, all these films are still examining questions about agency, embodiment, and corporate ownership.

We usually think of a portal fantasy as a form of escapism: someone abandons the responsibilities and cares of their workaday life and travels through a wardrobe, a magic door, or a police box into a land of adventure and fun. But the video game portal fantasy is a little different. When you're dealing with pixels instead of pixie dust, you always have to wonder who owns the code. Especially when your own body is made out of those pixels.

Free Will

Some heroes don't choose to go inside a game; they're pulled bodily inside. *TRON* and *Jumanji: Welcome to the Jungle* feature protagonists who are essentially kidnapped and given no choice but to become living game icons. But in other recent films, people decide to immerse themselves in a gamescape. In *Free Guy*, a coder and game designer ventures inside the multiplayer crime-spree game *Free City* to find proof that her code was stolen. *Ready Player One*'s heroes go inside a virtual world called OASIS and play games to win a kind of scavenger hunt, with ownership of OASIS as the ultimate prize.

It scarcely makes a difference whether the protagonists of these stories choose to venture inside a video game: either way, they are constrained by its rules, no matter how bewildering. Even in supposedly open worlds like the ones in *Free Guy* and *Ready Player One*, the protagonists have to overcome specific challenges in order to move forward. In *TRON*, it's fun to watch the cocky Flynn (Jeff Bridges) bridle at the notion that he must play whatever games the Master Control

Program has chosen for him. But to find a more incisive exploration of free will inside a game, one must turn to two dark-as-fuck indie movies: *eXistenZ* and *Gamer*.

In David Cronenberg's 1999 *eXistenZ*, Ted Pikul (Jude Law) is the "everyman" who gets dragged into a game along with its creator Allegra Geller (Jennifer Jason Leigh) in order to playtest it. A huge part of the horror for Pikul is that he has no choice but to take certain actions. He feels compelled to assemble a strange gun out of the bones in his food and use it to shoot a waiter in a Chinese restaurant. Allegra has to remind him that the NPCs—non-player characters—he encounters won't respond to him unless he says or does the thing they're expecting. At one point, Pikul observes, "Free will is obviously not a big factor in this little world of ours." To which Allegra responds, "It's just like real life: there's just enough to make it interesting."

In the underrated *Gamer* from 2007, prisoners and debtors are coerced into letting sadistic gamers remote-control their bodies. Kable (Gerard Butler) is a living avatar piloted by a wealthy teen named Simon (Logan Lerman) who controls all of Kable's actions inside a game called *Slayers*. At a certain point, as he is being steered in deadly combat, Kable gets into a tight spot and has to beg Simon to relinquish control: "I can beat them, but not with you controlling me. You want to win? Turn me loose." It turns out the creator of *Slayers*, Ken Castle (Michael C. Hall), wants to use this same technology to control everybody in the world. After a bizarre dance number where Castle controls a mob of people with his mind, Castle and Simon fight over control of Kable, and Kable only wins by using Castle's own mind games against him, getting Castle to visualize a knife sliding into his body.

Both *eXistenZ* and *Gamer* feature underground resistance movements against video games. In *Gamer*, the Humanz, led by Brother (Ludacris), warn that "mind control is slavery," whereas in *eXistenZ*, the Realists are more concerned that overly immersive VR games will erode our sense of reality: we'll believe our bodies in the games are actually our bodies. As flawed as *eXistenZ* is, there's a certain brilliance in making explicit the connection between free will and embodiment—because after all, so much of what we call "mind control" is actually bodily control, a matter of making your body move without your own volition.

Embodiment

Like most trans and queer people, I've known the feeling of being alienated from my own physicality, but I think it's actually a common sensation among straight cis people as well. The world is constantly putting expectations on us and requiring us to perform actions that aren't our own, so it's easy to feel kind of lost in our own flesh. (I always connect pretty strongly to that line from "Birth of Serpents" by the Mountain Goats about someone dwelling inside their own body like an uninvited guest.) So perhaps it's not surprising that a lot of these movies play around with the notion of losing control not just of your actions but also of your whole body.

The original gamer portal fantasy, *TRON*, starts with a macho hero who goes out of his way to let us know he's definitely had sex before. When we first meet Flynn, he can't help teasing his ex-girlfriend, Lori, in front of her new boyfriend, about her habit of leaving her clothes all over the floor. But once Flynn passes into the game realm, he's suddenly clad in a neon leotard covered with schematics, making him look like a dancer in a campy music video, and he is no longer in control of his own actions. He is forced to play a racing game in which he rides on a light cycle, a type of computer-generated motorcycle. The evil overseer, Sark, presses a motorcycle icon on his screen, and then a yellow handlebar appears right in front of Flynn, who looks at it in surprise but involuntarily grips it with both hands. A second later, Flynn is hunched forward, and a light cycle forms around him, as if it is now part of Flynn's body.

There's no overt body horror in this moment, but of course the notion of one's body becoming part of a piece of hardware without any explicit consent is inherently disturbing. And not surprisingly, David Cronenberg mines this rich seam of squick for all it's worth in *eXistenZ*, where the game controllers are strange biological entities that squelch and writhe. These fleshy controllers connect via umbilical cords to "ports" installed at the base of your spine, which look like anuses (and people are constantly fingering, lubricating, and even licking these holes).

While he's inside the game, Ted Pikul worries endlessly about what's happening to his body back in reality. Over time, this leads to a kind of dissociation that verges on dysphoria. Right before he commits involuntary murder in a Chinese restaurant, Pikul says, "I'm feeling a little disconnected from my real life. I'm kind of losing touch with the texture of it, you know what I mean? I mean, I actually think there's an element of psychosis involved here. I mean, I don't know where my body really is, or where reality is, what I've actually done, or not done." Allegra responds that this is good, because it means his nervous system is starting to engage with the game architecture.

Then there are those video game movies that explore the idea of having your body transform into something you don't recognize. That's the source of a lot of the humor in *Jumanji: Welcome to the Jungle*, in which four teenagers end up as cartoonish avatars in a video game. A scrawny kid named Spencer becomes Dwayne "The Rock" Johnson, a big football player named Fridge becomes a diminutive Kevin Hart, and Madison, a popular girl, is stuck being the dweeby Jack Black. "What happened to the rest of me?" demands Fridge as he surveys his much smaller body. This is pitched as comedy, but also provides a literal means of cutting Fridge "down to size" and forcing him and Madison to confront a whole new set of limitations, in the name of making them more empathetic and accepting.

Years ago, I became obsessed with another weird movie subgenre: gender-swap fantasies, in which someone is forced into a body of a different gender (e.g., *The Hot Chick*), or has to pretend to be a different gender (e.g., *Tootsie*). These movies almost always involve the protagonist learning an Important Lesson from walking in someone else's (usually high-heeled) shoes, while mining all the awkwardness that goes with this for laughs. *Jumanji: Welcome to the Jungle* and its recent sequel feel as though they're exploring a lot of the same territory as these films, with similar results.

Steven Spielberg's 2018 film version of *Ready Player One* keeps reminding the audience that people's real-life bodies might not resemble their avatars inside the virtual OASIS—to the point where it occasionally flirts with transphobia, as characters fret that a seemingly hot woman might really be a "three-hundred-pound man." But part of the fantasy of both gaming and virtual reality, of course, is that you can have whatever body you want. (Long before I figured out I was trans, I always played *Super Street Fighter II* as Chun-Li or Cammy.) As Wade (Tye Sheridan) explains, "People come to the OASIS for all the things they can do. But they stay because of all the things they can be. Tall, beautiful, scary, a different sex, a different species, live action, cartoon. It's all your call." Sure enough, Wade's avatar, Parzival, has elfin features and perfect boy-band hair, in place of Sheridan's more regular-shaped face. His love interest, Art3mis a.k.a. Samantha (Olivia Cooke), also looks like a punk fairy princess inside the game, but she keeps warning Wade that he'll be "disappointed" if they meet in real life. When they finally do, Samantha turns out to have a birthmark on her face, and Wade's acceptance of it is made out to be a sign of what a good guy he is. In one memorable scene, Parzival and Art3mis dance in midair, their bodies the only splash of color inside a teal-saturated nightclub. At its best, *Ready Player One* consciously explores the dichotomy between the idealized bodies in the game and the (only slightly) more realistic ones in the real world, cutting from Parzival's graceful movements to Wade's awkward reactions as he experiences his avatar's physical sensations.

Then there's 2019's *Serenity*, which somehow beats out a David Cronenberg film for the title of Weirdest Video Game Portal Fantasy of All Time.

Matthew McConaughey spends a fair amount of *Serenity* strutting around naked as Baker Dill—and the viewer is very much invited to admire the body that helped make *Magic Mike* so magical. Baker lives alone, on a mysterious island full of sugarcane fields and fishermen. His commitment to nudity reflects his yearning for freedom—because, much like Pikul in *eXistenZ*, he is at the mercy of compulsions he doesn't understand and cannot control: first, to catch the giant tuna that broke his heart (which he names Justice), and later to murder Frank (Jason Clarke), the new husband of his ex-wife (Anne Hathaway). An NPC finally tells Baker that his "compulsions" represent his tasks inside a video game, and he learns that his real-life son has nonconsensually resurrected him inside the game after he died in Iraq. (It's never entirely clear how Baker's son managed to upload or recreate his dead father's consciousness virtually, but it makes as much sense as a laser disintegrating Flynn's body and reassembling it inside a game in *TRON*.) Despite Baker's fairly clear in-game objectives (fishing and murder), he spends a lot of time scrambling to make money to cover fishing supplies by taking tourists out on fishing trips and doing sex work. His main (only?) sex work client is Constance (Diane Lane), who teasingly calls him a hooker—to which he replies, ruefully, that he's "a hooker who can't afford hooks." Even as the movie invites us to fetishize Baker's nude body, it keeps reminding us that his physicality is part of the prison he's trapped in.

But the movie that most exploits the potential for distorted bodies in virtual gamescapes is actually 2021's *Free Guy*, the story about a coder who enters a game to find out whether her code was stolen. The film's actual protagonist is an NPC named Guy (Ryan Reynolds), who finds some glasses that show him the options presented to players in the game, and that allow him to gain self-awareness and defy the game's ingrained tendency toward mayhem. In the film's climax, Guy faces Dude, a nightmare "upgraded" version of himself who's absurdly jacked—as if a bodybuilder ate another bodybuilder. Dude speaks in incomplete catchphrases (full of "TBD") and personifies the ultraviolent toxic masculinity that Guy has spent the entire movie rejecting. In fact, Dude represents the opposite side of the fetishism/repulsion coin from Baker Dill's buff nudity: the sheer volume of his muscle, and the lack of personality behind it, are meant to be disturbing. In a featurette released alongside the movie, Ryan Reynolds jokes that he got Dude's body (which isn't actually his, though he provided the voice and facial motion capture) by drinking a daily "protein bomb made out of pure human muscle" and that "life is about growth . . . hormones."

Dude and Guy represent two warring ideals of what a video game body could look like, and Dude is Guy's final boss fight in his quest for agency and liberation. Much like *TRON*'s eponymous hero, Guy fights for the users—as well as the NPCs—who are being abused for the sake of a sadistic fantasy. And Dude? Dude fights for the evil corporation that wants to own and control absolutely everything.

Capitalism

If one theme unites the video game portal fantasy from *TRON* all the way up to *Free Guy*, it's ownership and control.

In both *TRON* and *Free Guy*, a genius programmer has had their game stolen and repurposed by a slimy manipulator. And in both films, the programmer goes inside the system to find the evidence that will allow them to reclaim ownership. (In the case of *TRON*, as previously discussed, the journey is somewhat less voluntary.) *TRON*'s villain, the corporate sleazebag Dillinger, is such a control freak that he actually names his security software the Master Control Program, and he's openly contemptuous of the customer base of EnCom, the company he works for. At one point, the cofounder of EnCom, Walter Gibbs (Barnard Hughes) tells Dillinger, "User requests are what computers are for," to which Dillinger responds, "Doing our business is what computers are for." Once Flynn goes inside the system, he sees user-facing programs such as accounting software being turned into NPCs and forced to compete in gladiatorial games, and belief in "the users" is dismissed as a false religion—until Flynn reveals that he's a user himself.

In *Free Guy*, the villain Antwan (Taika Waititi) has stolen the code from the friendlier, more complex game *Life Itself* and turned it into the crass, ultraviolent *Free City*, where bank robberies and mass murder are the best way to rack up points. Much like Dillinger, Antwan doesn't care about his users, lying to them constantly and serving up a product full of bugs. He tells his developers that it doesn't matter if the sequel to *Free City* is a mess that lacks the characters everyone loved in the first game, because all that matters is intellectual property and brand recognition. When the creator of *Life Itself,* Millie Rusk (Jodie Comer) describes the game she created, it sounds idyllic and beautiful, full of NPCs who "grow and change and feel real," not to mention waterfalls, butterflies, and unicorns. The backstory of *Free Guy* is all about sensitive creators trying to make something that breaks the gaming mold, only to have it distorted and ruined by commercialism.

Ready Player One features a very similar storyline: Wade and his nerdy friends are competing with corporate sleazeball Sorrento (Ben Mendelsohn) for control over the virtual OASIS, which was packed full of references to classic video games and 1980s pop culture by its creator, James Halliday. Wade's love for those cultural touchstones gives him a reverence and appreciation for this virtual dreamscape, while Sorrento only sees it as something to be monetized, with loads and loads of advertising. Sorrento also has found a way to use OASIS's virtual interface to turn debtors into indentured servants, trapped in a dehumanizing virtual workspace. But it's obsessive knowledge of 1980s trivia that allows Wade to solve challenges and figure out what Halliday had in mind. In one scene, Sorrento pretends to be a true fan of *Robotron, Ferris Bueller's Day Off,* and Duran Duran, but Wade can tell he's faking it. As the film develops, Wade's nostalgia seems to serve a function similar to the magic glasses Guy wears in *Free Guy*— making him a player instead of someone to be played.

Players vs. NPCs

I love portal fantasies, in part, because they allow someone to visit a strange world and yet bring the familiar with them. The hero in a portal fantasy keeps one foot in everyday reality, even while journeying through strange, colorful realms. And in the context of a video game, this means the hero is part player, part NPC.

And it's no accident that so many of these films intentionally blur the player/NPC line. In *eXistenZ*, all of the supposed NPCs turn out to be players from the playtest group, who have been stuck with extremely limited roles in the game. *Ready Player One* starts out telling a story about ownership over a virtual space, but then peels back the layers to reveal that it's actually about indentured servitude. On the face of it, the conflicts in *TRON* and *Free Guy* are just internecine battles over laying claim to intellectual property and the corporate power that comes with it—until you realize that the NPCs in both virtual worlds are self-aware, which means these battles are actually over the ownership of people. Just as Flynn in *TRON* is a user who's constantly mistaken for a program, Guy in *Free Guy* is a program who keeps getting mistaken for a user. And Guy's magic glasses feel very much like a metaphor for the question at the heart of all of these films: How can we be made aware of and keep fighting for our own personhood and that of others?

For forty years, video game portal fantasies have been warning us about what happens when corporations control the stories that shape us. When we worry about capitalism ruining our favorite games, we're not just defending a beloved story or world: we're defending ourselves. Truly great gameplay makes us feel immersed and therefore embodied, and we infuse the characters in a game with parts of our own identities. The anxiety inherent in any portal fantasy is that the hero will become lost, or trapped, in the world on the other side, unable to return home—and that anxiety is doubled when the hero is in danger of becoming an avatar with no control over their own actions and bodies. So just like with any other cautionary tale about technology, we're worried not only about corporations owning beloved imaginary worlds in these films but also about corporations owning a piece of us.

Cathartic Warfare

JAMIL JAN KOCHAI

In first person, I—the gamer, the soldier, the American—stand over the virtual corpse I have just slaughtered. With his dark complexion, little black beard, and fallen machine gun, the digital corpse is supposed to resemble an Afghan insurgent. Though there are more objectives to complete, more buildings to purge and Afghans to shoot, I linger in this room, in this bombed-out, digital rendering of Kunar Province, Afghanistan. The corpse does not fade from the field of play, and in his face I'm forced to acknowledge what I have denied up to this point in my playthrough: that the enemy I have killed is me.

Released during my freshman year of high school, *Call of Duty 4: Modern Warfare* quickly became something of a cultural phenomenon in the United States. Not only a tremendous financial success, *Modern Warfare* was almost universally praised by video game publications for its storyline, gameplay mechanics, graphics, and its highly addictive online multiplayer format. Video game consoles (PlayStation, Nintendo 64, and the often-forgotten Sega Genesis) once bound gamers to their living rooms, but Microsoft's Xbox Live online multiplayer mode opened console gaming up to a whole new space of play and interaction. Aptly enough, *Modern Warfare*, whose central thematic subject was global military combat, turned into a globalized experience. My friends and I were absolutely obsessed. Instead of meeting at someone's house after school, we played together from the comfort of our individual homes. Both isolated and interconnected, we created our own competitive teams and fought opposing parties on digital battlefields. We were rewarded with higher rankings and unlockable content. We played late into the night, cursing and humiliating strangers, feeding off the exhilaration of another kill streak, of earning another cruise missile or a precision strike, of winning an entire match all on our own. *Modern Warfare's* online multiplayer mode turned into one of the main platforms through which teenagers at my high school interacted, communicated, and developed bonds. All this is just to say that to be excluded from *Modern Warfare* was to be excluded from an increasingly significant cultural experience.

Of course, before taking part in the incredibly popular online multiplayer mode, many children would start off with the story or "campaign mode." I was no exception.

All of the *Call of Duty* video games can be categorized as first-person shooters. The player sees the game from the perspective of the main playable character, usually an American or British soldier. But while the first three *Call of Duty* games are set during World War II, and the playable character takes part in actual historical battles, the storyline of *Call of Duty 4: Modern Warfare*—as the title suggests—is set within a "modern" historical context.

There is a caveat: although the weapons are updated (the player is allowed to switch between AK-47s generally reserved for the "insurgent" characters, standard military-issued M4s, stinger missiles, and, at one point, a drone) and the campaign takes place in a few concrete geographical locations (Chernobyl and Moscow), large swaths of the game are located in unnamed Middle Eastern territories. The weaponry, the uniforms, the landscapes, and the graphic images are awe-inspiring in their detail, but the setting, the historical timeline, and the geopolitical dimensions are oddly ambiguous. Certainly, the game is attempting to engage with the "War on Terror"—it is safe to assume that the unnamed Middle Eastern setting in *Modern Warfare* was Iraq and that the enemy being fought was a fictional counterpart of Al-Qaeda—but no real figures or organizations are written into the game's narrative.

As a fourteen-year-old Afghan American immigrant, I felt strangely comforted by this ambiguity. These aren't Iraqis I'm murdering, I kept telling myself. They might not even be Muslim. I was able to construct a barrier between myself and the virtual enemy. They and I were different. They and I were opposed. It was just a game. Just play.

In the sequel, however, *Modern Warfare 2* (which far surpassed its predecessor both in terms of its critical and financial success, making over a billion dollars in sales within a single year), the historical, geographical, and racial categories within the campaign mode (and even the online levels) became much more transparent. Its release roughly coincided with Barack Obama's first "troop surge" to Afghanistan in late 2009. By then I was a senior in high school and had followed Obama's campaign closely. I was delighted when he won and then devastated when he began pouring troops into Afghanistan. I was entering a new stage of political consciousness: reading historical texts, arguing with teachers about the Soviet and American occupation(s), following the news from Afghanistan, and researching past war crimes committed by American soldiers (the torture of Dilawar, the Uruzgan wedding bombing, and the Shinwar Massacre, to name a few). And yet, none of this stopped me from purchasing *Modern Warfare 2* and playing the first mission, which is very clearly set in Afghanistan. So there I found myself, in Afghanistan, playing as an American soldier, getting ready to kill Afghan insurgents.

Years later, in college, I would be reminded of this experience while reading Frantz Fanon's first book, *Black Skin, White Masks*. In his chapter describing the concept of collective catharsis, Fanon writes, "In every society, in every collectivity, exists . . . an outlet through which the forces accumulated in the form of aggression can be released. This is the purpose of games in children's institutions, of psychodramas in group therapy, and, in a more general way, of illustrated magazines for children." He suggests that Tarzan stories and comic book adventures of colonial heroes served as a release for the collective aggression of white society. The magazines "are put together by white men for little white men." Furthermore, the cathartic violence envisioned is always directed toward a colonized figure. Consequently, when a child in the colony is brought up to read these stories, they will inevitably identify with the hero and find themselves taking up the position of the white explorer as opposed to the barbaric native. The colonized child subjectively adopts a white man's attitude. But if that child saw herself as a European colonizer might see her—that is, as a racialized object—this revelatory and traumatic experience may cause a rupture in the psyche, or, as Fanon states, "a collapse of the ego." No longer able to identify with the white explorer, the symbolic manifestation of white aggression, the child is forced to acknowledge himself as the object of that aggression, the thing to be destroyed.

The campaign mode of *Modern Warfare 2* begins in the American Firebase Phoenix, located in the Korangal Valley of Kunar, Afghanistan. The main playable character, an American soldier named Private Joseph Allen, is tasked with training a platoon of NPC Afghan recruits. These Afghan NPCs speak Pashto throughout a mini training game that introduces weapons mechanics to the player. Here I was—the gamer—trying to figure out how to aim and toss grenades, and as the squad commander was instructing me in English, an Afghan interpreter translated everything the commander said into Pashto. This was an oddly disorienting experience. Though the Pashto is never translated with English subtitles, I felt uneasy that I could understand it so clearly. Pashto was a language that I almost exclusively associated with my homelife. My mother's jokes. My father's stories. My grandmother's curses. Sitting in my bedroom, door locked, zoned in, I wasn't prepared for this troubling association between myself (my language, my background, my family) and the NPCs in the video game.

After another short training session, I learn that a nearby bridge has been attacked by enemy forces, and so I am hurled into the heart of a battle between American military forces and Afghan insurgents.

In the first firefight, my enemies are located across a vast river, merely specks on the screen I fire upon from a distance. Neither their facial features nor their clothing can be distinguished. As the battle moves forward into the inner workings of an Afghan city, civilians can be spotted scurrying across roads or alleys, hunched over as if on the brink of trotting on all fours.

Shortly afterward, a rocket explosion throws me, Private Allen, from the Humvee. I am now fighting on foot. My platoon and I move from street to building, from room to room, finally up close to the enemy. Most of them wear black military fatigues, keffiyehs, and black ski masks, but occasionally one or two of the enemy combatants will not wear a mask at all. In *Modern Warfare 2* the digital corpses of enemies remain in the field of play for long after you have killed them. These corpses can be mutilated. You can stand over them and keep shooting, or you can stab them and they will wriggle and writhe and splatter blood. I remember very early in the mission, after I, Private Allen, killed an Afghan insurgent, I stood over his digital corpse and examined his face. Playing the game from the position of the white American soldier, in the first-person point of view, I am tasked with killing Afghan fighters to such a degree of realism that I am even able to sidetrack a mission and look at the features of a dead man's face and see how much he seems to resemble my father. Or me. I see me in him. In that moment, I stand in two positions at once. The white American soldier *and* the dead Afghan corpse. Suddenly, the virtual dream of the game collapses onto me. I put my controller down. I close my eyes. I stop playing.

In *Black Skin, White Masks*, Fanon mentions that "each type of society, of course, [requires] its own specific kind of catharsis." Just as comic books and children's tales were important tools used in the "collective catharsis" of white Europeans—giving them a medium through which they could express their collective aggression, their violent fantasies, upon a colonized people—*Modern Warfare* seems to be taking part in a similar process of collective catharsis for white Americans. The colonial fantasies of comic books and children's tales seem to have been superseded by the more immersive neo-imperial fantasies of the modern military video game. Though the *Modern Warfare* series is supposed to be restricted to "mature audiences"—that is, ages seventeen or older—their campaign narratives are essentially children's tales. The good American must destroy the bad Muslim, not only for the sake of their country (or whatever other geopolitical objectives are tied into that), but for the sake of the world. By the time a young gamer is finishing high school, they've been imbibing these narratives for years, and so these games become an effective recruiting tactic for the US military. I remember watching my friends in high school line up during lunch to play *Modern Warfare 2* at a recruiting station. The army recruiters had an Xbox and a flat-screen TV set up out of the back of a van. The line, mostly boys, stretched across the quad. Three kids I used to play *Modern Warfare* with ended up joining the military. Their participation in virtual violence prepared them for a career in actualized, geopolitical violence. Fantasies turned to flesh.

While playing the campaign mode of one of the most popular video games in the country, I was tasked with participating in the cathartic fantasies of white men destroying/mutilating Afghan men, and thus was also tasked with the civic duty of cathartically destroying/mutilating myself. By accepting the role of the American soldier while also identifying with the Afghan enemy, I fell into some ruptured space between the first-person shooter and the third-person corpse. This rupture was further intensified by the outlet through which it occurred. Playing a video game, especially a first-person shooter, is an immersive experience. The senses are assaulted on so many levels—the eyes, the ears, the hands. In a war film, at least it is Mark Wahlberg or Jeremy Renner or some other famous white actor who is slaughtering all of these Afghans, these Muslims. But in *Modern Warfare*, I am more explicitly implicated in my own destruction. I aim my rifle, the rifle of the white American subject, and I push the button, and I obliterate the Afghan, who is also myself. I obliterate myself. Because it is not enough that I must watch the white soldier murder me in films and on television shows. Now I, in the body of the soldier, in the skin of the white aggressor, from the perspective of the imperialist, I am tasked to murder myself, over and over, for the sake of the country, and in order to complete the cathartic mission of the white subject. If I am to exist within the narrative dreams of America, I, as a subject, must destroy myself, as an object, forever. It is not a choice; it is a duty. I must wait for me in the killing fields of the American imagination.

The Cocoon

ANDER MONSON

Alien vs. Predator

The first time was in a friend's rented apartment. I wish I could remember whose. This would already be a better essay if I remembered, and this is only the third sentence! I know I could make it up and you'd never know, but the answer matters. Was it Matt's? Dane's? Ryan's? Two of our moms had died, either just before or way before, or maybe just after. The others were still alive. It wasn't my apartment, or I'd remember it differently. But I don't remember. Just the CRT screen, an old TV, nothing special. No sense of what was around the screen. I remember the darkness and the throbbing sound as we walked or crept around whatever space station we were supposed to be in, being hunted by or hunting aliens or men. I felt sometimes then that I was an outsider in the world of men (by which I mean the world of humans, but also, really, the world of males and their exploits and behaviors): the way I understood masculinity in my high school and in action movies didn't always make it seem possible, appealing, or even human.

I remember the sudden jump scares, too, as you came out of an airlock or around a corner and anything could be there. It was cheap but effective: more visceral than you'd think, considering this was 1994. Video was ascendant, not games, which of course still came on cartridges. My friends and I consumed a ton of both, often in whoever's apartment had the system we wanted to use. It was walking distance

\ 83

to downtown, I think. Someone or someone's brother worked at Very Video in Hancock, across the bridge, and was allowed to bring home for the weekend whatever systems they hadn't rented, one of which was this new one: the Atari Jaguar.

I think playing *Alien vs. Predator* on that system was my first experience living in the atmosphere of a game. I mean being put in that state of dread and mystery and wonder by a game so that even when I left it, it's never left me. I've lost a lot of other stuff, but not that feeling. I remember that feeling better than any other feeling that year.

I'd been in this state before, I think, but only as a consequence of my own imagination. Older games required me to summon my own world from the box art and just some 8-bit blips, some dots, some letters. The *D* was a dragon. An *e* was an elf. From there I had to do my own work, and I did. Glyphs amid darkness: that was plenty to work from. But *AVP* for Atari Jaguar was the first game that seemed to me to have it all: the first-person point of view that would become so familiar to anyone playing games in the decades to come; the enveloping, atmospheric sound; that sense of losing myself in the action to the point where the thing onscreen became the only real thing, if just for a moment.

Skepticism vs. Jaguar

My friends and I were skeptical of the Jaguar and its titles. This was the comeback Atari, after the dominance of the 2600 in the first age of games, but it already seemed like nobody cared about it. A lot of stuff had happened since. Nintendo and Sega Genesis and Neo Geo and we'd all got driver's licenses and shot guns and blown stuff up and got drunk and arrested for dumb shit off-screen. I'd been arrested for some dumb shit on-screen, but I wanted to believe that was behind me now. It had been a while since we really played games. I was on the back end of a dark time in my life, though I didn't know I was through most of it yet, and at the same time it seemed like nothing much had happened, like nothing ever happened in our small town, snowbound for most of the year. I had just turned nineteen.

If the camera zoomed out from the apartment to the city block and then the city, it'd look pretty. Everything covered in snow. It mostly was. Some people liked doing stuff outside. Not me so much those days. Besides, being inside gave me more time for books and telephones and screens.

The Jaguar is an unloved video game system, probably not much remembered except as a misfire en route to the Xbox and PlayStation era. Billed as the first 64-bit system (because it had two 32-bit chips in it, this was something of a fudge), it sold poorly and was discontinued after only a year or two. I never played any game on it other than *Alien vs. Predator*. But *Alien vs. Predator* was totally great. There's a reason it's almost certainly the one game you've played or heard of if you've played or heard of the Atari Jaguar.

I'd seen *Alien* and *Aliens*, of course, and *Alien 3*, and 1987's *Predator* had marked me so deeply I would end up watching it over 150 times and writing a book about its depths. I was aware there was an Alien vs. Predator mash-up coming out of the comic book world, but I didn't read comic books. Alien vs. Predator? Like the Atari Jaguar, it sounded dumb. (It is pretty dumb.) It's also pretty fun, the kind of thing you get when adolescents start pitting things against each other because they're imaginative and bored. Who would win? A spider or an earwig? Your brother or your dad? The USSR or the USA? Our dreams or what we'd settle for? So sure, it made sense to set these two near-unstoppable aliens against each other and see what happened. But wait, you could play *as* the Alien? You could play *as* the Predator?

Ander vs. Other

If you haven't seen the movie *Predator*, don't let me ruin it for you. It's great. You should read my book about it. One of its many wonders is these long shots where we are in the Predator's point of view. It sees in infrared, so: heat. The outlines of gradations of heat. What the world looks like to an alien. It takes awhile to recognize the shapes of things. We're forced to try to make out what it's looking at. Many of the movie's most moving shots are ones in which we're not knowing what we're seeing, seeing as the creature, and only gradually putting it together. And then it looks at us, and here we see ourselves in red and orange and yellow coronas. We see our body heat. It's not that often that a movie gives us the opportunity to really *see* ourselves—I mean men; I mean humans; I mean Americans—from outside.

The game *Alien vs. Predator* takes the movie's best feature and takes it further. *Seeing* as an alien is one thing. *Playing* as an alien levels that experience up. If you play games, you know *playing* something is (often) *becoming* something. *Watching* something only occasionally is. Or it is, but in a lesser way. *Reading* something does this, too, and powerfully. As a technology books do this extremely well, powered as they are by the human machine running someone else's software (the story) on our hardware. But I'd never seen this attempted—and pulled off—in a first-person game. It's still not that common, twenty-five years later! Games remain so human oriented that even our attempts at playing aliens are humiliatingly unimaginative.

As a white straight cis guy it was a useful experience to have, though I would not have noted this at the time. I don't remember feeling that feeling at the time, that feeling of being something else, of moving through the world in a different body. I mean, I was aware that my body was pretty different than the bodies of the high school sports guys, and of the Schwarzeneggers of the world. What that would be like, I couldn't totally know. Of course I knew it would be cool to be *something, someone* other than I was. That's what we'd been doing playing D&D. But this was different: it wasn't just imagination. And it wasn't as if, when I moved Pac-Man around on the screen, I *felt* like Pac-Man, searching obsessively for dots, never ceasing until he dies. Playing that, I didn't see *as* Pac-Man. I wasn't inside his body doing the only thing he knew how to do, chased by ghosts, hungry, hungry, hungry.

Someone later told me *ander* means *other* in German.

Use vs. Preservation

In "Computer Game Archiving and the Serious Work of Silliness," Ken McAllister and Judd Ruggill, cocurators of the Learning Games Initiative Research Archive (LGIRA, basically an epic and open-ended video game library sited in part at the University of Arizona, but as they explain, it's a *distributed* library sited in hundreds of different institutions, including people's homes and storage units) put forth an unusual theory of digital preservation, arguing that instead of *preserving* games, people should *use* them, even if that results in the degradation of the games themselves:

> While we believe that the material preservation of computer gameplay's artifacts is vitally important to the extension of cultural memory, we also believe that it is just as important to facilitate that memory at the levels of experience and experimentation . . . such unorthodoxies being LGIRA's privileging of experiential over artifactual preservation. . . . The operative principle for LGIRA . . . is that deep human memory of the archive's artifacts can be both more timeless and more accurate than less experiential forms of study. . . .
>
> Whereas many archives limit access in order to preserve the artifacts therein, LGIRA encourages regular and substantial use of its collection, even when that use threatens to significantly degrade—or even destroy—a given artifact. In many important respects, memory, particularly when its contents are shared widely and deeply, is far more durable than what most game-related artifacts are constructed from: cheap papers, unstable plastics and chemicals, sloppy circuits, and other materials designed to turn a quick buck and then be guiltlessly supplanted. For this combination of reasons, the LGIRA mantra is not use *rather than* preservation, but use *as* preservation.

When I first read it, this whole idea seemed crazy, like a convenient fiction born from a lack of institutional funding. It is not well funded. Though LGIRA does have an official space at my university, it's only barely a real space, sited in the Transitional Office Building, the building's name demonstrating how marginal LGIRA's existence really is.

Having professed my skepticism about its ethos, while trying to write about *Alien vs. Predator*, I'm amazed at how vivid and physical my memory is of playing the game, of just how easy it is to access the feeling I used to get playing the game, even without playing the game itself.

For instance, I'm writing this essay while watching a two-plus-hours-long playthrough of the *AVP* game on YouTube. The Atari Jaguar itself is long obsolete, though you can buy a probably functional Atari Jaguar online for around four hundred dollars if you really want one. There are no emulators for this generally unloved console. It sold fewer than 150,000 units. Compare that to its contemporary, the original PlayStation, which sold more than 100 million. Game-changing Super Nintendo (1990) sold around 50 million in a much smaller video game market. PlayStation 2 (2000) remains the all-time best seller, with 155 million units.

An old copy of *Alien vs. Predator* can be purchased for around fifty dollars. Hooking it up to a contemporary television is possible but nontrivial. LGIRA does not have it. So the experience of actually playing the game is pretty much inaccessible now unless you're a real obsessive, but five minutes into the YouTube stream I'm brought back viscerally to exactly what it felt like to play it in 1994.

That feeling is one of slow mystery and tension, whether you're human or Alien or Predator. It's a pretty rudimentary game with limited resources to work with, but the sound is well done and creates a lived-in atmospheric effect: as I walk through corridors and open doors I hear the slow churning of the engines, or maybe it's the low cyclic hum of the ventilation system. Maybe it's that empty mall feeling I'm getting with added Aliens and the occasional Predator. The sound changes as you play different creatures, since I guess they experience that sound differently, which is a cool verisimilitude. There's the sense of alien dread and the wonder of exploring a mysterious space. I get that in real life, from exploring the storm sewers of Tucson, for instance, which are remarkably like the video game dungeon corridors I remember creeping through as far back as *The Bard's Tale* (1985). Being in this state is a sublime experience: I can't recommend it enough. You don't need the processing power of the newest system to get it either; even *Larn* or *Rogue* on the 8-bit IBM

PC can do it if you first played those games when you were willing to do that work. It's the same feeling I used to get accessing a system I wasn't supposed to be in by wardialing and running through possible passwords, my modem singing its weird warbling song into the night.

Research shows that every time I access a memory, I reexperience it and I rewrite it in the context of the current story I'm telling myself about myself. This enriches it—makes it myth—and even though I feel as if by my writing about it I'm probably diminishing its truth a little, I can feel it growing in me. This is the point McAllister and Ruggill make: the game is preserved most strongly in the visceral, emotional memory of playing it, not by trying to save the ROM or trying to preserve the crappy plastic cartridges these games came on. That's a losing battle anyway, as they well know in the Transitional Office Building.

I began to get the feeling that there may be something to this idea of preservation in memory.

Cocooning vs. Killing

Each species starts in its own distinct area: the Alien base, the Predator ship, and the Colonial Marine barracks. You creep around and try to kill the other two before you are killed yourself, a familiar interaction to anyone who's played video games since 1994. As the Alien, you cocoon the bodies of whatever you kill so as to spawn more Aliens and eventually overrun everything. The instructions are brief: "Queen is gone . . . Find Queen . . . Rescue . . . Cocoons vital to survival . . . Cocoon enemy with claw-tail-claw . . ." For the Predator, the humans are beside the point: "Claim the Skull of the Alien Queen. Attack when visible to gain honor and points. Lose points by killing without honor. Points gain access to superior weapons." As the underdog, the humans have to kill the Aliens *and* the Predator, which is a lot harder, but at least there are a lot of humans and at least they all have guns. The only civilians in the game are already dead, so you don't have to tell the difference between the two.

As the Alien, I remember the cocooning, how you can quickly spawn more of your species, and how the game quickly starts to become littered with the cocooned bodies of the Colonial Marines. I think they even persist after you leave an area. This is one of the mechanics I'm most interested in, how nearly all games let you forget how many other creatures you've killed. In most of these sorts of games the killing is the point—it's a way to solve a problem (how to get by X and Y) and a way of keeping score. But we rarely encounter the residual effects of all that killing. What if every time we returned to this crossroads we saw the bodies piled up of all the marauders we'd killed before? How many bodies do there need to be before we start to wonder what it is we're doing?

That kind of thinking is rarely fun for humans, so we rarely have to do it.

Brian Tomasik, a philosopher, ethicist, and author of *Essays on Reducing Suffering*, thinks about these kinds of questions all the time. He's written thoughtfully about whether it's moral to kill non-player characters in games. You can read more on his website reducing-suffering.org, but in short, killing an NPC in any video game you might be playing is of very little consequence, as you'd expect, but because of the sheer number of people killing NPCs in video games all day, every day, for years, these kills add up. And the more complex NPC behaviors and preferences and goals are, the (very slightly) less moral it becomes to kill them because they are that much closer to being alive. Tomasik says in a 2014 interview, "On any given occasion [killing an NPC] is not a big deal, but aggregated over [time], it does begin to add up to something nontrivial. That said, I don't think violence toward video-game characters is currently among the world's most pressing ethical problems." Since 2014 the number of NPCs killed must have increased by several orders of magnitude. I wonder sometimes at what point this becomes a problem, and if so, whose. In the past week as I worked on this essay (November 9–16, 2021), America registered fourteen mass shootings in which sixteen people were killed and fifty-one were injured.

Killing "alien" NPCs bothers me less than killing "human" NPCs, but the Alien deaths in this game are more consequential. When the Aliens are killed their bodies also remain until you leave the area. When you walk on them as the Predator or the Colonial Marine it hurts you a little on account of the Aliens' acidic blood (which, if you've seen the movies, you know is powerful enough to eat through the hull of a ship).

I wonder whether it's better to remember these actions, or whether it's better to forget. Keep in mind that especially at the time, the Atari Jaguar was only working with two megabytes of RAM, so you had to balance out every mechanic you built into a game versus the amount of processing power and memory it took to execute it. Video game making, particularly in the first twenty years of the industry, was largely an art of seeing how much you could do with the hardware constraints on offer. So every decision like this, choosing to let the bodies persist, has its technological cost.

I think a lot about LGIRA and to what extent its ethos is a function of these same constraints.

And what about us, as the engines and loci of games' preservation? How much space does playing games take up in our memories? I'm always annoyed when a game expects me to remember some crucial early detail, like a code I found on a keycard, in order to open a later door, as if I'm playing with a journal at my side, penciling everything down as I run across it. That kind of memory work I do not find fun, but I remember the demand it placed on me and my annoyance every time I encountered it in, for instance, the later game *Alien: Isolation*. I also wonder, having played a lot of games in my life, how much memory games take up against demands on my hardware. Like how much memory do games take up versus how much memory books take up? Does every night I spend with *Outer Wilds* nudge out some bit of *Dubliners* or *Mrs. Dalloway*, and am I okay with that? Are there costs to the user of use as preservation? Sometimes I wonder if I should be cocooning others to try to distribute these processing loads across multiple minds and memories.

Is what I'm doing here—writing about the experience of this

memory—a cocooning of you the reader, or is it cutting through my own cocoon in hopes of getting out?

Alien vs. Alien vs. Alien vs. Alien

- Let's start with the very first *Alien* or *Predator* game: *Alien* for Atari 2600 (1982) is a *Pac-Man* knockoff that is not very good. Cheap cash-in for sure.
- *Alien* for C64 (1984) is a more tactical top-down simulation. Shows a little more imagination, but not a lot.
- *Aliens* for C64 and Apple II (1986) is a first-person shooter way before systems were up to the task. Ambitious but not very playable.
- *Aliens: Alien 2* for MSX (1987) is a side-scroller.
- *Predator* for Amstrad, C64, Spectrum, Atari ST, NES, and Amiga (1987–89) is a side-scrolling game similar to *Contra*. I'm not sure why you're just shooting birds for a sizable chunk of the game, however. Eventually you get to blast some guys, I suppose approximating the plot of the movie. It is not remotely scary.
- *Aliens* for Arcade (1990) is a shoot-'em-up in the style of the movie.
- *Predator 2* for PC and Amiga (1990) is a first-person-ish shooter where you're just blasting dudes. There are so many men shooting at you in this future version of LA! They shoot and shoot and do not seem to hit you, or if they do, just do a little damage. I love watching the bullet counts go down (one of my favorite features in one of the scenes you can only see in the extended cut of the *Aliens* film). Most of the game is just you shooting guys, with the Predator clearly visible in the background also killing guys, I think. It's like you're on a guy-killing team, though eventually you know you'll have to fight each other.
- *Predator 2* for Sega Genesis (1991 and 1992) is a very different kind of game based on the same movie property. It's kind

of like a more violent *Paperboy*, done in the isometric style. After you kill each helpfully identified "drug squad" and I guess free a hostage, they say "yeah" with a speech bubble. It also makes a "yeah" sound. It's very easy to forget this has anything to do with aliens or predators.

- *Alien 3* for Sega Genesis (1992) is a more sophisticated side-scroller prioritizing guns. The Aliens are very easy to kill.
- *Alien 3* for Game Boy (1993) is a top-down 2D.
- *Alien 3* for NES (1993) is also a side-scroller, as was the C64 version of this game, also in 1993. Who was still using a C64 in 1993? They also made a number of other versions of this game for the SNES and Sega Genesis.
- *Alien vs. Predator* for SNES (1993) is a *Double Dragon*–style fighting game that didn't make much of a dent then, and it doesn't make one now.
- *Alien vs. Predator: The Last of His Clan* for Game Boy (1993): I'm not sure what to make of this game, but it's cool to play the Predator here as a sympathetic character just fighting for his right to perpetuate his bloodline. Since all the humans are dead (as the game tells us), I'm not *all* that invested in what happens.
- *Alien 3: The Gun* for Arcade (1993) is a machine-gun-oriented first-person shooter, which, at least, like most of these FPSes, gives you that sense of wildly firing at on-coming Aliens. When you blast a facehugger (the second stage in the Aliens' life cycle, in which they have to attach themselves to a creature's face in order to reproduce in the host), and you blast a lot of them, they make kind of a wild yipping sound. This game is about the carnage.
- *AVP* for Arcade (1994) is a fighting game.
- *Alien vs. Predator* for Jaguar (1994) is probably the best in the first twenty years of either franchise, which is why I'm four thousand words deep into it.
- *Aliens: A Comic Book Adventure* for DOS (1995) is a point-and-clicker (it looks more like Windows than DOS to me),

a weird hybrid of different kinds of games that looks very annoying to play.

- *Alien Trilogy* for PS, Sega Saturn, DOS (1996) is a smoother FPS.
- *Aliens Online* for Windows (1998) is also an FPS, presumably an online multiplayer.
- *Aliens vs. Predator* for Windows and Mac (1999) you play as whichever of the three familiar competitors you want. It's got stronger graphics than we've seen so far but doesn't have a lot to add to the franchise. Maybe its only innovation is introducing the motion tracker mechanic that the movies got so, so right. It looks very playable.
- *Alien: Resurrection* for PS (2000) is a very similar-looking game with a little different narrative frame.
- *Aliens: Thanatos Encounter* for Game Boy Color (2001) is a weird top-downer. Looks kind of wonky and kind of cool, clearly limited by the system's capabilities. It turns out the music—or the lack thereof—really adds a lot to the experience. Compare the dorky chiptunes soundtracking your play here to the excellent ambient sounds of *AVP* from seven years earlier.
- *Aliens vs. Predator 2* for Windows/Mac (2001) is an FPS with a lot of Alien screeching.
- *Aliens vs. Predator 2: Primal Hunt* (2002) is more of the same with even more emphasis on the gore, which I suppose is something.
- *Aliens vs. Predator: Extinction* for PS2 (2003) is a top-down tactical/strategy game. It's cool to see the franchise taken in an *X-Com*-like direction. For some reason all the comments on the YouTube longplays are in Spanish.
- *Aliens: Unleashed* for Java (2003) is barely playable. This game super sucks. I mean I'm obviously not going to play every game on this here survey, and this is why.
- *Predator* for mobile phones (2004) is hard to find much information on, probably because it is a very bad game. But

you do get to hunt a lot of humans for no real reason except that they are there and they have a lot of guns. There's no pure footage of anyone playing this game I could find. When you complete each level, your score is based on the number of "Soldiers Killed" (three hundred in just one example I found), your "Skulls Bonus" (750), and so forth.

- *Predator: Concrete Jungle* for PS2 (2005) takes this idea and pushes it further. It's a fighting game in which you kill street thugs and drug guys and "fight crime," I guess, whatever that means, but you also kill cops, I mean future cops, and you skin them too. This is mostly set in 2030 and seems to be one of the more entertaining *Predator* games. I mean, all these games are pretty aggro, but this one pushes it harder than most.
- *Aliens: Extermination* for Arcade (2006) is another blast-'em-up that would probably be fun to play in the arcade with your kid.
- *AVP Requiem* for Java (2007) is a top-down strategy sim in which you play as the Aliens.
- *AVP Requiem* for PS Portable (2007) you play as the Predator, and it's pretty compelling. I guess every video game system generation has its own Aliens and its own Predator and finds a way to pit them against each other. Do not watch the *AVP: Requiem* movie, though. It's by far the worst one in either of the *Alien* or *Predator* series thus far.
- *Predator: The Duel* for Java (2008) is a platformer, but I couldn't figure out what you were dueling the whole time I was watching the playthrough.
- *Aliens: Crucible* for Windows, PS3, Xbox 360 (intended but canceled before release in 2009) is an FPS.
- *AVP* for PS3 XBOX (2010) has lovely graphics and seems like it makes good use of narrative. Its fire effects are fantastic. I spent a half hour watching a playthrough in German.
- *Predator or Prey* for online (2010) is one of the very few games on this list I could not find evidence of anywhere.

Perhaps because its title is so ungoogleable it has simply disappeared.

- *Predators* for iPhone and Android (2010) leans into your pedatory instincts in an isometric way. You hunt humans through "24 levels of killing frenzy." The trailer tells us that "collecting heads unlocks new weapons and sharpens your skills," but this is definitely not canon.

- *Predators: The Great Hunt for* mobile/Java (2010) is a dumb *Mortal Kombat* sort of adaptation. It seems like the 2010 movie *Predators* (which is pretty good) spawned a ton of weak games.

- *Aliens: Infestation* for Nintendo DS (2011) is a fun-looking side-scroller.

- *Aliens: Colonial Marines* for PS3 Xbox (2013) is definitely an *Aliens*-y FPS.

- *Aliens vs. Predator: Evolution* for Android/iOS (2013) does a lot with the phone OS, though it's mostly a fighting game. It really likes its DOUBLE! and TRIPLE KILLS! It is also really invested in its equipment upgrades to a dumb degree, like you can unlock Praetorian's Tip Razor Whip, Lifescythe Razor Whip, and Shiucutter Razor Whip, which gives you an idea of where we are here. The more I read about this game (in one of the few reviews I could find online) the weirder it got: "In this game you will see that on a distant planet there is a blood feud between two clans the Predators. This feud leads to a final attempt to eradicate the Jungle Hunter Clan. The Super Predators secure the capabilities of the Aliens. As an alien, you will have to destroy the Super Predator clan in order to get freedom from Slavery. And if you play as a Super Predator then you have to kill the Alien queen so that it prevents the Super Predators from Extinction." As the first movie said, whoever wins, we lose. I assume we end up just whipping one another with our supercool whips. I hope that goes on forever.

- *Aliens: Armageddon* for Arcade (2014) is a shoot-'em-up. Stop me if you've heard this one before.
- *Alien: Isolation* for PS3 and Xbox 360 (2014) is great, full stop. It's certainly the best iteration of any of the *Alien* games. In my view it's nearly on a par with the original film. I mean it's really good, largely because you're not a jacked-up Marine or a Predator or an Alien. You're a human, a scared human, just a human, and a lot of the game is spent running and hiding. But it gets the atmosphere of the movie just right. All this broken analog future buttressed by treacherous corporations feels very of the moment too. If you have to play one game other than *AVP* for Jaguar, this is the one.
- *Mortal Kombat XL—Alien vs. Predator* for PS4, etc. (2016) is exactly as dumb as it sounds and probably also as fun. Those things rhyme for a reason.
- *Aliens vs. Pinball* for consoles (2016) is pleasantly a virtual pinball machine!
- *Alien Covenant in Utero* for Oculus Rift (2017) looks pretty weird, beginning in utero, as the title suggests, with you playing first-person as a baby Alien. I would play this game but no way am I buying an Oculus Rift and entering Zuckerberg's Metaverse.
- *Alien Covenant* for Arcade (2017) is a fun blaster.
- *Alien: Offworld Colony Simulator* for Amazon Alexa (2018) is a weirdly wireframed first-person simulator that looks pretty fun.
- *Predator VR* for Arcade (2018) is a pretty tough watch, since the twitchy camera's always moving, and the game is kind of based on the 1987 *Predator* movie, which at first is really cool, but mostly it ends up as yet another FPS in which you're blasting other humans when you play as a human. As usual, the real jam is playing as Predator, which is, I have to say, pretty compelling if you can take that much camera movement.

- *Alien: Blackout* for Android/iOS (2019) I can't quite tell what it is: Are you ordering the team about and watching them through the security cams?
- *Predator: Hunting Grounds* for PC/consoles (2020) may be "dumb fun" as one review suggests, but as it's only playable in groups, not solo, I can't confirm that yet.

Deep breath. That's fifty. It's a lot of Aliens and quite a few Predators, which are also, of course, aliens. Imagine how many NPC aliens and predators and humans get shot or sliced or cut or blasted or burned in the course of all these games. How many times do the players' characters die?

America vs. Jaguar

There are many fewer jaguars in life than aliens or Predators in games. The Atari Jaguar is extinct in the wild, just as the wild jaguar nearly is in America. In 2009, Macho B, the last confirmed American wild jaguar, was killed accidentally about an hour away from my home by— to put it conservatively—idiocy at the hands of Arizona Game and Fish. Maybe *hubris* is the better word, as the cover-up after his death revealed: he'd been lured and trapped intentionally, on the wrong side of the border, a victim of the struggle over the multi-million-dollar grants that would come with study for the border fence that George W. Bush had approved. As in the movie *Predator*, the work the agency did was officially unapproved, clandestine, and deniable. The players were expendable, disavowed, and fired. Prosecuted, actually. One was convicted. The other was not. At least they were not hunted down and shot. Or not yet.

Have I ever seen a jaguar? Certainly not in the wild. I would have remembered that. Encounters with animals in the wild, while rare and getting rarer, are memorable. I can still remember the speckle pattern of all three Gila monsters I've seen, and I remember the cadence of the bear I saw last summer in Michigan loping across the road. It's possible I may have seen a jaguar in a zoo, but that encounter wasn't enough to leave a memory trace. Is seeing an animal in captivity similar to playing an old game on an emulator? Is playing a game in its native environment a wild encounter? And what does it mean exactly that the only jaguar I can remember was made by Atari?

Twelve years later there are signs that wild jaguars might return: two young ones, El Jefe and Sombra, have been sighted in the Sonoran borderlands on motion-detecting trail cams. I watch them move on YouTube. It remains unclear if or how far north they will range into America, or what that will mean if they do.

Game vs. Time

Why can I remember so little about the *time* I spent playing *Alien vs. Predator*? I can locate it in time by looking it up, and I can locate it in space if I do some math. I remember what it felt like to play it, but I don't remember what it felt like to be me playing it, what it felt like to be with my friends playing it. You couldn't actually play *against* your friends in it. This wasn't *Goldeneye* or *Quake*. Though we had 1993's *Doom*, we'd have to wait a couple more years for the technology to mature to make that kind of co-op or deathmatch play possible for most of us.

It may be I can't remember because 1994 was a transitional year for me. I was serving out the terms of my probation after being convicted of computer crimes as a sixteen-year-old, after a half decade of phone phreaking and hacking, operating a bulletin board system that I unsubtly called Datacrime International, and breaking into banks and credit bureaus and extracting credit card numbers for my friends to use to order shitty Detroit pizza or go see Ozzy Osbourne fail to bite the head off bats in concert. These weren't wise crimes, but they were fun crimes, and they culminated with a memory of opening my dorm room at boarding school to find a mound of all my possessions on the floor, with a copy of the search warrant left on top like a cherry. I never got my computers back. As a result of my probation I was allowed to use computers only "for good," according to the judge. That didn't apply to video game systems, and I didn't have one anyway, nor did I have a computer during this time in my life, on account of I was not allowed to. I was finishing up a year at the local college, since my admissions to other schools had been rescinded, and was not on great terms with my family. I was coming off a year or two of Prozac and therapy, and this was before I found myself at my new college and moved away from the computer science world, the direction I had assumed for years that I was likely heading. I mean to say my life was in a solid shambles at the time, so maybe my memory is hazy on account of self-protection. I wasn't who I used to be, and I wasn't who I was becoming either. I was in self-gestation mode, both cocooning and being cocooned. Because *Alien vs. Predator* took me out of myself so fully, it makes sense that I remember more game than self that year.

Alien vs. Scale

If you zoom out a little from the screen, though, what you would see is a handful of guys around nineteen. They don't know that much about the world, but they know some things about helplessness and grief. They know some things about cold and meaninglessness and how hard it is, they think, to really make an impact in the world. They know some things about each other and about themselves, though not nearly as much as they think they know, which has got them into trouble and will continue to get them into trouble. They think they will be friends forever. A few of them will still be friends twenty years on. All of them will still *be*, twenty years on, at least, but others they know but do not often talk about will not. One of their mothers would die by suicide a year or two from then. Another had died twelve years before, not by suicide but of cancer. Another friend had almost died making a homemade bomb. Another's dad would die by suicide another fifteen years on. Another dad died by suicide six years before. Everything dies, baby, that's a fact, including seemingly unkillable creatures like the Alien and the Predator. All of them would (will) die eventually, taking all of these memories with them. I mean *us* is what I mean by *them*. Look at my POV slipping this late in the essay. It might be a bug or a function of decay.

Human vs. Aliens vs. Predator

Playing as a human—a hot Marine manlily named Lance J. Lewis—
mostly involves furiously backing up as the aliens charge at you, firing
at them, and hoping that you land enough shots to kill them before
they kill you. It's about seeing the bodies of so many other humans
laid out in front of you as you roam the levels and wondering what the
point of this endeavor is. It's reassuring to be doing what you end up
doing in pretty much every other first-person shooter, which is shooting and reloading, shooting and reloading, collecting weapons and
ammunition, killing before you're killed. It's a conventional game,
if also a tense one. The sway of the gun barrel in front of you as you
move gives you a sense of much-needed swagger, outclassed as you are
among such aliens.

Playing as a human becomes a game of collection. Shotgun rounds
collected. Food collected. Medkit collected. Pulse Rifle rounds collected. Security card #03 collected. Collecting is central to many of
my passions: I collect for pleasure. But here you collect to survive.
The Aliens collect for reproduction only. The Predator collects too. It
keeps skulls as trophies. It seems to be having the most fun, which is
probably why it's most fun to play as it. After all, it doesn't *have* to be
here. This isn't about survival. It's about *sport*.

What is fun is the Alien area, with its labial doorways, its green-
and-black palette, its gooey strands of whatever, its weird reptilian
wall textures. For an early game, the design is well done. It's weird
enough to convey the alienness. The Predator area is similarly distinc-
tive, if a little less so on account of there being less Predator decor on
offer to work with from the movies. Its yellow-and-brown tie-dye-
looking textures gives the impression of being inside some kind of
psychedelic animal ship or a college dorm room circa 1995.

Essay vs. Memory

I'm not sure if memory is use or preservation. I mean, who am I kidding? It's both. But where are my memories of actual human interaction

from this time? Of connection with my friends? We played the game together, I remember, at least a few of us huddling together in the dark. We spent a lot of time playing it and doing other stuff together, only some of which was breaking the law. At least this wasn't. When an alien pounced from behind an airlock door we all jumped, didn't we? I haven't asked my friends about what, if anything, they remember of that game, of that time. Maybe I should. I remember us jumping, echoing one another in the darkness. I assume it was winter, since it is almost always winter in my memory in Michigan. But that could be the wall of one memory letting something else in. It can't always have been winter. For at least a couple of months it was summer there, too, as I reconfirmed when I was up there last July with my wife and daughter.

My wife has never been one for video games, though my daughter definitely is. Living through a pandemic may have accelerated her initiation into the life of screens, but I think it was inevitable, on account of her dad. Sometimes I feel a sense of guilt about her love for games, how many hours she's put into playing *Outer Wilds*, a game she's a bit too young for but that she loves with her whole heart regardless. But then I play them with her too. Together we found the Vessel. We located and landed on the Quantum Moon. It led us to an encounter I don't want to give away if you haven't played it, and again to another one with the great expansion: *Echoes of the Eye*. Playing together, the two of us reached the eye of the universe. When that game ended I wept. I think she did too.

She talks about the world of *Outer Wilds* all the time now. Driving her to school, she wants me to be an alien: a Nomai or a Stranger. She plays the Hearthian or the Prisoner. We act these stories out over and over, expanding on them and reinscribing them every time. I don't think I'm giving too much away by telling you this.

She tells me I can only buy the next generation PlayStation if she can still play *Outer Wilds* on it. For the moment she can, since PS5s are backward compatible to the PS4, but with the next generation that won't be the case, and a couple more iterations and soon enough *Outer Wilds* will be as hard to find and play as *Alien vs. Predator*, more easily accessed by memory than by technology.

Except: memory is a technology, isn't it? The way memory works in *Outer Wilds* is essential to your experience of the game, in which you repeat the same twenty-two minutes a hundred or more times. In the game, and in my life, memory collapses time. It collects it. You'll have to play the game to see how it works exactly. I mean, I know eventually time takes everything—consoles, emulators, trail cameras, aliens, Predators, all of it. But until then at least we have memory, in which we and games are stored.

Recently my daughter got super into watching me play *Alien: Isolation*, one of the pretty recent titles in the Aliens list above. It's a great game, a throwback to the tense analog horror of the original movie, though it's definitely not okay for kids. In spite of that, what she *really* liked was when I would not just let her watch me play and get spindled by an alien, but when I would occasionally let her play my characters herself. She'd run me around in an insufficiently stealthy fashion until the Alien found and grabbed me and stabbed me through the heart or eyes with its whippy tail or its face within a face. When I died it was spectacular. Then she would laugh and laugh and laugh, and demand that we repeat it. This is a secret my wife doesn't know about—until perhaps this sentence, if she's reading it. In fact until this paragraph this scene only exists in memory: my daughter's and my own.

VIDEO GAME BOSS

BY MARINAOMI

2002 > I HAD RECENTLY RE-ENTERED THE VIDEO GAME INDUSTRY AFTER A BRIEF HIATUS. THINGS WERE NOT GOING WELL.

ANXIETY LONG COMMUTE

EXISTENTIAL DREAD

I'D COME A LONG WAY TO GET HERE, BATTLING MISOGYNY AS I FOUGHT TO GAIN FOOTING.

I WORKED MY WAY UP FROM TESTER JOBS...

1994

Hey, Mari. Hey, Mari. Hey.

MENU BUTT-

...TO ADMIN POSITIONS...

You're not a guy.

Your opinion doesn't matter.

I GOT TURNED DOWN FOR ART AND DESIGN JOBS...

The hiring manager doesn't think its a good environment for a woman.

...AND FINALLY LANDED A LOCALIZATION PRODUCER JOB MAKING GAMES FOR THE SEGA DREAMCAST.

1999

DREAM COME TRUE!

AS A LIFE-LONG GAMER, I WANTED GAMES TO BE MORE GIRL-FRIENDLY, AS THAT WAS A DEMOGRAPHIC THAT HAD BEEN ACTIVELY IGNORED BY THE U.S. MARKET. AT SEGA, I COULD FINALLY MAKE A DIFFERENCE.

> SPACE CHANNEL 5 <

Hey there, space cat!

The Japanese wrote you sweet and giggly, but in the American game I'll make you cool and confident.

Groovy!

> SEAMAN <

Sure, you can be offensive, but I won't make you a misogynist.

I appreciate it.

BUT IT WOULDN'T LAST. A COUPLE OF YEARS LATER, DROWNING IN DEBT, I WAS LURED AWAY FROM MY DREAM JOB BY A HIGH-PAYING START-UP.

I can't match their offer, Mari.

If only you'd asked for more when we offered you this job...

Damn.

WHEN THE TECH BUBBLE BURST, I WAS OUT OF A JOB AND SEGA COULDN'T TAKE ME BACK. NOR WAS THERE WORK ANYWHERE ELSE, IT SEEMED, SO WHEN A PAL REACHED OUT TO ME, IT FELT LIKE A MIRACLE.

It's a producer position reporting to a woman boss.

Very cool!

We're all fans of you here at Spamco.*

* NAME CHANGED BECAUSE

UNFORTUNATELY, MY NEW BOSS WAS NOT VERY COOL. NOR WAS SHE A FAN OF ME.

You need to get through this game faster.

I'm trying, but it keeps on crashing—

NO EXCUSES!

Why does she pick on me? She's nice to all the guys.

I HAD BEEN COMMENDED FOR MY HARD WORK AT MY PREVIOUS JOBS. HER CONSTANT DISAPPOINTMENT IN ME WAS DEVASTATING. NOTHING I DID MADE HER HAPPY.

EVEN WORSE, WE DIDN'T SHARE SIMILAR OBJECTIVES.

We ought to remove the sex scene between the grown man and the little girl.

Relax, they're just robots.

Have you still not gotten past that level??

I don't understand how you got this job.

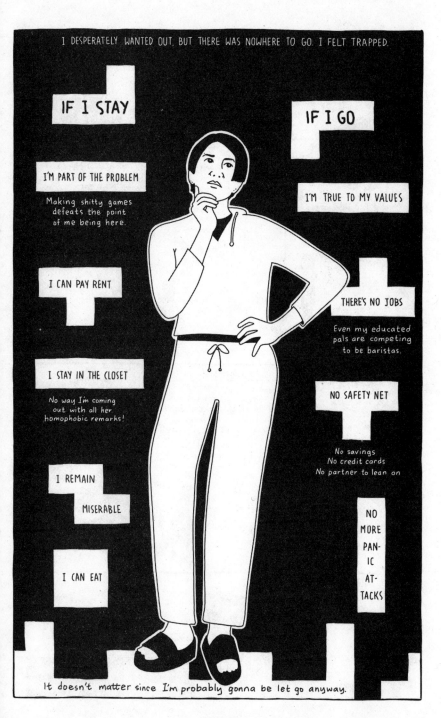

In the Shadow of the Wolf

VANESSA VILLARREAL

> I lay in dark and dreaming sleep while countless wars and ages
> passed; I woke still weak a year before I joined you. . . . I will save
> the elven people. Even if it means this world must die.
>
> —SOLAS/FEN'HAREL, *DRAGON AGE: INQUISITION TRESPASSER DLC*

The Dread Wolf Fenrir, son of the trickster god Loki, lies in wait beneath the earth, bound by a magical rope. According to Norse mythology, Odin bound the wolf, who is prophesied to appear at the dawn of Ragnarök, the cosmic battle of the gods against invaders at the end of the world. When the long winter comes and all humanity is at war, the black wolf will break loose of his bondage, and with fire streaming from his eyes and nostrils and his jaws open from earth to sky, he will devour everything in his path and swallow the sun, moon, and stars. The mountains will crumble and the oceans will rise to drown the world, until nothing is left but the void, ending the cosmos, the gods, and all human memory of what once was.

But before all of this, Fenrir bites off the hand of the Norse god Tyr.

I had not connected the Inquisitor's severed arm at the end of *Dragon Age: Inquisition*'s *Trespasser DLC* to Sigurd's severed arm in *Assassin's Creed Valhalla* until recently, when I finished both games back-to-back. It's too specific an amputation to be a coincidence, with too-specific circumstances—both the Inquisitor and Sigurd lose their arm to an apocalyptic wolf. In *DAI*, elf mage Solas—trusted companion, friend, and, in my case, lover—turns out to be the ancient trickster god Fen'Harel, or the Dread Wolf of elven lore who sabotages the Inquisition and, with a final kiss, disintegrates your arm. In *AC Valhalla*, siblings Eivor and Sigurd are led astray by Basim, leading to the loss of Sigurd's arm, echoing the loss of his arm to the wolf Fenrir in his former life as the Norse god Tyr. (It's a long story—the siblings are also Norse gods; we'll get to that in a minute.) But the similarities don't end there: Both Solas/Fen'Harel and Sigurd/Tyr are dual characters who are revealed to be gods, repeating their fates in their human lives; both are from races or cultures oppressed by a monotheistic empire. And both games—crucially—draw from the myth of Ragnarök as an allegory for a race war at the brink of apocalypse and extinction.

Please, Follow Me to My Normal Viking Conspiracy Wall

Historical high fantasy in earthy, medieval settings might be my favorite genre of visual storytelling. When done well, it can bring us back to the elements, be a refuge from the crises of modernity, and clarify a confusing world by reforging our problems with simplicity and possibility, centering friendship, self-discovery, and coming together to vanquish a great evil. But it can also be a haven for reactionary politics, which is why I've long been troubled by the turn to Vikings in popular culture and media. Historical Vikings themselves are not the issue—what is troubling is *why* they're back, what deeper political rumblings their return might signal, and what myths endure in our present racial imaginaries. It's alarming to see the blond, blue-eyed, all-powerful white Viking warrior archetype in media produced for mass consumption. I'm disturbed by ahistorical depictions of Vikings as a white ethnic group, and the investment in maintaining that myth with all-white casts. Viking contact with North American indigenous people in Greenland has a delicate history, and I wonder about how depictions of Vikings' tribalized whiteness enable fantasies of white indigeneity to be rendered as historical.

Vikings have long been a site of white projection, most recently to provide a convenient historical precedent to claim Black and indigenous cultural practices, from wearing locs and braids to dressing as shamans in animal skins. And while I appreciate textured, attentive representations of historical Viking dress, body modification, material culture, and lore, I worry about how fantasies of white indigeneity supplant the stories of Native American and indigenous people, who continue to be starkly underrepresented and reduced to crude stereotypes in media. Beyond all this, I wonder about fantasy's preoccupation with Ragnarök—the cataclysmic end of the cosmos, memory, and the gods—and its variations on apocalyptic urgency, reimagined as the Long Night, the Wild Hunt, the Eternal Winter, and so on.

And it's not just in *Dragon Age: Inquisition* and *Assassin's Creed Valhalla*—these are simply two massively popular games among many. Here is a short list of Viking- and Norse-mythology-themed media properties from the last fifteen years: *Dragon Age*, *Assassin's Creed*, *Frozen*, *God of War*, *Valheim*, *Hellblade*, *Game of Thrones* ("The Long Night"), *The Witcher* (Skellige and Ragh-nar-Roog), *Thor*, *The Last Kingdom*, *Norsemen*, *The Northman*, *How to Train Your Dragon*, *Vikings*, and its recent Netflix spin-off *Vikings: Valhalla*.

Why do Vikings and Ragnarök dominate twenty-first-century cultural production? What drives the demand for them, and what anxieties do they reflect about our own world? These things were all connected, but I couldn't grasp how. Until the severed arm.

Nordicism, the nineteenth-century theory of racial hierarchy that would serve as the prototype to the Aryanism of the Nazis, marks the evolution of white supremacy from "biological fact" to social-moral imperative. Arthur de Gobineau's *An Essay on the Inequality of the Human Races* (1853) posits that Nordics—hardened by the severe mountains and harsh winters of the North—are the superior race, defined by their whiteness, intelligence, natural leadership, and grit. For Gobineau, only the blond Germanic Nordics, purest of Aryans, could be leaders of the world, and when Aryans diluted their blood through interracial mixing with the so-called lower races, it brought about the "downfall of civilizations." (Nordicism is exclusive to Anglo-Saxon and Germanic peoples, however. Groups that have survived generations in even more extreme conditions, such as Tibet, Siberia, or Inuit lands, supposedly lack the correct ancestry.) According to Gobineau, Mediterranean and Southern Europeans cannot count as Aryan, because of their racial admixtures with North African and Semitic populations.

Nordicism is still going strong in our racial imaginaries, though—at its most benign, it appears in our praise of Sweden's education system, Norway's health care and bike lanes, the "progressive" politics of Scandinavian countries and their off-grid co-ops. At its worst, Nordicism is codified in our policies that place no restrictions on immigration from Scandinavian and Northern European countries, and in our media, which reinforce the notion that Nordic, Germanic, and Anglo-Saxon people are "good" immigrants and assets to our country, and that people from the Global South are dangerous strains on the economy. Nordicism is a primary racial logic of white supremacy in the Western world; its ideas are so standard, so deeply ingrained they're foundational to the concept of white American identity and heritage, which reproduces itself in our national imaginaries, which shape our collective futures. America's long history of ethnic cleansing and eugenics projects—from Jim Crow to the Chinese Exclusion Act to Operation Wetback to Indian boarding schools to the mass sterilization of Black, Latina, and indigenous women—reflects attempts to shape that future, motivated by the imagined threat to whiteness. As the "border surges" and "immigrant caravans" and "woke-ification" of our time threaten whiteness, the very core of American identity, what better hero than a Viking to defend it?

"Wait, Am *I* the Drama?"— Historical Vikings Just Finding Out They're White

The grand irony is that Vikings could not possibly be homogeneously white. Vikings and related Norse Germanic tribes lived between the ninth and eleventh centuries, predating the invention of race by more than five hundred years. They would not understand the concepts of whiteness, Blackness, indigeneity, Orientalism, etc., and would there-fore have no "whiteness" or "purity" to maintain.

Instead, Vikings were among the most culturally heterogeneous, ethnically mixed populations in antiquity. As explorers, raiders, and pirates, they survived by pillaging other lands, kidnapping brides and children along every known coast. Archaeological findings show that early Vikings thrived precisely *because* of their ability to trade and in-tegrate a wide range of cultures, spanning the Northern Hemisphere all the way down to Africa. It was only in the seventeenth century in Western Europe that the emerging sciences began the colonial proj-ect of classifying ethnic groups into racial hierarchies, constructing European whiteness as the physical and intellectual ideal. Although the Vikings were long gone by then, the myth of the pure white Viking as the symbolic European ancestor took hold in the racial imaginary. The Viking represented the physical and social ideals of whiteness and masculinity—intrepid explorer, conqueror, warrior, symbol of seafaring expeditions and discovery—and thus became the archetype used to justify colonial domination as the inherent nature of white people and, therefore, white supremacy as a scien-tific fact.

"To be white is to be a striver, a crusader, an explorer, and a con-queror," said Richard Spencer, American neo-Nazi and ideologue of the alt-right, in a speech upon the election of Donald Trump. "We build, we produce, we go upward. . . . For us, it is conquer or die. This is a unique burden for the white man, that our fate is entirely in our hands. And it is appropriate because within us, within the very blood in our veins as children of the sun, lies the potential for greatness."

In January 2018, just months after the Unite the Right rally in Charlottesville, where white men gathered with tiki torches to cry out, "You will not replace us," Donald Trump stated that while immigrants from affluent European nations such as Norway or Sweden were wel-come in the United States, immigrants from "shithole countries" such as Haiti and El Salvador were not. "Why do we need more Haitians?" he said. "Take them out." This anti-immigrant, ethno-nationalist language would escalate in the following months to his calling immigrants "animals" and vermin who "infest" the country.

In 2019, white men in El Paso, Texas, and Gilroy, California, carried out mass shootings, with both citing the "invasion of Hispanics" and "hordes of mestizos," or mixed-race Latines, as their targets. The El Paso shooter wrote a manifesto espousing replacement theory: the myth that white men are being replaced by minorities at the dawn of a mass white extinction. On the day of the shooting, the Gilroy shooter posted a photo of a Smokey Bear fire warning sign instructing his followers to read *Might Is Right*—a fascist manifesto from the late nineteenth century by an author calling himself Ragnar Redbeard, who viewed the pure white Viking as the pillar of strength on which great nations are built.

Texts like *Might Is Right* are shared often on 4chan, a massive gaming network and nexus of radicalization. Users post neo-Nazi propaganda, white supremacist misinformation, and misogynistic memes, sometimes going so far as to organize alt-right demonstrations and instigate acts of violence. Both the El Paso and the Gilroy shooter copied language from the widely shared manifesto of the New Zealand Christchurch shooter—who livestreamed his assault on Facebook in the style of a first-person shooter video game—which closed with, "I will see you in Valhalla." In 2022, a copycat shooting in Buffalo, New York—which explicitly targeted Black people—was streamed on Twitch, a gaming videochat platform, until it was quickly removed. The shooter's gun and armor were covered in Norse symbols, such as the Sonnenrad (Black Sun) and the Othala rune. The connective tissue of these mass shootings is the alt-right, gaming, and Viking imagery and symbolism.

Cut to the January 6th Capitol Insurrection, where the QAnon Shaman, bare-chested in Party City Viking cosplay, displayed three Odinist tattoos any white supremacist would recognize as dog whistles—Mjolnir, or Thor's Hammer; Yggdrasil, or the Tree of Life; and, over his heart, a valknut, or three interlocked triangles representing the "knot of the slain," a runic symbol sometimes interpreted as indicating a willingness to die as a warrior in Odin's army at

Ragnarök. While the three symbols are not necessarily racist in every context, the mass use of Norse symbols at the Capitol Insurrection *was* the context.

The conception of Ragnarök as a modern-day race war is rooted in toxic masculinist fantasy. There is ample evidence that Dane settlements across Europe assimilated peacefully into agrarian life and converted to Christianity of their own will. But for the rising alt-right, Ragnarök is a convenient metaphor for waging war against the white apocalypse—the invasion of nonwhite others that will bring about white extinction and the downfall of American civilization.

And this is historically when the Viking has been resurrected—when white supremacy is threatened by social change.

Rewind to 2011: President Obama is completing his first term and campaigning for the second, a presidency that will serve as the catalyst for the backlash of the Trump era. That same year, *Thor* is released in theaters; *Skyrim* redefines fantasy role-playing video games; while on television, *Game of Thrones* airs its first season and is catapulted to overnight success. *Vikings* will also begin production in 2011. Since then, the Viking has reemerged in full force, Disneyfied, even yassified,[1] stripped of explicit white supremacist associations while fulfilling a deeply reactionary cultural response to a changing world.

Lord of the Races

Race is not just part of world building in fantasy. It *is* the world.

J. R. R. Tolkien's *The Lord of the Rings* and *The Silmarillion* borrow heavily from the creatures and worlds of Norse mythology—Middle-earth is based on Midgard, Mordor on Muspelheim, and so

---

1. Take Chris Hemsworth and Tom Hiddleston—Thor and Loki, respectively—of the Marvel pantheon of Viking gods. Although Heimdall and Valkyrie are played by Black actors, Thor and Loki's features tell an older story: Thor is blond, blue-eyed, handsome, muscular, true to his word, and so morally upright he is worthy enough to wield Mjolnir, the lightning hammer; Loki is pale, with a large nose and greasy, slicked-back, black hair, and constantly goes back on his word to betray Thor, going so far as to ally with Thanos to bring about the extinction of half the universe.

on. But Tolkien applied a twentieth-century lens to a ninth-century cosmology—what were once Yggdrasil's "creatures" (dwarves, elves, humans, giants) Tolkien called "races," each with particular physical and moral characteristics: Elves are fair and intuitive, Dwarves are ruddy and proud, Hobbits are earthy farming folk, and Orcs—black-skinned, socially dead, corrupted—are an unpaid labor force representing a great evil.

Race is so foundational to Tolkien's world building that even Galadriel's opening monologue for the film adaptation of *Lord of the Rings* (2001) establishes race as the frame for the story (emphasis mine):

The world is changed. . . . It began with the forging of the great rings. Three were given to the Elves, *immortal, wisest, and fairest of all beings*. Seven to the Dwarf lords, *great miners and craftsmen of the mountain halls*. And nine, nine rings were gifted to the *race* of Men, who above all else, *desire power*. For within these rings was bound the *strength and will to govern each race*. But they were all of them deceived, for another ring was made.

In Tolkien's time, the world *had* changed. Written between 1937 and 1949 during World War II, two years after Nazi Germany implemented the Nuremberg Race Laws and at the height of Nazi Aryanism, *LOTR* captured industrialization, war, and the rise of fascism in the Western postcolonial world. Race was not only the West's primary way of organizing the world; it was Nazi Germany's primary concern. Although Tolkien intended only to write a mythic retelling of Anglo-Saxon history and strongly denied that *The Lord of the Rings* was an allegory, Middle-earth—from its moral geographies (West good, East evil) to its races and their metaphors—is undeniably a reproduction of his Europe.

As the blueprint for "high fantasy" literature, *LOTR*'s racial allegories have endured, reproduced across the genre in books, role-playing games, video games, television, and film. In *LOTR*-inspired fantasy, race structures the social hierarchies, geographies, and conflicts of the world. It's even the first decision (race, gender, class) a player must make in creating a character for any campaign in the iconic *Dungeons & Dragons* role-playing games.

When done well, fantasy's core racial archetypes—elf, dwarf, man, hobbit, orc, to use Tolkien's schema—subvert their stereotypes to perform a more complex relationality, using difference to provoke difficult conversations about our world. At its best, it can act as a radical critique of the larger, more abstract politics of structural power. Done poorly, fantasy races merely replicate the racial logics of our world, reentrenching stereotypes through the reenactment of oppressive narratives. The reemergence of the Viking in popular media is often here to do the latter; not even the queerest, most diverse portrayals of Viking culture and Norse mythology—like *Assassin's Creed Valhalla* and *Dragon Age: Inquisition*—can improve upon this model. In fact, maybe they make it worse.

White Apocalypse: The Story We Keep Telling

First, quick recap of Ragnarök's story beats. The Norse gods have become arrogant, gluttonous, and tyrannical, at constant war with other realms. Odin, head of the Norse gods, is given the prophecy of Ragnarök, or "the doom of the gods"—a betrayal that would see a Dread Wolf bring about the fall of Asgard, realm of the supreme Æsir gods, and, as a result, the end of all creation. In an attempt to cheat fate and prevent Ragnarök, Odin issues a decree to kill all the wolves. But as it turns out, one of the wolf pups is Loki's son Fenrir, a mongrel and abomination he sired with the giantess Angrboða, an enemy Jötunn and mother of monsters. Loki begs Odin not to kill his son, so Odin agrees, leaving the pup to be raised by Tyr while Odin devises a plan to tie the black wolf into a state of unbreakable bondage. By the time he returns with the magic rope, Fenrir has grown to a terrifying size. He doubts Odin will not try to bind him, so Tyr places his hand in Fenrir's mouth as an oath that the wolf would not be bound. Odin tricks both of them and binds Fenrir anyway, causing Tyr to lose his hand to the beast. Once bound, Fenrir will remain hidden in a deep cave until Loki breaches Heimdall's gate to the rainbow bridge (literally a border patrol checkpoint), allowing all kinds of giants and sea monsters into the highest, most guarded gated community of Asgard. After Fenrir breaks loose and the tides rise and swallow the earth, Loki leads a caravan of ships invading from the lower realms, steering the ship carrying Muspells, black lava-giants from the fiery South. The Norse gods refuse defeat and wage war against their fate, only to fall to the loosed wolf Fenrir, a mixed-race abomination out of bondage come to end all creation.

Although Odin loves Loki, the Æsir clan has never trusted the trickster god, depicted throughout history as a dark-haired, Semitic-coded outsider who shape-shifts and deceives, and will eventually sabotage Asgard from within.

The original myth of Ragnarök is a cautionary tale against arrogance, and sees extinction as cosmic fate, urging those who would fight it to accept defeat and instead live fully, knowing it will all be gone soon. In our time, however, Ragnarök has become an allegory for the coming race war, and a rallying cry against white genocide. As it is read today, it is a warning not to trust racialized outsiders, who will infiltrate the promised land, conspire with other outsiders, and bring about the downfall of civilization and extinction.

"We must secure the existence of our people and a future for white children." These are the Fourteen Words, the slogan coined by David Eden Lane, a member of the domestic terrorist group known as the Order. The saying reflects the core anxiety at the heart of white supremacist readings of Ragnarök: "Unless immediate action is taken, the white race is doomed to extinction by an alleged 'rising tide of color' purportedly controlled and manipulated by Jews."[2]

Every aspect of Ragnarök seems to resonate with white supremacist fear—Loki as the Semitic infiltrator whose conspiracy with other races leads to Ragnarök; Loki as impure and interbreeding with other races; Loki at the helm of the warship leading the invasion from the South; Loki's son Fenrir as an abomination and evidence that racial mixing brings about the downfall of civilizations;

2. This language is from the website of the Anti-Defamation League.

the literal rising tide of outsiders and monsters invading the realm of the superior gods.

It is important to note that the myth of Ragnarök predates the invention of race and was never written as a race war allegory. It's just impossible to disentangle it from that reading on this side of history.

Assassin's Creed Valhalla: Odinism with Pronouns

The world's mythologies and their gods are a foundational part of *Assassin's Creed* lore. Long ago, the Isu—a prehistoric race of demigods—bred with humans, creating the Tainted Ones, superhumans with Isu bloodlines who pass down extraordinary abilities generation to generation and eventually become the Assassins. That's how we are able to play as Assassins in the game—the Isu-tinged Assassin DNA has a third helix, which creates a detailed simulation of history from collective memory stored in genetic material, accessible through a machine called the Animus, allowing users to relive their ancestors' memories.

Here's the problem: The idea of the Isu seems to be inspired by the idea of Root Races—a key concept in Theosophy, which is a form of pseudoscientific mysticism that originated at the beginning of the twentieth century. According to this theory, seven root races span the course of human evolution: Lemurian, Atlantean, Aryan, and so on. While Root Race Theory did not define any of the root races by skin color (its theories were more mystical interpretations of archaeological findings of prehistoric humans), its belief in a white variation of the Aryan root race, which evolved from the Atlanteans and became the Nordic-Germanic peoples, allowed the Nazis to establish a "scientific" basis for their idea of a racially pure master race with a direct lineage to Atlantis. The Aryan root race, co-opted by the Nazis as an ethnonationalist racial identity, became a white supremacist concept forever linked to Nordicism and eugenics.

In the *Assassin's Creed* universe, the Isu ancestors of the Assassins fit a little too closely with the *bad* reading of Root Race Theory. In *Assassin's Creed Odyssey*, set in ancient Greece, the Isu are a race of Atlanteans, and ancestors of the assassin Kassandra, who is human.

At face value this is harmless, until we look at the next game, *Valhalla*, which focuses on the assassin Eivor, who is not a descendant of the Isu but rather *is* the Viking god Odin in human form. This is where it becomes not so harmless: If the Greek Isu are Atlanteans, the fourth Root Race, that makes the Viking Isu the fifth Root Race, which is none other than—you guessed it—Aryans.

In past games, the Isu are the good-time gods of the Greek and Roman pantheon—Juno, Minerva, and Poseidon, depicted as ten feet tall with glowing armor and exaggerated features—and *ancestors* of the Assassins. Crucially, the Isu are a prehistoric race and Assassins are humans, who flat out say *they are not gods*. In *Valhalla*, however, Eivor, Sigurd, and other human characters are literally reincarnated gods. Unlike the Isu of previous games, the Norse gods of Asgard are not physically different from humans—instead, they *are* human, and look exactly like Eivor and Sigurd, the main characters of the game.

It is unclear why *Assassin's Creed Valhalla* breaks with the Tainted Ones storyline, but doing so unlinks Eivor from being related to other Assassins. Eivor is not an Assassin because they are a mixed-race descendant of the Isu god Odin—instead, Eivor *is* Odin reincarnated, both human *and* god and the recipient of Odin's memories. Eivor's blood is not "tainted," which means that they have no shared lineage with Bayek, the first Assassin, a Black Egyptian Medjay and founder of the Hidden Ones, the secret brotherhood of Assassins. This implies that the Norse gods never went extinct, and that Norse humans—unlike any other culture in the *Assassin's Creed* universe—are so genetically pure that some *are* gods who innately possess superhuman abilities. So long as they maintain their purity, being Norse is superhuman enough for the gods to reincarnate in them. That's a major deviation, and a meaningful one.

As if the "Vikings are literally gods because of racial purity" angle wasn't bad enough, somehow the politics of *Assassin's Creed Valhalla* get even worse. The story begins in Norway, until circumstances force siblings Eivor and Sigurd to set out and form their own colony in England. Once they arrive, they must grow their settlement, which requires the player to raid monasteries over and over throughout the game. The raids are play sequences with their own soundtracks and indulgently violent animations—aesthetically rich, culturally precise, intense, and rewarding, so well designed that they can even become fun, implicating the player in a kind of Brechtian moral bind. What does it mean to raid and burn down monasteries for reward? The raiding imagery and music calls back to the Norwegian church burnings of the nineties, when black metal musicians and neopagan heathens burned down medieval churches in protest, claiming that the Norwegian people were brainwashed by the Abrahamic religions and had forgotten their pagan gods. Modern-day Odinists and alt-right ethnonationalists still target temples, churches, and mosques today. Many gamers don't know this history, and yet by raiding the monasteries they are enacting these sublimated white supremacist themes.

I don't believe the *Assassin's Creed* developers mean to advance white supremacist views. In fact, I think they aim to refute them with accurate history—in the game, Black and Asian people live in Viking settlements, reflecting a more historically accurate medieval Europe. Our protagonist Eivor is canonically female but can be played as either gender and is referred to with they/them pronouns. They can have romances with any gender, as any gender. Their brother Sigurd (Tyr) is a Viking explorer who, early in the game, returns from a diplomatic expedition having made contact with many lands and traded with "people of all colors," bringing back gifts and people from all over the known world willing to settle among the Norse. To add to its credit, the developers took great care in designing a historical depiction of Vinland, the Viking name for the Americas, consulting indigenous language experts to write untranslated dialogue and voice its inhabitants. The Norse gods are also not depicted in the best light— they are excessive, proud, and boastful, and Valhalla, the great hall of fallen warriors, is a nightmare. Eivor often ignores Odin's counsel encouraging violence and domination, asserting their will over Odin's control. Although the reincarnation of the gods is a central narrative pillar, Eivor's story is ultimately one of leaving Valhalla, refusing to be tied to Odin. By reclaiming their soul from Odin's grip, Eivor severs their fate from Odin's fate, thereby ending the Æsirs' reincarnation loophole and liberating themselves from the cycles of violence that killed their parents and displaced their clan. It's a beautiful story, and a beautiful game.

Still, there is the problem of Basim, the mysterious, silk-tongued Assassin who returns with Sigurd from Constantinople. Basim is part of the Levantine Brotherhood of Assassins, and is also implied to be Muslim—a heavily racialized character against the backdrop of Vikings in medieval England, voiced by an actor who affects a vaguely Arabic accent. Despite Basim's being an outsider, Sigurd brings him into the Raven clan and treats him as a brother, much like Odin does Loki. Although Basim becomes a friend who trains Eivor in stealth assassin techniques and gifts them with the Assassin's blade, it is difficult to read Basim's intentions or know where his loyalties lie. It is a constant tension throughout the game—who is he; how much does he know; is he helping or luring Eivor and Sigurd toward danger? He turns out to be the game's principal villain—the reincarnation of Loki seeking Odin in medieval times to avenge his son Fenrir. Basim betrays Eivor and Sigurd in this life just as he did in Asgard, and just as Loki conspired with the lower realms to bring about Asgard's downfall, Basim's foreignness and connections to shadowy global networks are what make him dangerous. His ability to shape-shift—to move between worlds, play both sides, deceive, infiltrate, sabotage, and ultimately invade—represent the imagined threat all racialized outsiders pose to whiteness. Loki is only able to reincarnate into Basim[3] because he tricks his way into Odin's memory upload device. Basim/Loki's role as a racialized infiltrator, conspirator, traitor, and apocalypse bringer reinforces an age-old, deeply harmful anti-Semitic trope—that of the global Jewish conspiracy—that finds new life in every generation, and continues to fuel white supremacist conspiracy theories today.

On the surface, it may seem that Viking stories are an attempt to seek an authentic reconnection to European culture, but the ubiquity of Viking narratives implies a deeper cultural desire: the return of

---

3. Wild that Ygdrassil would choose to reincarnate Odin and Tyr as white and Loki as Levantine.

white male dominance, free from colonial baggage or accountability. White men are attracted to Viking narratives because they allow them to imagine themselves as both the victors and victims of history, both superhuman conquerors *and* oppressed rebels fighting against Christianity and empire. The Viking predates settler colonialism, and is therefore a representation of whiteness exempt from the racial reckonings of the past ten years—Black Lives Matter, responses to global migrant crises, abolitionist and decolonization movements—that attempt to hold white people accountable for their history. The Viking is a symbol of masculinity and aggression, but also extinction, and in our current political moment, it captures the rage of white men in social decline.

But perhaps *Assassin's Creed Valhalla* and other Ragnarök narratives speak to a different but related anxiety—of history repeating itself. The United States is just 247 years old; the Viking Age only lasted 273 years, between 793 and 1066 AD. The Vikings could not continue to raid and plunder as a way of life. In order to survive, they faced an existential choice: adapt, or die. Perhaps *Assassin's Creed Valhalla* is an old story reincarnated to help us learn from our mistakes.

There is no denying, though, that white supremacy is in the very DNA of Norse mythology and Odinism, and just as Odin can upload and reincarnate his memories into new bodies, so too can white men upload white supremacy into Viking narratives; so too can the gamer download white supremacist programming by consuming those narratives and embodying Eivor, the genetically superior Viking god, not just as an Assassin but as a vessel for his rage. It is up to the gamer what path he chooses with the material of Eivor's story—radical inclusion or reactionary aggression.

"I'm Really Sad, Therefore Everyone Must Die"—Solas, Probably

In *Dragon Age: Inquisition*, the events leading up to its Ragnarök are a bit more ethically and emotionally complex. An evil mage has torn a gash in reality called the Breach, allowing demons to come through from the spirit realm (the Fade) into the realm of the living. You, the Inquisitor, spend the majority of the game politically uniting the realms and their races, only to find out that one disgruntled white elf supremacist you thought was your friend has been plotting against you the whole time in order to eradicate all the other races but his and also to end the world.

Throughout the game, the rebel elven mage Solas is one of your primary allies until he disappears without a word, only to be revealed at the final cutscene as Fen'Harel, or the Dread Wolf, ancient elven trickster god. (Cue me, screaming and crying and throwing up.)

Solas only helped you because he means to restore Elvhenan, the magical prehistoric civilization of the elves, by ending the world for everyone else. Was he a megalomaniacal villain all along, or is he just a lost elf, bent on self-destruction?

The lore of the elves in the *Dragon Age* universe could fill an entire literature course, but for the purposes of this essay, suffice it to say that the elves are an allegory for both slavery and indigenous dispossession, once a great civilization connected to the land, now estranged from it and each other and cut off from their immortality, memories, and magic. Those who maintain ties to what's left of elven culture are called the Dalish, are identifiable by their facial tattoos, and live in nomadic tribes in the wilderness; those who choose to sever ties are city elves and live in alienages—marginal settlements for the magically oppressed. Although the elves are the most oppressed race, like Tolkien's elves they are mostly all pale-white, and maintain an impossibly ethereal, delicate physicality as tall, thin, graceful, intuitive creatures. Despite their rarity and magic, they are reviled rather than revered, and are a labor class who suffer constant racism, exploitation, and sexual fetishization.

In *Dragon Age: Inquisition*, the player can choose from four races: an aristocratic human, an exiled dwarf, an "exotic" Qunari (I know, that's another essay), or a Dalish elf. The *Dragon Age* games, especially *Inquisition*, have been widely praised for their inclusive representations of race, gender, and queer sexualities and romance storylines, as well as their robust avatar-building tool, where the player can construct their Inquisitor's features and race to the most precise, delicate degree.[4] In the *DAI* universe, skin color does not define race—only magical race is acknowledged.

In post-Tolkien high fantasy, however, elves cannot be disentangled from colonial history, which inscribes their whiteness with meaning. The elves of *DAI* are still derived from Tolkien's elves and from Norse mythology, described as demigods and luminous beings "more beautiful than the sun," who are earthly prototypes for the Æsir gods of Asgard. They are "of the purest white," as if "lit from within," although originally not in the racial sense. Their ancient genetic purity is what makes them immortal, telepathic, wise, and superior to all races, vulnerable to "fading" if they stay among humans too long. They are seen as a noble race going extinct as humans rise to power and corrupt the world.

So although the elves of *Dragon Age: Inquisition* are a colonized, dispossessed, and enslaved race, Solas and the elves are still based in Norse mythology and its symbolic systems, written as allegories for racial purity and superiority. Despite their colonial subjugation at the hands of empire, they can never be understood as allegories for indigenous or Black people, but as whiteness imagining its own extinction. The fantasy of white genocide is the desire to possess Black and indigenous histories of subjugation, where whiteness imagines its own history inflicted upon itself—a kind of reverse colonialism, where experiences of enslavement and colonial dispossession are imagined in white bodies. But those histories can never be possessed, not even in fantasy—when whiteness imagines its own subjugation, it is always in the context of apocalypse, where liberation means everyone must die. Ragnarök.

Before the events of *Dragon Age: Inquisition*, Solas—then the god Fen'Harel—lived in the Ancient age, when Elvhenan, the immortal elven civilization, existed as a kind of Eden, or a version of the world

---

4. It's worth it to add that *Dragon Age: Inquisition* was released in late 2014, before the HB2 North Carolina bathroom bill of 2016, and in the character customization menu, trans women can choose an Adam's apple for their female character—a subtle but meaningful option the developers could have left out or restricted only to male characters.

unified with the realm of the spirit. Fen'Harel grew disgusted with the elf gods when, in their quest for power, they began enslaving their own people. To save the elven people, Fen'Harel created the Veil between the mortal realm and the spirit realm, and banished the elven gods forever. This required such a huge amount of power and will that he fell into a deep slumber. Humans rose to power, and the elves became mortal and disconnected from their magic. Since then, nine ages, or thousands of years, have passed, bringing us to the Dragon Age, when Fen'Harel wakes up. Elvhenan has been renamed Thedas, and a mono-theistic religion reigns. Fen'Harel, now Solas, has to live in a terrifying world nearly devoid of magic, where subjugated elves do not remember their splendor, and all collective memory has been lost, surviving only in ruins and lost relics. The elves who did not die from human illnesses have been conquered and enslaved by humans.

Incognito as a common rebel mage, Solas joins the Inquisition to ul-timately fix his "great mistake"—the creation of the Veil—and restore Elvhenan. Tearing down the Veil between Thedas and the Fade is an apocalyptic plan, however—doing so would be like breaking Solomon's seal and opening the gates of hell, liberating demons that would effec-tively end the world for *everyone*. But that is Solas's fatal flaw: his noble intentions make love into a destructive force, and his hubris makes him unable to foresee the consequences of his actions.

But Solas is less like Odin or Thor and more like Loki, the outsider god. In the story of Ragnarök, Loki represents the "other" in the race war, the leader of the invaders who will topple the white supremacy of Asgard. Like Loki, Solas betrays the gods in retaliation for their tyr-anny. And just as Loki conspires with the Muspell fire-giants of Norse mythology, so too does Solas join forces with the shadowy Qunari, a horned, silvery, dark-skinned race known for its espionage and strict, militaristic, "backward" culture, outsiders who mean to breach the borders and take down the empire.

Throughout the story, there are moments that complicate our under-standing of Solas's motivations and resonate as postcolonial critique. Operating from a place of great sorrow, Solas is always acting on behalf of the elves' liberation and survival. He is an embodiment of ancient memory and a repository of arcane knowledge, which he recovers by crossing the Veil and sleeping in elven ruins, dreaming their history in an effort to record and restore what was lost. Whatever your relationship with Solas (it can easily go sour), he is also an archivist, painting heroic murals of your actions as the Inquisitor. If your Inquisitor is a female elf and in a romance with Solas (I was—11/10, highly recommend), he takes you to a beautiful waterfall at night and informs you that your facial tattoos, the Vallaslin, are actually slave markings, not gifts from the old gods, and offers to delicately, lovingly remove them with magic before mysteriously dumping you. Tortured, brilliant, unknowable, and ever-maligned as a duplicitous trickster god, Solas can be read as a tragic antihero who only sabotages and betrays those he loves because he is always opposed to the abuse of power, willing to sacrifice the world for the elves in order to restore Elvhenan and give the land back to its original people.

A very complicated, decolonial, genocidal boyfriend.

Solas ghosts you at the end of *Dragon Age: Inquisition* and we don't see him again until the very end of the *Trespasser DLC*. First, you must navigate a complex conspiracy and chase him through an interdimensional realm of mirrors, broken bridges (isn't that every situationship?), elven ruins, and a structure called the Shattered Library—floating half rooms of deteriorating books and records documenting lost elven science, poetry, great romances, and heroes. As you maneuver through the entropy of elven memory, you see the world as Solas does—already broken and lost to the fathoms of time.

Memory is a central theme in *Dragon Age: Inquisition*, if not its main battleground. One of the final quests in the base game is to find the Well of Sorrows, a fountain deep in a ruined elven temple that contains all the collective knowledge and memories of the ancient elves in its waters. The ruin is guarded by ancient elven sentinels—strong, graceful elves who have protected the well since the fall of Elvhenan, headed by an elf named Abelas, whose name is elven for "sorrow." These elves have witnessed violence and atrocity at the hands of men across the ages, as well as the deterioration of elven culture and the magic of Elvhenan. But they do not identify with the elves of Thedas nor seek to help them, and only allow you, the Inquisitor, to access the well in order to be freed from the heavy burden of remembering.

This quest hits different: I'm a descendant of indigenous Mexican farm workers on both sides of my family, and my history and indigeneity have been totally obliterated, with no surviving records I can use to trace back to my tribes. I remember indigenous members of my family and retain some of their healing rituals, but after they died, no record of their medicines, knowledge, or lineage survives. I feel myself ever disappearing into whiteness as time goes on, and would give anything to restore the path back to my ancestors. Solas's anxiety over restoring elven memory is recognizable to me as a kind of postcolonial haunting. He must watch as human mages study the elven history their kind obliterated, becoming self-proclaimed experts in elven ruins, language, and artifacts in order to appropriate elven magic. I get Solas, and his rage.

When you finally reunite with Solas at the end of *Trespasser*, the once slight and nerdy mage is now a gleaming god, elegant in smoky opal elven sentinel armor, wolf fur draped over his shoulder, solemn and resolute in his goals. Solas has had a glow-up, and now that he looks better than ever, he's going to break your heart *again*. Solas says, "I suspect you have questions," and delivers this monologue:

> I sought to set my people free
> from slavery to would-be gods;
> I broke the chains of all who wished to join me.
> The false gods called me Fen'Harel,
> and when they finally went too far
> I formed the Veil and banished them forever.
>
> Thus I freed the
> elven people,
> and in so doing
> destroyed their world.

. . .

I lay in dark and dreaming sleep
while countless wars and ages passed;
I woke still weak a year before I joined you.
My people fell for what I did
to strike the Evanuris down
but still some hope remains for restoration.

I will save the elven people.
Even if it means this world must die.

Those iambs, though! Solas, unmasked as the Dread Wolf Fen'harel, has become Fenrir, the wolf that brings on Ragnarök, and the consequence of a god's impossible love, who can liberate only through betrayal. This is how Solas loves the elven people, and loves the Inquisitor (only if in a romance—if not, he's a pretty clear-cut villain)—destructively. His deception is painful but necessary, although his feelings are real: "I would not have lain with you under false pretenses." (I am *bereft*.) The Inquisitor begs him to change his mind, but with a heavy heart and deep sorrow—"*Ir abelas, vhenan*," or, *I'm sorry, my heart*—he refuses to end his genocidal plan. And so with a final kiss, he cuts off her arm. (It's complicated—just know it was a kindness.) "*Solas, var lath vir suledin!*" the Inquisitor begs. *Our love will find a way to endure!*

Big "I can fix him" energy. Can he be redeemed? Find out in *Dragon Age 4: Dreadwolf*, coming in 2023!

Solas will return, and while it looks like he will again be the Big Bad, the likelihood of a redemption arc is unclear. The Solas-Inquisitor romance (Solavellan, if you want to spend hours browsing fan fiction and erotic fan art, not that I have) is the most popular romance in *Dragon Age: Inquisition*, with its tragic, star-crossed-lovers storyline complicating the finality of Solas's Ragnarök plot. The Inquisitor, the woman he loves, is an elf who stands for the cooperation of all races, all lands, all realms in the fight against tyrannical evil, and allows him to imagine another kind of future, consider another way to survive.

But Solas's romantic standards do raise an eyebrow. Of all the romanceable characters in *DAI*, Solas, a straight white male elf, is the only character with rigid racial and heterosexual desires: female elf only. Every other character is open to other races and sexualities. Solas's sexual preferences could be read as racist, but as an elf—a fetishized, oppressed race—his desirability politics are murkier. Does Solas not mix races in an effort to preserve his elven racial purity? Or is it because Solas is a god that he does not mix with mortals? However you read his romantic preferences depends on how you want to read Solas—genocidal villain or rebel liberator.

There's also the problem of elven slavery as a metaphor. In *Scenes of Subjection*, Saidiya Hartman writes that slavery is incomprehensible; it is such an unintelligible, unfathomable violence that it can never be represented or understood. No attempt to represent slavery—neither explicit depictions of violence and brutality, nor revenge fantasies—can capture or convey the material, bodily, lived, generational suffering of slavery, and to try is to indulge a desire to consume and possess Black pain. Representations of slavery meant to inspire empathy require the white viewer to imagine Black suffering as their own, resulting in a slippery empathy that exists only when Black suffering is visible and intelligible on a white body. This is why representations of white enslavement are dangerous: they do not increase empathy for Black descendants of the enslaved, but rather allow white people to imagine themselves as slaves.

Even in fantasy worlds where skin color is neutralized and race is magical and metaphorical, fantasy races function within the same racial imaginaries as our world, just abstracted and distanced from history. Without a historicized racial context, the enslavement of white elves has no proximity to colonial violence, and therefore cannot motivate a politics of liberation. Instead, it validates white reactionary rage.

In *Dragon Age: Inquisition*, slavery is the narrative device that justifies Solas's genocide, framed as a kind of retributive, decolonial apocalypse. Is Solas's destruction of the Veil a revolutionary act of liberation and justice for the elves? Or is he an arrogant, tyrannical god, always acting on behalf of others without their consent, working from an ideology of elven supremacy? The only thing that saves Solas's campaign from fascistic vibes is ultimately his *magical* race, lacking structural, institutional, and political power. That, and love.

What If the End Is Actually the Beginning

So we're back at the severed arm. How do they connect? *Dragon Age: Inquisition: Trespasser DLC*'s and *Assassin's Creed Valhalla*'s respective visions of fantasy use the same repository of images from the same Norse and Viking symbolic systems: wolves, gods, apocalypses, whiteness, race, severed arms. But despite their efforts to rehabilitate those systems, they end up in the same place with the same problematic implications: Ragnarök, or the race war at the end of the world.

Viking stories are often about fighting extinction, with extinction defined as the physical obliteration of a people. This is a difference between stories told from the perspective of the dominant culture and those told from a colonized or lost culture: extinction is the obliteration not just of a people but of memory, the shared cosmos of knowledge systems, language, gods, myths, and culture of creation—forcibly lost to the history of invaders.

What's unique and tragic about both of these games is how clearly *AC Valhalla* and *Dragon Age: Inquisition* worked really, really hard not to be racist, sexist, or homophobic, and went to great lengths to attempt radical inclusion. Ubisoft's disclaimer before all *Assassin's Creed* games has evolved and expanded its scope over time, from *This work of fiction was designed, developed, and produced by a multicultural team of various religious faiths and beliefs* to . . . *various beliefs, sexual orientations, and gender identities*. They are really trying! And still, just by virtue of its mythology, its history, how that history is situated in the present, who it engages, and what its racial imaginaries motivate, these games easily lend themselves to white supremacist interpretations.

If the stories we tell about the past are really the stories we are telling about the present, then the fact that Norse mythology and Vikings and European monarchs and British accents maintain such a stronghold on fantasy is *already* a racial conversation, and should be critiqued on its implications. (And the absence of such critiques accounts for the length of this essay!) As the white-dominant mono-culture of the twentieth century fades and content diversifies around smaller, more niche audiences, historical fantasy remains one of the last "universal" genres—code for default whiteness in a Western European setting—and one of the last holdouts employing all-white casts. In traditional fantasy, whiteness is canonical, a standard set in the source material, and therefore exempt from critique. But this is changing, in baby steps. The first phase has been to diversify characters and casts, with some attempts more successful than others. The recent back-lash against the "woke" casting of actors of color in shows like *The Witcher* and Amazon's *Lord of the Rings: The Rings of Power* goes to show that fantasy is one of the last, unspoken realms of white domi-nance, ripe for radical new visions. The next phase will perhaps de-center the West.

In some versions of Ragnarök, after Fenrir consumes the sun, the ruins of the world will sink into the sea and nothing will be left but the void, the end of all creation. Other versions imagine a lush, green world emerging from the waters, healed and repeopled by survivors who strive for life. Odin's obsession with his own extinction was rooted in ego and arrogance all along—as it turns out, the end of the world is ultimately a failure of the imagination.

"We've already survived an apocalypse," says Rebecca Roanhorse, Black and indigenous author of science fiction novel *Black Sun*, in the *New York Times*. "I set [my book] in the future specifically so I could say hey, Natives exist, and we'll exist in the future." What fu-ture does the survivor imagine when the end of the world has already happened? Fantasy has long been ready for narratives that transcend the limitations of white, Western, European history, whose timeline will always end in apocalypse and violence. "Whose fantasy" becomes a question of "whose imagination," and what characters, geographies, and histories that entails.

I desperately want to see fantasy and video games from different re-lationships to history, and different relationships to empire. *The Witcher* books and games, written by Polish author Andrzej Sapkowski follow-ing the fall of the Berlin Wall and the end of the Cold War, are just one example of how folktales from countries with histories of colonization, enslavement, pogroms, and genocide, decentered from Western European narrative conventions, breathe new life into high fantasy. What if lost mythologies and suppressed sagas from the Global South were to be given the budget of an *Assassin's Creed* triple-A game? What kind of histories and futures could Black and indigenous fantasy help us imagine? Fantasy, after all, is the space of the imaginary, and the imaginaries we collectively engage create our futures. Rather than resurrect and relive oppressive European colonial histories, why not spend time with people who have survived that history, and can evolve our sense of collective possibility? What other heroes can save us from these new monsters? And if we change our imaginaries, what are our stories capable of? What do they make capable in us?

Clash Rules Everything Around Me

TONY TULATHIMUTTE

Something in my pocket is killing me: a suckling tick, a phone-borne horde of barbarians. Have you played *Clash of Clans*? It's a mobile strategy game in which you cultivate a base of tiny soldiers to destroy other people's bases of tiny soldiers. Released in 2012 by the company Supercell in Helsinki, which puts the Viking pillage mechanics into some kind of approximate cultural context, it's free to download and nominally free to play—yet as of 2018 had the highest revenue of any app on Apple's App Store: $6.4 billion, $9 million of which went toward a Super Bowl commercial starring Liam Neeson.

I want to talk about how this happens, but right now I'm busy playing *Clash*. Would you like to see my base? Here, flea-sized people teem around in an isometric village, in shades of nuclear green, concrete gray, mustard yellow, and turd brown. Little tunic-clad builders swing teensy hammers at scaffolded barracks, while info bubbles importune me to brew spells, research upgrades, and collect resources. Every tap of the screen brings on a new funny plip or jackpot chime or orchestra hit. My defenses are a mix of military industriousness and high fantasy: house-sized mortars, pink-haired archers in flak helmets, wizards poised atop mountains ready to send fireballs streaking from their fingers. My wealth is housed in enormous bins of gold doubloons and globes of magenta elixir. I will spend it all today and get it all back again tomorrow.

Clash isn't especially addictive (I know what *that* looks like), but it puts me in constant low-grade anxiety. Is my shield depleting? Are my builders idle? Which upgrades do I pursue? It is a persistent itch that's pleasurable to scratch. Every fifteen minutes or so a notification informs me that my troops are ready for battle, or that my village was wiped out by someone called "dank nuggs" or "rektum." The threat of invasion from other players is constant, as is the opportunity to invade them; a "Revenge" button appears after someone attacks you. Pressing your fingertip to the battlefield makes a gush of wriggling troops surge out, absorbing bombardments from the enemy's defenses. Your troops either get wiped out or successfully raze your enemy's base; the more total the destruction, the greater the spoils of gold, elixir, trophies, and sadistic glee.

Not everyone is your enemy. You can create or join clans of players, enabling you to request reinforcements and battle other clans. Little distinguishes one clan from another besides stats and names, names like Pinoy Guns, $DA BEASTS$, BLOOD FOR WAR. In an aspirational mood, I searched for any clans called "Happiness," but they were all either empty or invite-only. Clan Prestige kicked me out immediately; Clan Friendship kicked me out for donating weak troops; Clan Love communicated mostly in Arabic. So I stayed awhile in the dead-silent Clan Maturity, left a week later for Clan Corgi Butts, and ended up where I always suspected I belonged: in the Trash Clan. Never mind—everyone is your enemy.

Clash belongs to the "resource management" subgenre of strategy games, which are descended from *SimCity*, *Starcraft*, and *XCOM*, and which the likes of *FarmVille* and *Tiny Tower* have networked and miniaturized. Resource management games have you balancing various types of currency and resources. Construction and warfare lead to more resources, which leads to more construction and warfare: *Clash*'s simplified mechanics boil the resources down to troops, gold, and elixir (read: oil—you extract it from the ground).

There is a trite-and-true political argument that's often made about such games: how they're capitalism simulators, models of military-industrial neoliberalism, ideologies encoded as entertainment—*SimCity* favors regressive taxes, while Molleindustria's *To Build a Better Mousetrap* demonstrates how automation and incarceration are used to exploit labor. In *Clash*, everything is military, purchasable, and replaceable; the battle reports tell you how many troops you "expended." Unlike other cartoon-style games, where characters are "knocked out" or "eliminated," there's no ambiguity about death. When killed, troops turn briefly into skeletons, then gravestones, and tapping on the gravestones converts them into elixir (read again: oil).

This capitalist angle gets a lot more interesting when you consider that *Clash*'s purpose is to extract the world's most important resource from its player base (now read: money). Gameplay largely involves waiting for things to finish building. If you don't want to wait, you spend. Gems allow you to bypass the wait times for constructions and upgrades, which ordinarily take hours, days, or even weeks to complete. The bright green color of grass, greed, and envy, gems can be earned a few at a time through gameplay but can be purchased with real money to the tune of $4.99 for 500, or up to $99.99 for a 14,000-gem war chest; each gem is worth somewhere between one and twenty minutes of time.

Once you've arranged your base—and there's no end to the possible arrangements—a typical session of base maintenance and raiding lasts about five minutes, and the wait times to train new troops enforce a limit on your gameplay; without gems it'll be another fifteen to thirty minutes before your army is ready for battle, and that will suit most casual players fine. On an online forum, one user calculated that it would take about 952 days—just over two and a half years—to fully upgrade your entire base (provided you have only one builder; more builders can be purchased with gems). He also figures that it'd take 343,000 gems to rush the whole thing, which comes out to roughly $2,450. Many of the top players are wealthy, disproportionately Middle Eastern folks who've spent upwards of $16,000 on the game; game developers call these high spenders "whales," and one Saudi whale in particular was rumored to have spouted over a million dollars on the game.

Clashing on the cheap imposes a discipline on your life. I like to start upgrades right before bedtime to exploit the natural eight-hour waiting period called sleep. One high-level player on YouTube stressed that the most important element of fully upgrading your base for free is scheduling. "Yes, you actually *do* have to do something in real life to farm a fully maxed-out base," he says, and continues:

> Can you clash at work? Can you clash at school? Do you have breaks? Are you your own boss? Do you have long periods of inactivity, just because that's what happens—can you raid there? The first thing you do when you wake up is you play *Clash*. . . . You can clash in the shower, on the toilet—not recommended, if you don't want to damage or get your phone dirty, but you can do that.

Not recommended, but also not hypothetical: the former no. 1–ranked player George Yao would bring five plastic-wrapped iPads into the shower with him to keep multiple *Clash* accounts going.

So the most interesting thing about *Clash* isn't how it's an allegory for late capitalism. (Isn't everything? Isn't that the point?) It's that *Clash* makes especially clear how interchangeable everything becomes under such a system, and how technology obscures transactions between real and virtual. *Time is life is work is play is death is money is property is time.* Like almost every game with a death mechanic, the true currency of *Clash* isn't virtual gold but actual time. Dying in a game forces you to waste your time trying again, "spending" part of your limited lifespan on a failed effort. Money can help you enjoy your time more, but there's no changing that every session brings you five minutes, a hundred thousand coins, and dozens of deaths closer to your death.

Anyone who grew up playing as many video games as I did wonders about the life they might've led if they'd learned to speak fluent Thai instead. When we call something a "waste of time," we usually mean something outside of the narrative of whatever you've called your real life, some menial and unproductive activity that doesn't amass wealth, deepen your relationships and quality of life, or improve you. Something that makes time pass without changing anything else. *Clash* lends itself to being played casually in captive or idle moments—train time and toilet time—and thus positions itself as a superior waste of time.

It is some wonder how a decades-old, $21 billion industry that outperforms Hollywood could still be considered culturally marginal, but there's no games critic at the *New Yorker*, is there? One can discern in mainstream game writing a common strain of anxiety, quick to reassure us either of gaming's artistic legitimacy and utility or else its corrupting effects (recall the "hand-eye coordination" vs. "Nintendonitis" think pieces of the nineties). Most efforts to make games respectable noisily advertise their seriousness: conferences and college degrees called Serious Play and Serious Games; or the irreverent theme of *Kill Screen* magazine's inaugural issue, *No Fun*.

All this defensiveness seems awfully unnecessary. These days, video games are a thirty-something with a steady job and a *New York Times* subscription. They're used mostly to entertain, but also to train surgeons, soldiers, and pilots, to alleviate pain in hospitalized children, to fundraise for charities; I can also personally attest that I achieved peak fitness from playing an hour of *Dance Dance Revolution* every day in college. (It wasn't worth it.) Games are just too broad to generalize about.

You wouldn't know this from watching TV or movies, though. It's always instructive to hear one medium's opinion of another, but it's especially interesting how TV and movies treat video games, given that the latter were until recently the whipping boys of culture. On film, a character playing video games alone is understood to signify that he—almost always "he"—is lazy, neglectful, depressed, antisocial, unambitious, and/or emotionally stunted. (A few games have cheekily internalized these archetypes—consider *Grand Theft Auto V*'s insufferable gamebro Jimmy De Santa, or *Uncharted 4*'s Nathan Drake, who dismisses the PlayStation as a "little TV game thing.") *House of Cards* stands as an exception: Frank Underwood demonstrates range, erudition, and hipness in his fondness for both *Call of Duty* and *Monument Valley*, though he also demonstrates multiple murders.

The suggestion is that all virtual life is an immersive escape fantasy, one in which your humdrum assigned existence is exchanged for other, more interesting, powerful, or liberated ones. This is no more true of *Clash* than it is of *Tetris*. As your village's Chief, you have no backstory or identity, your troops don't speak or have relationships with one another, and there is no motive to destroy other than destruction itself; your adviser, a concerned-looking brunette, is all business, and so are most of the other human players.

But more often, video games, in the way they structure our behavior and obtrude into our lives, are less escapes from reality than they are metaphors for it. If modern life often seems like it's about making money for large corporations just to pull in enough resources to buy things, collect experiences, form good connections, have fun, and improve yourself, all against a backdrop of nonstop worldwide violent conflict and plunder (especially in the Middle East), then *Clash* is more lifelike than life itself.

In that sense, it's not just a war simulator played on your phone but a success simulator played on your life, one whose achievements can be more consistently rewarding than what our suboptimal social reality offers. Is it at all surprising that some people would decide the play's the thing, and use their lives as resources for the game? "My day job was a means to an end, paying the bills, and my real life was the game," George Yao said of his career pinnacle. The more time, money, effort, and emotion you invest in the game, the less sense it makes to separate it from life—especially if the simulation theorists are right and we're all living in a more advanced civilization's video game anyway.

Nongamers never fail to be amused by people like Yao. Why spend dozens of hours chasing a rare armor set or decorating an in-game house when you could be grinding at work or achieving orgasm? Then again, why achieve orgasm? You expend all your sexual energy today and get it back tomorrow. The stuff of *Clash* may be intangible, but so is most wealth, not to mention status, relationships, accomplishments, and the concepts of God and the nation-state. The pleasure of games like *Clash* is not joy, excitement, or catharsis, and certainly not material gain. It's the steady drip of progression, of constantly gaining and spending currency. Like cultivating a bonsai, building your base is a means of externalizing self-improvement.

Though you lose battles quite often, in *Clash* there is no concept of loss. Destroyed buildings are rebuilt in seconds, troops can be replaced with identical ones in minutes, and stolen resources can be regained with a bit more killing. *Clash* guarantees that your property only improves; nothing ever breaks or obsolesces or depreciates. Upgrades are conspicuous, inviting you to compare your dingy stone walls with other players' purple crystal bulwarks, or your rickety wooden towers to another's iron parapets—here, luxury is not just power but military power. The only irreplaceable thing is the time you spend, the time you *kill*, playing it.

Maybe it is a waste of time. Yet many wastes of time are classified as meaningful work or enjoyable experience, despite seeming to me intuitively pointless: camping, going on walks, sitting at the beach, team sports, fishing, and having and raising children. Then again, I also think reading and writing fiction are wastes of time, and those are mostly what I do. If I were to mount a utilitarian defense, I could wax poetic about how games and novels offer vivid vicarious experiences and broaden your worldview by putting you in the minds and roles of other people, but that's disingenuous. I read and play games because I want to and nobody is making me stop.

The fact that people still *do* make utilitarian cases for art is a good example of people's need to rationalize their preferences. In a *Wired* profile, one wealthy "whale" reasoned that spending a thousand dollars a night on *Clash* actually saved him money, since he'd otherwise go out and spend six thousand dollars drinking with his buddies. I suspect this attitude has something to do with sunk cost and cognitive dissonance: you might stick to a particular activity because you don't want the hours and cash you've spent to "go to waste," which then encourages you to retroactively imbue that activity with all sorts of heavy meaning to assure yourself that your time was well spent. Compulsion gets reframed as passion, hobbies become identities, and life seems like something more than the process of becoming a beached whale.

Is calling myself a writer or gamer just a way of dignifying my habits? One reason the loser-gamer stereotype persists is precisely the notion that games are *easier* than reality—that people who play lots of them can't cope with the real world's challenges, risks, and uncertainties, and opt for the soft electric blanket of an impoverished simulation. Or they can't do human interaction and have to settle for the companionship of weak AI. Or they're addicts who lack imagination and purpose. Sounds good, except: games, especially online competitive ones, are way hard and failure-prone and full of tedious chores and complete assholes. Compulsive gaming is real enough, but there's a difference between simply preferring to spend your time gaming and being unable to stop, though not a mutually exclusive one. It's a lot easier to call gamers (or readers, or art lovers) weak-minded misfits than it is to countenance the idea that art, even bad art, is richer, deeper, more meaningful than what's available under certain shitty conditions of life: poverty, oppression, exclusion, illness, or even plain old distaste.

What I'm saying is, depending on what your life looks like, either *Clash* is as good a way to spend your time as any, or everything is equally a waste of time. At least enjoy wasting it.

The other day I had my blood drawn, and to distract from the needle I was reading Leonard Michaels's *Sylvia*. As the second vial was drawn I hit a scene just a few pages from the end where a major character dies, and the nurse started wiggling the needle in my arm, asking me to open and close my fist. "Nothing's coming out," she said. "It was coming out fast before, and now it's stopped." After a few more nauseating wiggles she withdrew the needle and told me she'd have to try the other arm.

When the needle went in again, my forehead went damp and my hearing cotton-balled; from somewhere I heard a shrill distorted remix of a Beach Boys song, then I came to with my clothes soaked, a pair of latex-gloved hands supporting my head by the mandible, and a nurse fanning me, saying, "You're waking up. You passed out. What's your name?"

My mouth replied, "Was I dead?"

They'd moved my book and glasses out of reach, and I was made to sit tight for half an hour, infantilized, sipping a cloying orange electrolyte solution and sitting in the phlebotomist's high chair with my legs elevated. I got bored immediately, annoyed that my stupid vasovagal reflex was eating into the time I could have spent at home playing video games instead of writing. I asked my nurse if there was anything I *was* allowed to do; she said I could use my phone. With ash-gray hands I took out my phone and went to war.

The Great Indoorsmen

ELEANOR HENDERSON

Black Friday, 2020. I showed up at my local GameStop at 5:30 in the morning for a 6:00 a.m. opening. Grumpy. Tired. It was dark, and a line of thirty people was already waiting ahead of me on the sidewalk in front of the strip mall. These were serious gamers, with folding chairs and beer cozies. Stupid, to think I could arrive so late. The Sony PlayStation 5 had been released two weeks before, and because of wild demand and supply chain issues, they were nearly impossible to find. I sipped coffee from my thermos while a fight broke out at the front of the line. Voices raised. Swearing. Cops were called; they arrived and subdued the fight. At 6:01 a.m., the weary teenage employee unlocked the door and handed out two vouchers to the first two people in line: that was the number of PS5s they had in stock. I got back into my car and drove home.

On Christmas morning, my two sons pretended not to be disappointed, and I pretended not to be relieved.

I wanted to report that I'd *tried* to obtain the PS5—I was at the store before the sun rose! Basically the greatest mom ever!—but I had not been totally sorry to be turned away from GameStop. I was disappointed with myself for participating in the capitalist tradition of Black Friday doorbuster madness, where the threat of not getting the chance to spend hundreds of dollars on a machine made of thermoplastic and silicone and metals that had been mined from some faraway mountain made Americans threaten bodily harm to their fellow citizens. What's more, I was painfully ambivalent about the dominant role of video games in my children's lives. I didn't want to have to decide whether to be the kind of mother who continued to enable their gaming habit. What was I teaching them about what was important? That it was worth spending your Saturday slaughtering zombies? Would they be any different from the other young white men, isolated and brainwashed, who committed acts of terrorism with AR-15s?

The failed acquisition of the PS5 felt like a tipping point, but it wasn't completely. My kids survived without the PS5 that year because they had plenty of other game systems already. It was dizzying to admit how many: a PS4 they had played so hard it now sounded like a helicopter taking off, a Nintendo 64, a Nintendo 3DS, a Nintendo Switch, a Game Cube, an Xbox One, and an Oculus Quest, as well as the dozens of Atari and Nintendo systems their father had collected since he was a teenager playing *Pac-Man* and *Paperboy* at arcades on the streets of the Lower East Side of New York.

I grew up on video games too. We had an Atari in the early 1980s, and my two older brothers sometimes let me play *Frogger* or *Donkey Kong* or *Pitfall*. It was electrifying. I remember the first time I heard the word Nintendo, as I jumped on our neighbor's trampoline in 1988. I heard it as "Intendo," and I intended to find out what the fuss was all about. I first played *Super Mario Bros.* when I was nine at my friend Andrea's house. I fell in love. She had brothers, too, but they weren't home: what a thrill, to spend the afternoon with a friend, no boys around to tell us it was their turn or we were doing it wrong, just hopping from block to bridge all day, squashing all the Goombas we wanted.

But we didn't stay inside all day when I was growing up. Christmas morning was spent riding your new bike in the street. We rode our bikes to the oak tree that had been lightninged in half, climbed it until our moms called us home for dinner. We built forts in the woods and played baseball in the backyard and football in the front. In the summers, we stayed in a cabin with no indoor plumbing and swam and canoed and pitfalled into the lake from actual rope swings. The flickering screen of *Mario* (of course, the way to show you knew how to fix the flicker was to carefully blow into the game cartridge as though into a delicate wind instrument) was for rainy days. We took real risks, leapt from real branches. My cousin injured the palm of the same hand three times—a wood stove, a fishing hook, and, in the barn when we were visiting, a BB shot by his brother. Even my husband rode his skateboard to the arcade.

My sons, Nico (thirteen) and Henry (ten), have barely had a scratch. They are proud indoorsmen. In the summer, they opt for the media arts camp, making stop-motion videos, while their friends go to basketball camp, swimming camp, camp camp. My kids don't play video games the way I used to, for an hour here or there. They live there, in their digital reality, and occasionally they visit the reality I live in.

Actually, Nico has had a scratch. Henry once cracked a PlayStation controller across his brother's eyebrow, drawing blood.

Nico was three years old when he beat *Lego Batman* on the Wii. Like, the whole game. His tiny fingers were barely big enough to grasp the controller. But as he grew, and as his tastes evolved with his increasingly advanced graphics cards, his hands and his brain grew around games. His muscles, his synapses, began to fire in megahertz and teraflops. With the alphabet, he also learned the language of gaming. His childhood might be best cataloged through his Christmas and birthday lists, which were always penned months in advance and marked by the titles whose release dates he'd memorized: *Disney Infinity*, *Skylander*, *Lego Marvel Super Heroes*, *Minecraft*, *Fortnite*, among many, many more. Then, as he polished his skills of negotiation, the M-for-Mature games, when he was eleven or so, like his all-time favorite, *The Last of Us*. In a puddle of parental surrender: *Grand Theft Auto*.

Nico has logged, for some of these games, hundreds of hours. He has beaten most of them multiple times, in various iterations, with various "trophies" to show for it. Some parents go to cello concerts or soccer tournaments. (He quit both after a year.) We hear about our son's accomplishments, some of which we pretend to understand, while sitting around the dinner table. How was your day? "Great! I two-hundred-forty-percented *Batman: Arkham* on the hardest difficulty." Or "I'm ranked twenty-fifth-fastest *Resident Evil 8* speedrun on Xbox." Or "I beat *Breath of the Wild* with no clothes and only a stick!"

When I start to add up all the hours my kids have spent speed-running and hundred-percenting, not even counting how many hours they've spent watching *other* people play games on the Internet, I end up in a tailspin. They could be spending those hours reading books! Drawing pictures! *Making* worlds, and not just consuming them. I worry that I'm raising kids who know only how to seize re-sources: eat up pellets, plunder coins. Even when I do convince them to take a walk in the woods—I'm forbidden to use the word *hike*—Nico will inevitably say, admiring a gorge, "This really reminds me of *Death Stranding*."

We know the risks. Every year, their pediatrician gives them a lec-ture, and sometimes a handout, on limiting screen time. We've read the *Scholastic News* stories and the CDC studies.

We've tried moderation. A series of feckless rules we've applied for a few days or a few weeks, some that we still half-heartedly enforce. No gaming after the timer rings, no gaming until homework's done, no gaming if you hit your brother upside the head with a PlayStation controller.

The American Academy of Pediatrics encourages kids to give "sales pitches" to their parents if they want to play a certain game. Nico needs no encouragement in this area.

"It helps my problem-solving skills. Fine-motor skills. It helps me learn patience. Grit! It helps me with archery. It'll help me be a better driver someday. I won't look at the prostitute parts."

Henry, for his part, is less obsessed with the latest and greatest games and has a more nostalgic attraction to the games of generations past. He has a love for vintage systems, an appreciation of the old as well as the new. This characteristic was no doubt planted by my husband, who regales our kids with stories about the first time he played *Pong*. "It was like . . . just a ball . . . that went back and forth . . . and that was *it*."

Henry loves, to my great satisfaction, *Super Mario Bros.* We play on his Switch, taking turns. He lets me do the swimming worlds; I let him do the fire ones. Almost everything I know about video games can be performed in the first four worlds of *Mario*, and when my kids first saw me whiz through the first stage—I could still remember the hill peak where the 1-Up mushroom was hidden, still knew how to do a badass run-shoot-slide combo, still knew, from muscle memory, how to leap from the top of the stairs, when the last number in the remaining time changed from 0 to 9, in order to land at the top of the flagpole when the last number was 6, triggering six spectacular bursts of fireworks—they were a little dazzled. And I was breathless with a certain kind of packed-away joy, the joy of childhood, of being back at Andrea's house with adrenaline pumping through my little body.

"I always wanted to save the princess," I admitted to Henry. My older brothers, the keepers of that secret wisdom, the finders of the warp zones, had both made their way through the eight worlds of the Mushroom Kingdom, had battled Bowser eight valiant times to rescue Princess Toadstool. But I had never gotten past the fourth or fifth world. I was terrified of the turtles with the ninja stars. The GAME OVER screen taunted me. Some combination of impatience, fear, and frustration, along with my brothers' monopolization of the Nintendo, caused me to put down the controller and go outside or find a book.

Over the years I occasionally attempted one of the increasingly 3D versions of *Super Mario*. My kids love *Super Mario Odyssey*. They'd invite me to play, and for five minutes and only for five minutes I'd be content dog-paddling in the crystal-blue waters, hopping and racing and climbing out in the open world. "Just relax," Nico would say. "Just explore."

"But what am I supposed to *do*?" I asked. My sons' minds are packed with more codes and combinations than I could hope to memorize in a lifetime, but they're also content just *wandering*.

"See what's through that door," they suggested.

I missed the side-scrolling gameplay, when the world was closed and two-dimensional, when you couldn't turn back, when the only direction was toward the flagpole. What did it say about me, that I needed a script, the narrow path of an obstacle course? Real life had too many open doors, too many hidden traps. What appealed to me about my *Super Mario Bros.* was the knowability of the world, that if you tried hard enough you could learn the steps, execute them, and win. If not, you died. There was no coming back. You had to hit the dreaded Reset button and return to the beginning.

Pretty cool, though, just to roam. I watch my kids in admiration, while they turn over leaves and throw cars and jump from buildings to see if they might fly. Sometimes they do; sometimes they disappear into ghosts and then drop out of the sky, reborn. They are mapping out a far larger terrain than I ever did, learning what works, what they can do, what gravity feels like.

When Henry learned that I'd never saved the princess, he was determined to do it. Together we tag-teamed, warping our way to the advanced levels. We got closer and closer. The sixth world, the seventh. Then one day shortly after he turned nine, when we reached the eighth and final world, I saw him do something. On his Switch, on the final stage, he pulled the two triggers at the same time. "What are you doing?" I asked.

"Saving our place," he said.

"What do you mean, saving our place?"

"That way, if we die, we can come back to this spot."

I was already uncomfortable with my kids' access to an Internet full of step-by-step guides, secrets, and tricks. Now you could save your place? "Do you think that's cheating?" I asked. I worried that, if we won, it would cheapen the thrill a little.

"We still got here on our own," he said. "We're just going back to try again."

It's a defining tension between my kids' generation and my own: the idea that they are protected, unrealistically, from disappointment, from consequences. No "Game Over" screen for them. No scratches. Unlimited lives. At the media arts camp they attend, everyone gets a trophy: a little golden Oscar statuette for best cinematography, best sound, best Claymation—dozens of categories, one for each special kid. When I got an all-star trophy when I was a nine-year-old pitcher for my softball team, it felt magnificent. Never mind what the ten non-all-star girls felt like. My kids were excited about their trophies, but they saw through them: "Everyone gets one," they said, shrugging.

But when I watched Henry save the princess, I didn't care if we'd cheated. I'd watched him try to defeat that motherfucker Bowser for hours. He lives in a world where there is a how-to video for everything, where YouTube can teach you how to grow a garden or build a go-cart or blow glass, where he can do more than I ever dreamed. Who was I to deny him that? The music was triumphant. "THANK YOU MARIO! YOUR QUEST IS OVER." I felt like I was nine years old all over again.

Nico isn't wrong about all the things gaming has taught him and his brother to do. When I'm feeling optimistic, I see my kids playing video games and I see them trying to figure out how to do something hard. I see them trying to improve their top scores. I see kind, smart, respectful, well-adjusted boys who care about justice and stand up for each other. I see kids with critical vocabularies and sophisticated fandoms. I see them weighing consequences and practicing self-regulation, making their own decisions about when to put down the controller. When I'm being honest, I admit that my own favorite methods of escaping from one reality into another—Netflix, Instagram, a glass of wine— are practices I sometimes have a hard time regulating myself.

When I was a kid, my preferred method of escaping reality was reading and writing books. At an early age, I developed a callous on the middle finger of my right hand, from gripping the pencil too passionately. When I hold my kids' hands—sweet boys, they still let me hold their hands—I feel the calacuses of their own obsessions, the dry and worn webs between thumb and forefinger, from manipulating their way through imaginary lands. How are these lands any different from the fictions I spend my precious hours in?

Our cultural understanding of video games is indeed fusing rapidly with our understanding of literature. The college where I teach offers a new major in writing for emerging media, including writing for video games. Games may feature more blood and gore than ever, but they also feature visually stunning and incredibly detailed environments, nuanced character development, rich backstories, strong dialogue, and intricate and emotionally resonant plots—all ingredients of good writing. Some, I have been late to discover, are as immersive as any novel.

One day, when I asked Nico to take out the trash—a chore he does obediently in order to earn an allowance that he immediately spends on games—he quietly sobbed all the way to the street. "What's wrong?" I asked him when he came inside. I couldn't imagine what had befallen him—Bad news from a friend? Was he being bullied? Had he been dumped by some girlfriend I didn't know about?

Warning: spoilers ahead.

"Arthur Morgan died," he said, still crying.

"Who's Arthur Morgan?"

"The dude from *Red Dead Redemption 2*." He explained how Arthur contracted tuberculosis from beating some guy to death, how his father figure and gang leader betrayed him, and how he was left to die for the last minutes of the chapter. Nico had been crying so hard he stomped his feet on the ground and accidentally knocked the sensor of the PS4, which was slowly dying, ejecting the disc. Then he had to play the last hour a second time, watching Arthur suffer all over again.

I gave a little laugh and hugged him.

When I'm feeling generous, I'll agree to sit with Nico and "watch" a game, which can last for hours. Observing him observing fictional characters fight for survival in some historical or postapocalyptic universe, I see him engaging in curiosity, in a human literacy. On the screen, I see the sunlight on the blades of grass and I see the goosebumps on the hero's arms. I see how attached Nico is to this world, how much he *cares*. And I see that video games may have the power to isolate young men in their bedrooms, but they also have the capacity to connect them to their most empathetic selves. And I remember that novels, too, the virtual reality to which I've devoted my life, were once criticized and feared for their craven powers of distraction.

Cool thing is: actually, you can always play again. And each time, you get smarter.

The next year, I didn't wait for Black Friday. I stopped in at GameStop a few days before Thanksgiving to check in with the dude behind the counter. He was probably thirty, and Nico had by then spent hours of his life chatting with this guy like old friends while he looked up game release dates and added points to his copious GameStop account.

GameStop Guy gave me the scoop on the PlayStation 5: Thanksgiving Day, 6:00 p.m. *6:00 p.m.*—the magic hour had been moved up, which meant if I wanted to try to get a PS5 (they'd post how many consoles they had available on the door the night before), I'd have to be there early in the day. On Thanksgiving. When I was supposed to be at home, making stuffing. Did I have the patience? Could I pull it off? Where would I tell my kids I'd disappeared to on Thanksgiving?

Around noon, I showed up with a book, a thermos of coffee, and a backpack of snacks. I thought I'd just drive by, see if the line was defeatingly long. If I had to leave empty-handed again, it was meant to be.

But only four folding chairs were lined up on the sidewalk, and I could see that the few cars in the parking lot were running, the people inside keeping warm. It was forty degrees outside. The sign posted on the door said that eleven PlayStation 5s were in stock. I parked directly in front of the store, took the chair I'd thought to bring and set it up, the fifth in line, then returned to my car. It was a system we all seemed to respect. Over the next few hours, more cars showed up, more chairs. We took bathroom breaks at the gas station across the street, got back into line. Around 4:30 p.m., when the line started to get long, I took a seat in my chair, which regrettably was a beach chair, low to the ground, so that the Camaro parked in front of me exhaled its exhaust directly in my face. The driver kindly shut off the engine. By now a series of people, mostly young men but also women, Black, Latino, white, Asian, college roommates, fathers and sons, were gathered around the open trunk of the Camaro, tailgating, trading stories of favorite games, of saving up paychecks, of searching all the Wal-Marts and Best Buys within fifty miles. It was getting dark. A joint was passed around. Merriment was in the air. No cops were called. A few hopeful flakes of snow began to fall.

At 6:01, GameStop Guy unlocked the door. I stood up, heart racing, and held my breath until the voucher was in my hand. When I walked out of the store carrying the PS5 from its little nylon strap, I felt like I'd saved the princess.

My kids didn't even realize I'd been gone all day. They were too busy playing video games.

On Christmas morning, we opened all the presents. Books and pajamas, candy bars and toys. The kids pretended not to be disappointed. Then I took the wrapped package out of the hall closet. Cautiously they began to peel back the paper. Then they lost their little minds. They leapt over furniture, knocked me over with hugs. My quest was over.

They didn't spend Christmas morning riding bikes, but they did save the world a few times. "Wanna play?" they asked me. I said no thank you. I opened a new book. From upstairs I could hear their shrieks and their laughter.

I Was a Teenage Transgender Supersoldier

NAT STEELE

When I was a child in the 1990s, I lived in a Navy town with a mostly white population. I played with the white boys on the playground, but I wasn't white, nor was I a boy, a fact I would not realize for many years. We played Army; we played Vietnam. We chased girls around the playground in a strange, gender-segregated game of tag. My best friend bragged about his father's Navy hat, citing years of service; he gloated knowingly about the "scrambled eggs" embellishment on the visor and how he would have a hat like that someday.

I wanted to be a soldier when I grew up. I was in the closet, or perhaps I contained a closet. I constructed for myself an armor to protect the feeling that I knew should not exist within me: the feeling I got the first time I played *Word Rescue* for MS-DOS at age four, the feeling of flight that arose within me when I played as the female character and saw her hair flutter in her jump animation. I understood that this was not an allowable feeling. I created for myself boxes within boxes, each padlocked.

I did not become a soldier. But I was a child who kept secrets to survive, and if a poem I once read by a trans poet is to be believed, that made me a "soldier in [my] soul." And I spent much of my childhood playing soldier in *Halo*.

343 Gamer Start

Released in 2001 as a launch title for the original Xbox, *Halo: Combat Evolved* was something of an adolescent rite of passage for many suburban and urban millennial men in the United States, Europe, and Australia. The *Halo* formula was a prime fit for a certain type of masculine upbringing: player vs. player combat with an arsenal of futuristic weaponry, a male soldier protagonist, a female sidekick, and hordes of aliens to slaughter.

I first encountered it one school night in 2003. My brother and I were among the students invited to a game night our math teacher was hosting at a nearby tech center. I had heard of *Halo* but had never played it. I had never seen an Xbox; I was new to consoles, our family having only recently purchased a Gamecube after much begging and pleading by me and my brother. My brother, my teacher, another classmate, and I loaded into a game of four-person Slayer on Blood Gulch, a canyon setting with squat fortresses on either end.

I was hooked from the first kill. I set out from my spawn location, stumbling across a rocket launcher in no-man's-land. Arriving at the other end of the canyon, I found a drivable vehicle crashed into the front of the enemy base. I got in, excited to drive, but it was the wrong side and I was trapped in the passenger seat. I turned to face the entrance of the base. A blue Spartan came traipsing out. I had my rocket launcher equipped. The vision of that kill is burned into my synapses with the fury of a hallucinogen trip. I went on to finish second on the leaderboard, a seemingly impossible feat.

My brother and I pleaded again with my parents with all our might, and an Xbox and a copy of *Halo* were not long in coming. At the time, I did not know *Halo* had a single-player mode; all I knew was this moment of multiplayer glory. Surprisingly, it was the single-player mode that captured my attention with a story that hit close to home.

The Faceless Man

Consider the origins of the SPARTAN program, which produces *Halo* protagonist Master Chief Petty Officer John-117: In the midst of a deadly war that all of society has oriented itself around, a group of special children are secretly abducted from their families, replaced by "flash clones" that die within months. The children are chemically castrated; cybernetic modifications remove their human weaknesses and neuter their emotions and biological impulses. Indoctrination destroys their human connections. They are reinforced with metals and trained to become precise and unfeeling weapons of war. Spartans are dissociative and "hyper-lethal," human but inhuman. They are tools inhabiting whatever roles they are assigned, and they play their roles perfectly. They are child soldiers who grow up to become adult soldiers. Their armor never cracks—those who break in the process are discarded.

In some ways, it's *Animorphs* with power armor. In other ways, it's a trans woman's childhood in allegory.

I played the *Halo* campaign relentlessly, daily. I progressed through the difficulty settings and pored over fan websites. In real life, I was an awkward teenager who hit puberty far too early, who didn't understand why I was so frustrated and unable to inhabit the social roles and relationships expected of young men and women. In *Halo*, I was a soldier in an armor suit who shot familiar aliens with familiar weapons. My real life felt like it had not begun and would perhaps never begin, for reasons I couldn't yet define as trans. In the game, I always knew where I was: the security facility in Silent Cartographer, the final bridge in Assault on the Control Room. (I still got lost in The Library.)

The Spartans' backstory is not present in-game. From *Halo*'s script, what you know about Master Chief is that he is a special soldier who is unfrozen right before a pivotal encounter with alien forces. He is a man (we presume) in armor that covers his whole body and head. He serves whatever role the AI in his head and the troops on the ground need of him. He's a shell that takes orders, who takes weapons his commanding officer gives him or picks them up off the ground. We don't know if he has friends or relationships other than the purely professional relationships he develops by necessity in the process of killing aliens. Game critic and developer Tim Rogers puts it bluntly: "Master Chief isn't a *character* or a *person*—he's an *icon*. He never takes off his mask, because, as one of *Halo 3*'s producers said, 'if he took off that helmet, it'd be you inside.'"

For a child like me, the idea that no one needed to know who you were inside was an escape. Inside, I had no clue who I really was. Deep within myself, I was furious at the way my childhood had developed. It was full of domestic conflict and weighed down by parental expectations for my social and career success. I was frustrated by aspects of my immigrant upbringing that held me unmistakably apart from my white American peers. Above all, I was *unaware* of my inner turmoil. My inner self was a black box, even to me. Common childhood injunctions to "follow your passions," the kind that my peers took seriously, felt impossible to understand. What passions? I thought the phrase must be a metaphor.

Master Chief had no such problems. He was not expected to relate to his peers; in fact, none outside the exclusive SPARTAN program could even consider themselves his peers. When he said, "Give me a weapon" at the beginning of the game, it was abundantly clear what would follow: shooting enemies. The problems of Master Chief's life all walked (or crawled or shambled) toward him, and the solution rested firmly within his right hand. No one asked Master Chief what his passions were; it was as meaningless a question for him as it was for me. He had locked up his feelings as a child, as had I. He was made perfectly for his purpose, in all the ways that I feared I was not. He was applauded for his professionalism; I wished my own professional distance from myself could be recognized as heroic.

A Welcome Grave

Halo 2 was the first game I ever preordered.

After its release in 2004, my parents vetoed Xbox Live. My father saw online gaming as a frivolous expense when I should be focused on studying and becoming workforce-ready. In retrospect, this wasn't necessarily an inaccurate judgment; the chances of a fifteen-year-old's becoming a pro gamer were slim (though not impossible: my high school's *Halo 2* tournament was won by a boy who would later become known as esports star and caster MLG Bravo).

Without consistent access to multiplayer, I turned to *Halo 2*'s campaign mode. This time, Master Chief was a defender of Earth and inadvertently fueled an alien civil war. Once again, all problems could be solved by shooting at them, by playing the role you were given. The alien Covenant, who are portrayed as fanatics of a religious cult, produce a key character who rebels against his mission and changes the arc of the series. In contrast, Master Chief never rebels. As the mysterious alien corpse-being known as the Gravemind notes of our protagonist, "This one is machine and nerve, and has its mind concluded."

It is hard to recall how I felt about *Halo 2*'s story at the time; after all, one hallmark of my time in the closet was that it seemed impossible to feel, as if the world was wrapped in gauze. What I do know is that I played the campaigns on repeat. They felt more real than my daily life, which was consumed with future planning: college, then career ambitions, then presumably the grave.

By 2005, I was aware that my problem was gender. I had seen a provocative gender-bending commercial on TV. That advertisement sent me down a rabbit hole, of googling "boy turns into girl," looking for more transgender content. The prospect of gender transformation made its sharp intrusion into my unfeeling life and showed me a glimpse of real emotion. I began searching for something: staying up late at night scrolling through transgender media, fiction and comic strips, memoir and allegory. I couldn't explain its appeal to me. It terrified me. At some point, I was sure, this terrible secret would come out and destroy my career and life prospects—even if I couldn't describe exactly what that secret was.

Playing *Halo 2* became a way to avoid feeling. Online reviewers pilloried the game's cliffhanger ending and how it avoided concluding Master Chief's narrative arc. These complaints made little sense to me: For me, *Halo* was an action to be taken and repeated, not a story with a destination. It was comfort food whose taste mattered less than its familiarity and safety. I grew fond of all the aspects of the game reviewers disliked: the abject polygons of the characters' faces, the Gravemind's apocalyptic intonations looming in the background of the action, the convoluted alien civil war which is never fully explicated in-game. I memorized enemy spawn locations. I started reading the *Halo* novels, committing lore to memory. "This is not your grave," the Gravemind told me, "but you are welcome in it."

My relationship to the series eventually waned, but always seemed to resurge whenever life gave me too much time to think about who I was. *Halo 3* found me in late high school, in the peak of college application anxiety. I caught up on *Halo 3: ODST*, *Halo: Reach*, and *Halo 4* in a spell of postcollege unemployment, connecting with the online speedrunning scene and eventually helping to found the speedrunning website HaloRuns. Much later, during the Covid pandemic, I briefly rediscovered my *Halo* fixation and indulged my completionist instinct to get every achievement. (I had begun my gender transition by this point. My old gamertag appears in a speedrunning achievement in *Halo: The Master Chief Collection*, the gamer equivalent of a deadname, I suppose.)

As written by Bungie, *Halo*'s original developers, the protagonists of each *Halo* game—the Chief, *Halo 3: ODST*'s Rookie, *Halo: Reach*'s Noble Six—are nothing if not dedicated to their missions. They are strong, silent, their personalities redacted, their presence itself a meaningful void. At the end of *Halo 3*, Master Chief becomes a noble sacrifice in service of a higher purpose, a loyal soldier to the last. Having successfully destroyed one alien enemy and achieved a tentative peace with another, his reward is to float in deep space, marooned aboard the half of his spaceship that did not make it through the slipspace portal back to Earth. It is possible he will perish out there. He does not seem to feel much at this state of affairs. "Wake me when you need me," he tells his AI companion, and climbs into the armored cocoon of his cryo-chamber. It is not his grave, but he feels welcome in it.

A Soldier in Their Soul

Depersonalization is a common phenomenon in trans people, as attested by trans writer and YouTuber Zinnia Jones in her writings on gender dysphoria. In a 2018 blog post, she wrote of her attempts to don armor against the world's injuries:

Depersonalization protected me even as it killed off the parts of me that made anything matter in this world, as if to shield me from some catastrophic personal collapse that was bound to happen. . . . There have been times when, feeling shamed or humiliated and without access to that protective inner core, I reacted by covering myself in as many layers of clothing as possible.

In her essay "A Maze of Murderscapes," S. R. Holiwell wrote of her time spent playing *Metroid II* while homeless in a women's shelter in Providence, Rhode Island:

These digital objects [missile-doors, shrines, map tiles] were my city streets, my landmark buildings. . . . I felt like an object myself, representative of something no one can ever know, moving through the city where people passed by me as unknowable figures that intrigued me just as I might intrigue them. . . . A delight and mystery in having nowhere in particular to be and exploring the world around me.

Holiwell is not writing specifically about the trans closet, but her remembrances show that, while the armor of dissociation can be alienating, it can also give one the freedom to explore and become. At the end of the first *Metroid*, Samus takes off her armor and reveals herself to be a beautiful woman. "Gotcha," she seems to be saying. "You didn't know who I was at all."

The dissociative armor of the trans closet itself is most incisively described in Isabel Fall's "Helicopter Story"—originally titled "I Sexually Identify as an Attack Helicopter" (a provocative riff on a transphobic meme beloved by extremely online young men in the early 2010s). Fall's story follows a character named Barb, a female-to-helicopter transsexual, and explores "tactical gender": our gendered passage through the world and its similarities to military indoctrination. It explores the ways in which we armor up, attack, and defend; our patterns of motion, shows of force, whether we announce our presence or go radio silent.

The story has since been withdrawn from publication but lives on in Internet archives. In it, Barb refers to her body as a "component in my mission," emphasizing how becoming a war machine was a welcome relief from the pain and threat of being a woman. Fall was castigated for writing her story: some supposedly progressive commentators claimed that such a deviant intermingling of gender and warfare could only be the anti-feminist work of a cisgender man. The vicious backlash caused Fall to withdraw her story. Her trans personhood retreated from the Internet. As she later told *Vox*:

> In this story I think that the helicopter is a closet. . . . Where do you feel dysphoria the hardest? In the closet. Or so I have to hope; I have not been anywhere outside it, except for [in publishing "Attack Helicopter"], which convinced me it was safer inside. . . . The story was withdrawn to avoid my death.

Barb's helicopter body is SPARTAN-117's armor. For me, the story of *Halo* gave me this same feeling that Fall refers to: the closet feeling, terrible and comforting. It is a joy to be a Hyper-Lethal Vector, like Master Chief and Noble Six of *Halo: Reach*. It is the joy of armor, protection, distance. It is the false freedom of remaining unseen and untouched.

I want to emphasize one word above: *false*. The *Vox* piece said Fall had "the option of retreating to the relative safety of her legal, masculine identity." This is an easy summary, but "safety" is far from the true picture of what the closet entails. Armor does not grow with the person it protects, as any hermit crab knows; it constricts and smothers. Despite the closet's promise of freedom, movement within it comes with limitations.

In "Helicopter Story," Barb's rising gender dysphoria poses a threat to her mission and existence. At no point in *Halo* can Master Chief put down his weapons and talk to the aliens. The campaign will always proceed the same way: he will crash-land on the mysterious ring world; he will fight his way across landscapes and spaceships; he will make the noble sacrifice, save the day, and float off into distant space. The trans closet functions for us as Master Chief's narrative constraints function for him. His freedom of choice is limited to cutscenes that we do not control. And no matter the strength of his armor, when his shields are depleted, Master Chief bleeds. The closet is not safety; the closet is a sense of false security, within which one continues to accumulate damage upon damage.

At the end of *Halo 4*, we see Master Chief's face. One of my trans comrades has argued to me that this is the moment where *Halo* betrays itself; after all, regardless of what canon might say, *that's you in there*. Master Chief has worn this armor since the beginning of *Halo 2*—approximately four years and nine months, per canon—and this is the first time we see it removed. We see technicians guiding specialized machines around his body, unscrewing and collecting and unclamping the tons of combat-grade metal plate. Like real armor, it does not come off easily. Like real armor, it is a process that takes time and requires help from others.

Under that armor, Master Chief was someone I did not recognize.

Wake Me When You Need Me

I have spent much of the past several years learning to take off my own armor. Medical transition has helped me feel more comfortable in my body. I have had help from therapists, friends, and loved ones. In that time, Master Chief has continued his own journey toward a distinctly male, market-oriented personhood. *Halo 4* leans into the relationship between Master Chief and his AI partner, Cortana. Games reviewer Erik Kain writes in *Forbes* of its "beautiful, tragic love story," propelled by Master Chief's emotion-driven need to find a cure for her incipient robot dementia, while noting the game's "odd sexualization of Cortana." In *Halo 5: Guardians* (which I have not yet played), Master Chief has gone rogue and must be hunted down by military forces. In both games, Master Chief disobeys direct orders from superiors in order to protect Cortana. It's clear that the future of *Halo* protagonists is one of complex human connections that tie them to specific identities, relationships, and character traits. The developer of

Halo Infinite, 343 Industries, promises that the days of treating the Spartan as an empty orders-following vessel are over; henceforth, he will have ample characterization and a "human story."

Perhaps my disconnect from the narrative of the later *Halo* games is simple: Master Chief's developers have decided to make him a person, and that person is not me. That person is a white male soldier, much like the other white male soldiers that populate the first-person-shooter market space. The AAA shooter fanbase skews toward young men, and developers need to market their content toward their customers. They generally don't make AAA video games about people like me.

Other people are the ones who get "human stories." Trans people like me get allegory, allusions, and headcanons. (Someday I'll tell you how *Halo: Reach*'s Noble Six is a he/him lesbian.) We get Internet listicles of "trans-friendly characters" as human and real as Birdo, the egg-spitting dinosaur from the *Mario* series. So trans people have to find ourselves in stories that weren't written for us. We make memes of popular video game characters saying "trans rights" while deciding for ourselves which characters we will claim as part of the community.

Given that reality, I'll take what I found in *Halo*'s story. I hold out hope that I can come around to John-117's new personhood, that I can learn to accept him on his own neutered-white-male-cyborg terms. But I doubt I will bond with him the way I did with the original *Halo* games and their faceless armored man. While I suffered in the closet, I am trying to build compassion for the kid who survived that closet. That compassion extends to closeted characters. To this day, I'm attached to helmeted characters and stories that don't tie them to emotional connections. The amnesiac, dysphoric, closed-off, and guarded will always find a friend in me.

Ninjas and Foxes

ALEXANDER CHEE

If you were to have asked me what I thought I was doing in the fall of 2006, playing several hours a day of the video games *Ninja Gaiden Black* and *Jade Empire* alone in my faculty apartment near the football field at Amherst College, I would probably have told you that I was interested in developing a course on video games. This would never come to pass. Alone with myself, I might have admitted that I still childishly wanted to be a ninja, and that I had always had dreams of seeing the fox spirit—though these desires had come to me much later than childhood. I might have said these games helped me hold on to those dreams.

The truth was something I couldn't have explained at the time, as I took my discs out of their sleeves and placed them in the Xbox, which felt a little like loading myself into a small but powerful gun. Something hiding on the other side of those dreams. The video games were an expression of my loneliness, even an investigation of it. I wasn't obviously lonely—I had friends, family, a busy professional life. But I was struggling with something in myself I didn't understand and for which I didn't want an audience.

I had just moved into town the summer previous, and after breaking up with a boyfriend. The job was three years long, with a fourth year possible if both they and I wanted me to stay. It came with faculty housing, and in that too-large apartment I'd rented to share with the boyfriend I had just broken up with—the attic apartment next to the football field—I first played in the vast, not particularly well-insulated living room. After a four-hundred-dollar heating bill that first January, almost as much as the rent I paid, I took to living mostly in a small room over the garage and moved my Xbox into the room too.

I'd purchased the console four years before to play *Halo* with another previous boyfriend, and I hadn't really done more with it since then other than use it to watch DVDs, like the entire run of *Six Feet Under*. And as playing *Halo* only reminded me of that ex and the foolishness of this purchase, I often couldn't find the point of playing that game alone. I told myself I was being practical, buying new games so as to use the unused game system and research a class. All of this seemed like a path into the more stable future I wanted. Of course, all of this was just me justifying owning the Xbox to begin with.

The two games had some nominal similarities but offered users very different experiences. If I were teaching that class that never came to be, I would say both of them were technically adventure games, full of levels—a gamer word for adventures, if you have never played these games—and both offered what were theoretically Asian-centered narratives, with what the culture would come to call Main Character Energy a little over a decade later. Both also made visible anxieties about race and authenticity that still surround us—and by *us*, for this essay's purposes, let's begin with me.

Ninja Gaiden Black is a hack and slash game, as the genre is called. The main character, Ryu Hyabusa, is a ninja clan leader armed with a sword carved from a dragon's tooth, called the Dragon Sword, created to keep the evil gods at bay. He is human in appearance but is part human, part demon, and is one of the most iconic of modern video game characters. He has a significant role in another popular game called *Dead or Alive*, which is heading toward its seventh edition, due out in 2024. I remember playing him in a Tokyo video game arcade back in 1999 when I visited my brother there.

Ryu does not look particularly Japanese, but instead resembles the Big Jim Doll I had as a child in the 1970s. Asian cosplay performers dressing as Ryu have used blue contact lenses and red hair tints to make their appearance match his dark blue or gray eyes and his auburn hair. The game is made by Japanese game designers and voiced by Japanese actors, and so it perplexed me that the main character and most of the game play characters had Caucasian features. The story also made no attempt to reconcile his appearance with his being the heir to a ninja clan with a Japanese last name. His father is named Joe Hayabusa, for example, and I could have enthusiastically accepted the idea that Ryu or his father was mixed, of Asian and white parentage like me, but that was never offered to me as an explanation in any materials I saw.

Ryu and his friends fought their enemies sometimes in traditional Japanese villages, sometimes in luxurious nightclubs, and sometimes in absurd temples like the ones found in any science fiction or fantasy franchise, and that also seemed indifferent to any concerns about cultural authenticity. All the figures looked like off-brand superhero characters from Western comic books—with exaggerated gender characteristics, either hypermasculine or hyperfeminine, dressed in revealing formfitting costumes. And yet this seemingly homogeneous Westernized aesthetic was something I recalled from many Japanese animated films, comics, and TV shows. It's a world setting made from a pastiche of European styles, with the towns in these stories and comics so often showing the red rooftops East Germans used to look for when they fled for the West.

The game was so hard at first that I nearly stopped playing. I distinctly remember thinking I didn't have it in me to remember the combinations for the different moves, until I did. I even went back to Newbury Comics and bought one of those game guides—a way to cheat formally, basically—just to play.

But even looking the cheat codes up now for this essay fills my heart with lead. From the highest-rated online guide from Gamespot, by user aaxe, we have this guide to the basic handset:

X - Light Attack: X Button
Y - Heavy Attack: Y Button
B - Projectile: B Button

A - Jump: A Button
R - Reset camera: Right Trigger
L - Block: Left Trigger
W - Karma Window: White Button
K - Map: Black Button
S - Inventory: Start
RC - Switch Camera Mode—Right-stick Click
        (Hurricane Pack only)
LC - Switch Encounter Timer—Left-stick Click
X+A - Wind Run—X+A Buttons
Y+B - Ninpo—Y+B Buttons

The controllers here had triggers on each side, a handful of buttons across the top, and a toggle switch, too, and were hard enough to use without this guide. I don't recall the Karma Window. Switch Camera Mode would sometimes happen accidentally, disorienting me—it meant changing the view, as if you were directing yourself in a TV show. I had forgotten, also, that the game changed with the difficulty levels, or that you could have a conversation, say, and have to give someone 49—not 40, not 50, but 49—golden scarabs, and the game would switch to arcade mode, a mode I never played in. Without the guide, I would have had to seek out this or that non-player character and tried paying them all the different amounts, a hopelessly dull task and not like an adventure at all. Tips included directions like "Triangle jump at the aqueduct." It wasn't at first clear what the aqueduct was.

Jade Empire felt like the opposite of this: an American-made game, set in a steampunk world with characters who all looked East Asian or South Asian, your main character is the last of a line of Spirit Monks who were wiped out by the Emperor because of their ability to speak to the dead. You have choices in two genders: Furious Ming, Lu the Prodigy, Radiant Jen Zhi, Scholar Ling, Tiger Shen, Wu the Lotus Blossom, Monk Zeng. The names may sound Chinese to you, and at this point you may also recognize that it is effectively a Wu Shu epic—and it takes inspiration, certainly, from that genre—but the main character can also have romances with non-player characters of the same gender. And this made the game strangely intimate to me, unlike any other game I'd played since my first in the late 1970s. After a lifetime of imagining myself in other worlds, here was one that seemed made for me.

Only a few of the non-player characters you meet are white, and you don't meet them for many levels. When you do, it is a bit of a shock. And they are not good or kind: they're would-be colonizers, either oafish or villainous or both. The linguist Wolf Wikeley was hired to create a language, Tho Fan, for the game which . . . was not my favorite part of it, but which I nonetheless accepted because of what the rest of the game offered.

You make decisions at key points along a moral matrix, and so it's a Choose Your Own Adventure game that becomes a Choose Whether You Are Good or Evil game, but with variations that allow you to be shades of belligerent, malicious, good, or even seemingly neutral. Your conversations with non-player characters are as important as, if not more so than, the battles because, like in life, you are always choosing to do good or evil, in everything you say or do.

Most, if not all, of the adventures were about learning the wisdom of ghosts, people who had died but still had lessons to offer the living. Companions joined up for as long as they could as you made your way to either saving the land from evil, or becoming the evil that would next rule the land.

I played the two games often one after the other, and so comparisons were frequent, and the irony visible in the contrasts was apparent to me each time: Japanese designers had made a game where ninjas were basically white. And white Americans: they had made a game where I could play a queer Asian main character in a Pan-Asian world with a romantic partner named Sky. I couldn't tell if it was a utopia or a dystopia, in the game and in the world around me.

Together, they were a part of some larger game I had been playing my whole life, of trying to find some part of this American world that I could claim. In a novel I might try and make this the Final Boss Challenge for a character like me, but in life it was not to be that way.

I knew I was enacting something from childhood. Or continuing something from childhood. I had bought a bicycle that I rode from Amherst to Northampton and back again on the bike paths, and when I did, I often felt like the kid I used to be, but I also felt like I was a main character looking for the place the game really opened up. And the place that I felt that most was, well, when I played these games. It was the wrong answer, so to speak—not the answer you want. But it was the answer I had.

I'd spent my childhood in Maine with a secret occult life, complete with tests from parapsychologists and a high school coven that had once been a Dungeons and Dragons game. I had retreated into that life as a way to escape from the way my real life felt impossible to me, the one where I was queer and chubby, biracial and Korean, finding novels and comics and reading rapaciously, especially if they included even the slightest mention of an Asian person. I was making a kind of ad hoc identity out of any Asian elements I found in the landscape—and, it should be said, Maine was the whitest state in the country at the time. Whether it was Gundam, or the Hawaiian restaurant out by the mall, where my father could order Chinese food off-menu—the one place near us where he could get chicken's feet served to him—I used this patchwork identity to feel an approximation of authenticity and affirmation.

If I felt abandoned, I was. As a teenager, a rift had opened between my family in Korea and my family in America, and it was in part a rift created by my father's assimilation into American culture. His decision that we would not learn Korean alienated his family, but because he was a favorite son, they did not blame him—they blamed my mother, and us. This in turn alienated us even more, and the schism grew only greater when my father died in 1983. I grew up around a Korean American community he had helped foster in Maine, but I could not understand Korean, and felt attempting to do so was disobeying him. It is a taboo I still feel, all these years later, even as I long to learn the language.

At the same time, I found there was a lot of pressure to like Japanese science fiction and manga as someone visibly Asian in America in the 1980s. It seemed to be one of the few Asian things that other Americans enjoyed, besides sushi and Chinese food and songs like "Turning Japanese." I was cautious, as I knew about the Japanese colonization of Korea, and it seemed like a betrayal of my family to like these things. I couldn't explain them either to people who really did expect me to be able to explain them, and this just made me feel worse about it, because these comics and shows were really, really popular with Americans, when I was not.

I had put that that kind of life behind me, had found another life for myself in communities in New York City and then Los Angeles, but now that I was again in a mostly white New England town with just one Korean restaurant, getting to which required a car or a bus ride, these games offered a new way to return to the pattern of coping I had once used to survive. I told myself I felt more authentic while playing the game. This wasn't exactly true, but it was interesting to think about. I think what I felt was a relief from my anxiety about authenticity. If Ryu Hayabusa could be a decades-old character across several game systems, popular around the world, who looked nothing like a ninja or a Japanese person, then I could be Korean just as I was. And while I didn't feel so authentic while getting a game guide in order to play *Ninja Gaiden Black*, I was used to the idea that I was playing a game with hidden rules—publishing, academia, being queer, being Korean American and biracial. Here at last was one that literally had a guidebook you could buy in a store. I thought back to when I was closeted, a kid of eight, nine, thirteen, fifteen. Back to when it felt like I needed a cheat code to pretending to desire women. Or, worse, a way to pretend to be more "Asian" in ways people could identify.

And *Jade Empire*, with the ersatz Asian culture fantasy that still allowed me to play as a queer main character . . . wasn't that just like being queer and Asian American in America? Playing a game designed by white people and wanting any validation from it at all, much less getting it—that felt like martial arts, sparring with swords I'd made from my own mind. Dream interpretation in therapy told me I was everything in my dreams. In this case, I was everything in the game.

These were the realizations emerging that fall and winter. And then I found my way to the fox in *Jade Empire* and I didn't care about any of this at all.

I had first encountered the fox when I was much younger, in the stories my father told me at bedtime, stories I imagined he had made up, about animals and how they came to be who they are. When I was writing my first novel, *Edinburgh*, I learned of Japanese myths of fox spirits, and the Chinese and Korean myths as well, and was moved to use one of them as the frame for the novel—a queering of an old story, done to make myself and my novel fit into the world. Fox spirits have since become very popular in manga and anime, but their inclusions in those stories often lacked for the sort of magic I felt when reading the older myths.

The Fox Spirit level of *Jade Empire* begins at an inn near the woods where the Foxes live. There's been an outbreak of cannibals, and as you fight them and flee, you make your way to a spirit realm, and almost immediately begin fighting on the side of the Foxes. There is a war between the Forest Shadow, as the Fox Spirit is named, and Mother, the evil spirit creating the cannibals. The Forest Shadow speaks to you in a gentle bell tone, translated into subtitles on the screen. The effect is a little as if she is speaking in your mind.

The animation here is quite beautiful, even if at times the Foxes seem like they are about to compete on *RuPaul's Drag Race*, with jewelry and long eyelashes. What I remember is just staring, full of joy, as the Forest Shadow spoke to me of my destiny. I told myself it was just a game, that my interest was purely intellectual curiosity, to guard myself against the shame I felt at my pleasure.

One night after a particularly intense period of gameplay with *Ninja Gaiden Black*, I turned it off, furious, and sat alone in the dark, the only light coming off the football stadium by my apartment, my pulse pounding. Humiliating as it was to play, it would be more humiliating to be found with my controller in my hand, dead on the floor. *You're not allowed to die alone in the dark playing this game.*

I had completed the game at ordinary difficulty. To advance, you turn up the difficulty level and play again, and as you do your adversaries become more complex. I was Ryu Hayabusa, on the Path of the Ninja, somersaulting backward, pressing the Y button repeatedly as I fought a boss, all on my quest to do something so vague I cannot recall it.

And so I gave up the Xbox a few months later to a friend's son, a boy who was having trouble settling into his new town. The very next week when I went over to visit my friend, a professor in Russian literature, we watched happily as her son headed to the basement with his new friends, emerging later from the basement with them to get snacks and sodas before returning downstairs. The system was so much better for him. I had made some narrow escape I wasn't sure I knew how to describe.

The draw to play is still there. I see games now that interest me, like *Ghost of Tsushima*, but I'm almost an old man now, and I'm getting along fine without them. More importantly, I feel like the main character in my life now. I don't need the game to offer me the cheap alternative.

As I think about what I've learned about the impulse to play in a world that is like the world I want but not that world, I ask myself: Why would I want to be a samurai, or a ninja, or a martial arts legend, in America now? And on whose terms? Is there something about being in this country that makes me long for that? My late father actually was a martial artist, and I think of the amused disgust he would feel at seeing me play this game from the afterlife, though it is maybe even the case that playing these games was and is a way of missing him. It may also be there is still something I need to figure out this way, and in the end, that is how I will think of it: each game just another mask to wear in search of the truth, whatever that truth might be. One truth might be this: it may be that now I could play a game like that just for the fun of it. At last.

No Traces

STEPHEN SEXTON

In 1998, my friend S lived in a terraced bungalow on the crest of a steep hill. It was called the Brae, in Lowland Scots. In a spare room opposite his bedroom, between an undressed single bed and a wardrobe, a Packard Bell desktop was installed on its own bespoke computer desk: sliding, retractable keyboard shelf; spaces for printer and scanner.

The computer was largely untouched, it seemed to me, and perpetually off-line. It was more of an investment than an entity, a machine whose relevance was for the future to discover. Its boxy apparatus seems so crude and cumbersome to think of now: the buzzing knee-high tower to which the mouse and keyboard were connected through redundant, color-coded PS/2 ports. Speakers snapped into the monitor like the ears of a square-faced elephant.

Everyone I knew was acquiring a home computer around that time, or rather their parents were. The mid-1990s home-computing boom reached Northern Ireland a few years after it reached the US and the rest of the UK, and it wouldn't be until June 2000 that my parents took the step. Neither of them was particularly computer-literate—what an ancient phrase—though my mother used one in her clerical job. She worked as a civil servant, mediating between foster parents and the government. The home computer would distract my brother and me through the long summer holidays, they thought, and prepare us, first of all, for secondary school, and then for the rest of our lives, which, my parents vaguely generalized, would be dominated by "computers."

The year 1998 was wild. In April, Koko, the gorilla who learned sign language, participated in the world's first (as far as we know) interspecies online chat on AOL Live. Members of the public put questions to Koko via text in a chat room. Then, over the telephone, these questions were put to Koko's trainer and caregiver, Dr. Penny Patterson, who would, for thirty minutes, sign the questions to Koko and interpret her response. Their conversation, available as a transcript, is not thrilling, except for the nature of its transmission and that the first question Koko was asked was whether she was going to have a baby:

DrPPatrsn: What about a baby? You going to have baby? She's just thinking . . . her hands are together . . .

LiveKOKO: Unattention

DrPPatrsn: She covered her face with her hands . . . which means it's not happening, basically, or it hasn't happened yet . . . I don't see it.

Host: That's sad!

The Good Friday Agreement was signed on April 10, 1998. It ended most of the violence of the conflict known as the Troubles, during which approximately thirty-five hundred civilians and members of the security forces had been killed since the late 1960s. In August 1998, I was playing *Super Mario World* at home in County Down when, on the other side of the country, the Omagh bomb—planted by the Real IRA, who opposed the peace agreement—killed twenty-nine people and injured hundreds more. From the radio in the kitchen, I heard these facts begin to emerge from confusion; the TV news that night and thereafter refined and corroborated the scale of the event. It's among the first and last memories I have of the period of violence that dominated almost every aspect of my parents' lives.

A few weeks after the bomb, I was back at school, preparing for the procedure known as the Transfer Test or the 11+: a series of exams that would determine which secondary school I'd attend two years later. As the stress and severity of the exam came into view, I cried myself to sleep many nights, knowing the little society of my friends would be splintered and scattered according to academic ability. I thought I'd never see them again, S included. We'd become something like best friends.

In September 1998, *Metal Gear Solid* was released on the Sony PlayStation. It's a sequel to *Metal Gear* (1987) and *Metal Gear 2: Solid Snake* (1990); all three were directed, produced, and written by Hideo Kojima and published by Konami. Throughout the summer before its release, I followed and studied the exclusives in *GamesMaster* magazine, and despite not owning a PlayStation, grew delirious with excitement.

The articles suggested it was a stunning achievement of graphics, mechanics, narrative, and gameplay. S had a PlayStation. I must have mentioned the game on the playground because S told me he had preordered *Metal Gear Solid* from a catalog. Or rather his mother had preordered it. This was bewildering to me. I'd never heard of anyone preordering games. I'd never heard of anyone getting new games. S was, however, a son between two daughters, and was obviously doted upon. Besides, it was his birthday in September. It was mine, too, which bonded us. I had my suspicions. I couldn't imagine asking for something like a video game *and* getting it.

Children have little sense of household economics or their class position, unless there are things they go without. My brother and I wanted for nothing, as the cliché goes, but my parents weren't well off. I was curious about S. Their house was smaller than ours. His mother didn't work. His father's job was a mystery, though most of his work was at night. I have a memory of seeing his father in the hall, bleary-eyed from sleep one Friday evening.

There was every possibility that no such preorder had been made. S had been known to tell a tall tale, which is one reason I liked him. We waited and waited. No game came. We waited. We waited until we forgot about it and fell into the rhythms of the school term. Halloween passed and Christmas passed. In those days, it turned out, as with CDs and movies, simultaneous international releases of video games didn't happen.

It wasn't until one morning in February 1999 that *Metal Gear Solid* was released in the UK. S brought the double-tiered jewel case to school, still in its plastic postal bag. Two discs, the thick manual; the protagonist Solid Snake, as rendered by Yoji Shinkawa, in a moody grayscale on the cover; tantalizing screenshots of gameplay on the back.

The Metal Gear franchise is notoriously convoluted. Its story arc runs over five decades from the 1960s. *Metal Gear Solid* is relatively straightforward, taken as an isolated text. Set in 2005 (seven years in the future, or six if you're in Northern Ireland), protagonist Solid Snake is coaxed out of retirement to confront a terrorist group that threatens to use a nuclear weapon if its demands are not met. Those demands are simple: $1 billion and the remains of Big Boss, an extraordinary solider, whose DNA they plan to develop, through gene therapy, into an army of genetically enhanced soldiers. Against the ticking clock, Solid Snake must infiltrate the secret weapons facility on Shadow Moses Island, Alaska, where the terrorists are based, rescue hostages, including the DARPA chief and the ArmsTech president, defeat the terrorists, avert a nuclear strike, and destroy the Metal Gear, a bipedal walking tank capable of firing warheads. Solid Snake will also encounter, do battle with, and defeat the terrorist leader, Liquid Snake, his twin brother.

Between S and me, it took many weeks to complete *Metal Gear Solid*. It's a single-player stealth video game, which is to say players are encouraged, as they carry out the mission, to proceed with caution and secrecy. Being spotted by one's antagonists causes an alert to sound; Snake will be surrounded and likely killed in the earlier stages of the game. We were impatient, blundering through bosses, barely paying attention to narrative twists and turns, entirely ignorant of its politics.

Neither were we aware of the game's themes: genetics and destiny, nature and nurture, violence and pacifism. Its major fixation is whether our fates are inescapable; if we are doomed to follow the course set by our parents. As with all the Metal Gear games, there is also the profound terror of the nuclear weapon, the risk of Armageddon at the push of a button either by a superpower or a rogue state.

S and I watched the cutscenes together, coached each other's game-play, refined strategies, resolved the puzzles of biometric key cards, and located the radio frequency for Meryl (a rookie soldier turned love interest), hidden in plain view on the back of the CD case. When she and Solid Snake encounter a sniper—the alluring Russian stereotype, Sniper Wolf—Meryl is shot. Over the soundtrack's swelling orchestral strings and an operatic vocal line, Meryl, dreadfully wounded, begs Snake to shoot her or leave her. For all the game's action movie swagger, this is its most poignant moment.

Because it was getting late, S and I stopped our session. All through the next week, he reminisced about the sniper's red dot moving over Meryl's body, bade me remember it with him. He was well on his way down the long slide of puberty.

The weeks we played *Metal Gear Solid* were a time of the most extraordinary intimacy. We became intertwined. And despite the intensity of the experience, it's strange to me that I don't remember who held the controller, and at which moments. We were both there in his bedroom, but we had transcended our bodies. It's an experience I had no words for until I was reading literature about video games and their receptions as objects of visual culture, particularly when it comes to how children experience them.

I'd just finished a draft of what would become my first book, *If All the World and Love Were Young*. An extended elegy for my mother, it maps her illness and death onto the levels of *Super Mario World*. Reading academics and cultural theorists like Johan Huizinga—whose *Homo Ludens*, first published in 1938, is a foundational text on play—expressed back to me what it was like to be in that kind of "magic circle" of play, beyond time and place.

In an article about Nintendo, Peter Buse says this:

The player manipulates the icon on the screen with a joystick and/or various buttons, completing the circuit of specularity. . . . The player sees herself or himself seeing herself or himself and, through this actual physical participation, gains control over the physical world as well as the image one.

The circuit of specularity! It's a phrase I love. To see myself seeing myself! Buse is, I think, talking about single-player games played by individuals alone. For S and me, the intimacy of our experience hung on the sense that, for hours on end, neither of us felt like we were physically present in the room. Even if only one of us navigated Solid Snake through the weapons facility, across the mined snowfield, up and down the communications towers, we were both him, in his sneaking suit, smoking his cigarettes. It was only when we saved the game and switched it off that we returned to our bodies and ourselves.

What was important, though, was not only seeing oneself as someone else—Solid Snake or whoever. What's important was that there was someone else there to witness it. That's what separates playing the game alone and playing it in company: someone else participates in your imaginative adventures, reifies them.

This is not an uncommon experience. For many people, it's an older sibling they watch playing a video game, enthralled by plot or action. Video game consoles, contrasted with the vast, coin-hungry machines of the arcade, put the experience of gaming into domestic spaces. It's for this reason, I think, that they seem to possess a kind of inherent nostalgia: they are representative of the home, and the moments of childhood one rapidly outgrows. That processors continue to develop at such a remarkable rate causes these moments of intimacy to be fixed in technological time as well as personal history: new generations of consoles make retro what was once the cutting edge.

One night about twenty years after S and I first played *Metal Gear Solid*, I was in bed, having trouble sleeping. I opened my laptop. Bored by the thought of Netflix, too weary for the algorithmic whims of YouTube, and nevertheless in the mood for company, I pulled up Twitch, the website on which hundreds of thousands of players stream their games to an audience. I wanted to tire my eyes.

I do this occasionally. Several people have told me they do this too. There is something about the real albeit distant presence of a person playing a game, somewhere in the world, that is more compelling than a recorded playthrough on YouTube. I had no wish to interact with the streamers themselves or the tens, hundreds, or thousands of viewers who might be online, but I liked that they were there. I wanted to watch a familiar game being played by a stranger.

Vicariousness is something video games offer, it's obvious to say. It's what Buse refers to: the moment "the player sees himself or herself seeing himself or herself." A vicarious experience is something experienced imaginatively through another. You're estranged from yourself, in the same way that, through the language and presence of a vicar, you might have an experience of God.

Vicariousness is something the Internet does very well too. As I'm writing this, approximately half a million people are viewing streamers on Twitch, typing messages into chat boxes, participating in a vast, international community of spectatorship. In this context, the audience's experience of the game strives to recover those first moments of imaginative intimacy: watching your friend play a game.

That sleepless night, I found someone playing *Metal Gear Solid*. I was captivated. I was wide awake. I did something I'd never done before. The streamer was stuck. Meryl had been shot and was bleeding out in front of the communications tower. Snake had to find a sniper rifle with which to do battle. "But where am I going to get one?" the streamer said out loud. Thinking it was a genuine question, I typed a response: I told him exactly what to do.

Immediately, I was bombarded with complaints and threats of sanctions. Other viewers chastised me. There was a strict *no hints* policy on this Twitch stream. This was a *blind playthrough*. In other words, the streamer hadn't played the game before: he was experiencing *Metal Gear Solid* for the first time, and he was doing so for an audience. I was red-faced. I was fascinated. The streamer had commodified *not knowing*, or at least the performance of not knowing. What attracted the viewership was a profoundly vicarious impulse: to recover what the first time felt like by watching someone else experience it.

What, I wondered, do such videos tell us about memory or friendship, or the acute and growing loneliness felt by so many people? What drives the impulse to experience something again for the first time? I thought of all those people watching the video with me, lonely or alone in their various ways, longing, on some level, for a moment of their lives—either recent or ancient—that they can't have again.

Once, S asked me if I'd ever seen a gun. He made me promise not to tell anyone. He took me into the spare room where the Packard Bell sat under the light switch. Gently, he slid open the door to the wardrobe, swept the tails of long coats to one side and nodded into the corner. First I saw the brass caps of what revealed themselves to be shotgun shells. He lifted the snug, leathery lid of a box, which had a handgun in it. I feel both awestruck and ashamed without knowing why. I wasn't to tell anyone, he said. His dad was in the police—the Royal Ulster Constabulary, to be exact. (This organization, accused of collusion with Loyalist paramilitaries and deeply distrusted by many nationalists, would be disbanded as part of the Good Friday Agreement and replaced with the Police Service of Northern Ireland.) These weapons were for protecting himself and his family.

S's father, as a member of the security forces, would have been considered a legitimate target by some paramilitary groups in Northern Ireland. Looking back now, I know that S, after playing *Metal Gear Solid* on a Friday night, having blown a hole in the armory with C4, would have been trained to check under the family's car on a Saturday morning for anything resembling a bomb. It's only now I realize how, as close as we were to each other, how unknowable we also were.

After the 11+ exam, we drifted apart: new friends, new interests, new lives. For a while, I saw him on buses or in Belfast City Centre. When I saw him in the street, I felt awkward and embarrassed, but for nothing really, except the intensity of our friendship. I haven't seen him in years, though we must move through each other's world all the time without leaving a trace, neither knowing the other was there.

It's been twenty-five years, a generation, since the peace agreement, since Koko barely spoke on AOL, since *Metal Gear Solid* in S's house on the Brae. I have withheld his name and kept his secret.

These days, I don't play many video games, but I write poems. Occasionally, I'm asked when or where poetry started for me. I remember when I wrote a poem for the first time, but that doesn't feel like an honest answer. The feeling I get from writing, from that imaginative labor, predates poetry for me: a poem is one expression of it; absorption in a video game is another.

The work of poetry, which often stretches into the early hours, is play. When it's going well, I feel outside myself, strange to myself, outside the usual flow of time. I don't know how to get there, but for the briefest time, I sense that circuit—subject and object, writer and reader, player and icon—complete itself through me. It's like catching your reflection in the glass of your front door as you reach for the handle, either leaving or coming home—you can't, for the moment, tell which.

Status Effect

LARISSA PHAM

As long as I've known pain, I've been fascinated by it—its malleability, its palpability, its density known only to me. In my early teens, and throughout high school, I was prone to migraines, searing headaches that started behind an eye and lit flares in my skull. I'd lie in the dark, head throbbing, sometimes to the point of nausea, coming up with absurd visualizations to try to capture what was going on in my skull: chrysanthemum-shaped fireworks; fields of flashing lights; white strobes that turned into little pips like dandelion fluff, scattering. Other times it was a dull, oppressive pain that persisted the entire school day and left my brain feeling waterlogged. I never figured out why the headaches came, and one or two years into college, they stopped.

What was interesting to me then, and remains interesting to me now, is how, on the surface of me, there was no difference between a migraine and no migraine. There was no mark above my brow to denote the pain below the skin. And yet it was there—invisible, like a ghost hand squeezing. This irked me. I wanted to suffer beautifully, like a martyr, or at least gain the sympathy that broken bones and a cast bestowed. Instead, I had a shut-in's malady, one that rendered me pinched and tense. On bad days, I learned to carry around foil packets of Excedrin. On good days, I forgot there were bad days at all.

But what was that line between good and bad, felt if not writ? That barrier—well, unwell. When a headache stopped it was like arriving at a stream of pure water. I promised I'd never take feeling normal for granted, but I'd soon forget that too. Not long after the routine of headaches stopped, another feeling arrived to take its place: flat blue like cellophane, gray like incoming clouds.

I started gaming during the first year of the pandemic, on a whim downloading *Genshin Impact*, a phone game to which I have now become hopelessly addicted. I was drawn in by the cute mascot, the surprisingly well-rendered visuals, and the promise of exploring a new, fantastical world: I wanted to climb trees. Prior to becoming a gamer, I spent most of 2020—the warm months, anyway—outdoors on my bike, riding with my partner the twenty-four miles to and from the beach. But then winter arrived, and everything returned to interiors. So, as a balm: my little phone game. An Isekai role-playing game with incredibly confusing lore and overdesigned characters with gravity-defying titties. I opted to play as the girl twin, on a quest searching for her brother in a fantasy land named Teyvat.

In the first playable scene of *Genshin Impact*, minutes after waking up on the beach, you're given a sword. You spot a slime by the water; you're instructed to fight it. Diligently, I attacked. The slime was felled, but not before it had bounced back and landed a hit on me. Blue numbers popped up—I'd taken a tiny amount of damage. My health bar shortened accordingly.

On and on I gamed. I explored the world, lighting up half the map on a night in which I stayed up until 8:00 a.m. My little character got stronger, her health bar fatter, as I leveled her skills, geared her up, and learned how to cook food that would restore my health points— that would heal me. I somehow convinced two of my roommates to start playing alongside me. We became gamers, sleep-deprived, draining our phone batteries. And in the course of this transformation, my vocabulary changed.

I grew up with the lingo, even as a nongamer, coming of age alongside *Mario* and *Final Fantasy*, *Street Fighter* and *Kingdom Hearts*, enough so that it feels self-explanatory to point out that the language of video games has provided an avenue for hyperbole that's permeated modern life. *You died! You lost a life!* Did we really die so much before we were given the opportunity to save at checkpoints, to leap back into action with our two remaining lives? When you die in a game, you don't die in real life. That's why we can keep saying it: *Oh no, I died, I died, I died!* But it's never really you dying, even in those games where you get to design your avatar. You respawn and you try again. Here's the beautiful separation games promise: you can become someone, even grow to love someone, a character that's both the result of your efforts and not yourself.

It happened suddenly: the way my mind blotted out days, even weeks. In retrospect, I can locate it with some precision to the fall of 2012, my first year living off-campus, in a house where I occupied a cavernous attic room that had no heat. At some point I noticed I was missing patches of October, the events gapped like jack-o'-lantern teeth. There was a hole where November had been. At the time, I'd noticed nothing outside of my usual vacillation between ecstatic and melancholic turns. I'd been doing things, most of them extreme, in order to feel the way I wanted to feel. In the way a lot of young people do, I was wrenching at my life, trying to make something happen. But then—I'm picturing something dense sinking into water, like an iron bar—finding the feeling, any feeling, got harder too. Whatever grip I had on agency had left my hands, and I was floating away.

There's nothing glamorous about depression. The only novelty was the novelty of it. I had known sadness, like anyone, with its resonant troughs; I hadn't known the dense, clogged lump that depression turned my brain into. Unlike other moods, it wasn't a low point I could see coming as much as it was an arrival. After the first time, I recognized its texture from the inside—like a layer of blue cling film had been wrapped around my life. Nothing seemed to penetrate it: not sex, not drugs. My mind soaked in it, relentless, like a print in a developer bath, until—just as mysteriously as my youthful headaches would wane—my mood would lift, and the usual colors of the world would return. I'd return missed calls. Be able to look at art again. And when I felt more myself, I'd research my symptoms, trying to self-diagnose according to the DSM-V.

The troughs and lost time arrived just as I entered my twenties. A pattern emerged, loosely aligned with my period, but not quite. Worse in winter. Some winters, much worse. In the years that followed that waterlogged autumn, I'd get frustrated with my own mental health, forgetting each year what happened to my brain. I came up with endless metaphors, trying to make it something outside me, wanting to separate myself from it. It wasn't me, I wanted to believe. *I'm having a bad day. A bad couple of weeks. It's my brain chemistry. It's my bad seed. It's my worm.*

There are several ways to get injured or die in Teyvat. You can fall off something high, which will decrease your health proportionate to the distance you fall. If it's from too high, you'll die—your body disintegrating into particles—and respawn as another character in your party. You can get burned by fire or struck by lightning. If you're swimming, and you run out of stamina before you reach land, you drown. You don't ever get hungry, but you do get cold, and in certain regions, you can freeze to death. You can get pricked by thorns and knocked over by exploding barrels. And you can take damage from enemies, who are legion, but unlike the obstacles of nature, you can fight back.

The combat, at least in the overworld—the lit-up map and the area where quests and treasure hunting take place—isn't particularly hard. It's not a game that's supposed to be difficult to play, like *Dark Souls* (I've never played *Dark Souls*). If you're leveled up appropriately and have a decently balanced team, you can go just about anywhere in the overworld and kill anything. For a while, that was fun—to get superstrong and take out enemies in just a few attacks, going God Mode. But as the game went on and the content grew sparser between updates, I found that I kind of liked being underleveled. I liked dodging and timing my hits, judiciously taking damage, seeing how low the health bar could go. Though you can eat food to heal, it's distracting during combat; it's better to have a dedicated healer in your party, whose skills allow you to regenerate health points, or HP. Sometimes, though, I liked to play without a healer. I wanted to see if I could do it—make it through the battle, damaged but not fallen, my team hanging on by the skin of their teeth. I liked waiting to patch up after the fights, standing reverently at the healing statue, watching the HP numbers rush back in a wave of little green sprites.

I wanted to be like that in life too—to go somewhere peaceful and watch my health flood back. It occurs to me now that in order to heal, you first have to take damage.

That initial pandemic winter was bad. The following year, which ended not long ago as I type this, was somehow worse. I couldn't handle reopening, couldn't handle the seesawing jerk of the intervals between variants. I wanted it all—the freedom, the parties, the return to crowded bars and noisy rooms—but I didn't know what was safe, or possible. I kept throwing up from drinking too much. My relationship deteriorated. It was a blur, of course, all of it—my jack-o'-lantern's mouth punched toothless, gaping and raw. By autumn of 2021, I found myself grappling for language to describe the mental badness I felt, which seemed both unique and utterly mundane. *A mental health crisis? In a pandemic? Groundbreaking.* Around this time, the developers that had crafted *Genshin* added a new game mechanic.

It was called *corrosion*. It was applied when you were hit with an attack by a specific creature, a Rifthound, which looks like a combination of a dog, a dragon, and a wolf. Purple splotches would shoot out of your body, and for as long as the state was active the lingering poison slowly drained your health. Unless you had a dedicated healer on your team, within a few undodged attacks, all your characters would be dead. It was a radical new mechanism—the polar opposite of the in-game foods and potions that increased a character's attack or made their defense stronger. And though players complained, it made the game better. A few months earlier, the developers had released a character whose shield was so good, it dwarfed the enemies' attacks. The game had become too easy, the content too quick to speedrun, and players were getting bored. There had to be another way to get hurt.

The first time I tried to fight one of the Rifthounds, I died instantly.

I tried again, and again, learning how to stave off the HP drain that the poison brought about. It was frustrating, but fun—the reason I kept returning to the game. Real gamers would refer to corrosion as one of many *status effects*, brought about by the increasingly complex game mechanics. A status effect is something that changes an aspect of a character—like a strength boost that makes their attacks hit for a higher number of points, or a speed boost that enables a character to outrun their enemies. Positive status effects are called *buffs*—an attack buff, a defense buff, a shield buff, a critical hit buff—and negative effects, like corrosion, are called *debuffs*.

When I learned the word *debuff*, I laughed out loud. Finally, a way to describe it—that spiritual depletion, the sense that something is gnawing away at your life.

More ways to die in Teyvat: You can get shot at by crossbows, blitzed by homing missiles fired from giant robots, knifed by treasure hoarders, and slashed at by rogue samurai. You can get stuck in a bubble and electroshocked into oblivion, or frozen and stomped on by the aforementioned giant robots. You can whittle down an enemy's life to nearly nothing, then get knocked off a cliff in their next animation cycle. As in life, there are stupid ways to die in a game.

But for the most part, you live. At least in the overworld. If you have a real desire to be wrecked—to plunge into battle without explanation, without the arc of a story or the moral satisfaction of a hero's journey; if you want to die over and over, not even valiantly, just for fun—there's something called the Spiral Abyss.

A player enters the Abyss through a portal on a forgotten island empty except for an eerie vortex of a gate. The in-game language used is dark and evocative: the Spiral Abyss is a "massive underground city constructed by an ancient civilization long gone." The Abyss is supposedly full of treasure, offering rewards for every chamber explored—from the description, one imagines a forgotten city, ripe for looting. But the Abyss has no map, no chests, no secrets. It's a bare-bones gladiator's arena—a never-ending battle with increasingly strong enemies and punishingly hard combat. The Abyss is structured as a series of floors in an inverse tower; a player descends deeper and deeper into it, unable to use potions or food, swap out weapons, or resurrect characters who fall. The first eight floors are easy; the ninth and tenth moderately hard. The eleventh is a challenge for all but the most dedicated player, and the twelfth, the final floor, is nearly impossible to beat within the allotted time. But it's not completely impossible—only nearly just. And in the Abyss, though you might die, there's nothing to stop you from picking yourself up and trying once more. All it takes is the tap of a button to start the trial again.

Of course I've gone into the Abyss. Of course I've spent hours there, mindlessly thrusting my characters into battle, dying and restarting and dying again.

Practically speaking, the Abyss is endgame content. *Genshin* is an open-world game, which means the fun is in exploring. But once you run out of quests and treasure, the game starts to feel repetitive—even boring—and even the most dedicated team of developers can't build out a map as rich and detailed as Teyvat fast enough to keep up with player demand. The Abyss is there for the no-lifers who speed-run the overworld, the whales who have money to blow on in-game transactions that allow them to collect the strongest weapons and rarest characters, which in turn makes the game easier and even faster to play. Spiral Abyss is absurdly hard because it has to be—it's there to soak up a player's time and attention after the rest of the game has been played through. It's like the hyperbaric training chambers in *Dragonball Z.* It's like the gym. It's a little bit like depression: time-sucking, completely numbing. Spending an afternoon in the Abyss, I look up from my phone and see two hours have passed.

In a recent Spiral Abyss cycle—it resets every two weeks—one of the battle chambers included a pack of Rifthounds. The trick was to forget about dodging and try to kill them all before they killed you, and hope that you had a good enough healer to sop up the damage after everything was done. I brought my strongest team and died. Then I did it until I didn't die. Then I went into the next chamber and did it all over again.

There's something strangely alluring about the starkness of the

Abyss. Even the design is bleak: you fight in a circular arena, hemmed in by an invisible barrier. At the periphery are ruins and columns, glimpses of that unknown city, though by the deepest floors, you hardly notice the landscape, fighting for every second against the ticking clock of the time trial. At the beginning of the descent, you choose your teams. Once inside, all you have is all you've brought: it's a lesson in endurance, in trying and failing. The only gift the game gives you is that before each challenge, you're allowed to choose from one of three randomly selected buffs.

Playing Spiral Abyss, I don't feel joy. My entire body tenses up; it's probably partly why I'm constantly on the verge of developing carpal tunnel. My brow furrows, my shoulders hunch, and I tap on my phone like a maniac. At the start of each cycle I try new team compositions, regear my characters, trying to figure out how to make it through the chambers. I've lost hours this way—they swirl mindlessly into the Abyss, like foam disappearing down a drain. But stay in the Abyss long enough, deep enough, and something starts to emerge from the mundanity of the constant combat. You start to notice patterns, attack rhythms, which enemies to kill first—all little things that allow you to shave seconds off your time. The endless battle turns into a ballet. And somehow—with a little bit of luck, and one of the better buffs—you can manage to clear it. To make it to the bottom of the Abyss.

Each time I clear it, I feel triumphant. That strange, savage joy that I've made it—I've suffered enough and pushed through.

It's nearly spring as I write this. The Abyss reset a week ago and I have yet to clear it. I'm nursing a new wound. The second pandemic winter punched a hole in me, the cartoonish kind, where you look down and can see right through. My relationship of four years ended just as the days began to lengthen in Brooklyn, and though it was for the right reasons, I'm grieving still. Some days it's a dense ball I feel in my gut; other days, so gauzy and ephemeral I imagine I've been crying, only to realize my cheeks are dry. But there's not much for me to do except keep going. I game, check off my daily commissions, fight my battles, level my mains. Soon, in patches of soil around the city, the crocuses will be peeping out. I've always thought it felt particularly cruel to be sad in warm weather—I've always wanted the outside world to match how I felt inside.

But there's one place where I can go to fight those battles, where I can chase storms across Inazuma and seek heat while hiking through Dragonspine. There's a place where everything becomes literal: strength, poison, health, death, dying.

I like the palpability of a health bar. The green when it's full, the red when it's empty, the neat, round number of HP. The stakes are so simple—you live until you die, and then you respawn and try again. The numbers are proof that something's happening. Though some games make the screen flash red or paint blood onto an avatar's face, in Teyvat my little heroine just keeps on going. She fights on and on, even when she's got fewer than a hundred HP left. But I, her god, her controller, know I need to heal her. Especially if she's under a debuff, her health draining away.

Gaming, with its endless, ever-evolving mechanics, its optimizing and min-maxing and strategizing, has its own language. There are ways to talk about how you got stronger, and perhaps even more ways to talk about the ways you can get hurt. There are debuffs and different kinds of damage—physical, psychic, stamina reduction. There are characters that get nerfed and enemies that shred defense.

At first, tongue in cheek, I brought this language into my daily life. Nothing describes the way depression feels quite like a poison debuff. Now I embrace it, leavened as it is with the bleak humor that makes depression itself bearable. After all, the pain I was so enamored with when I was younger has shifted locations. It's still in my head, still invisible, though maybe legible in my messy room and unmade bed. But now there's more language for it, and a debuff is just a status effect—it's not a permanent state. For every debuff there's a buff, and in real life, a buff means—however briefly—I'm blessed.

Ruined Ground

J. ROBERT LENNON

In the spring of 1974, my uncle Joe Mirenna left Pennsylvania, the state he grew up in, to join some friends on the twenty-three acres of remote hillside they'd bought thirty miles north-northeast of Charleston, West Virginia. An itinerant fiddler and leatherwork artisan, my uncle had chafed at the constraints of polite society and longed for a new kind of independence and self-sufficiency; he'd moved from job to job and relationship to relationship since dropping out of college, occasionally clashing with his mother and stepfather—my grandparents—over his apparent aimlessness and perpetual poverty. It was time for a change.

Joe describes his arrival on Green Creek in an immensely entertaining 2019 memoir, *The Making of a Field Hippie*:

> I'll never forget that mid April day when I drove my van to that place where the hard road ends and the dirt road begins, loaded with gear, a thousand dollars to my name. . . . As I started my descent on the twisty road toward the Hart farm five miles away, heavily rutted from the end of the March rainy mud season, I was struck not so much with the litter of old refrigerators and such at the gully bottoms, but with the stunning beauty of the white dogwood blossoms and their horizontal structure, contrasted with the rosey blooms of redbud dotting the landscape. The rest of the

forest had not leafed out, so here stood a view reminiscent of a Japanese painting.

I will also never forget my own, rather less dignified arrival in West Virginia, on my own patch of hillside, which also occurred on an April day, this one in 2103, inside the online multiplayer video-game *Fallout 76*. I woke with a hangover in the subterranean vault where I had spent my life cowering in terror of the postapocalyptic wilderness outside. I'd overslept; everyone else had left before me. I gathered some supplies and stepped out into the sunshine—only to be attacked and killed by Chinese Liberator robots, artifacts of the war that had further devastated the plague-stricken, genetically engineered world of the late 2070s.

Revived, I tried walking the other way this time, and encountered two friendly women. They directed me toward a bar that had just opened—presumably the first new business in West Virginia in decades—and I made my way there, dodging giant rats and moles, and pausing to pick a few blackberries from a bush. It was inside that bar, the Wayward, that I would be given the first assignments of my new life off the grid.

Outside the bar, outside the game, outside my house, humanity had been stricken by its own, mercifully less severe plague, to which I had reacted with surprising—to me—extremity. Writers on the internet cracked wise that spring about how little the coronavirus pandemic was likely to affect their lives: Never leaving the house, you say? Drinking alone? Shunning humanity, having food delivered? Why, that's what I've been doing for years!

But I am not an introvert. I like to rub elbows with strangers, share meals, talk for hours. COVID-19 transformed me into a shirking, flinching coward who crossed the street to avoid children, who trembled with rage any time an unmasked jogger passed too close by. One writer of my acquaintance, barely older than I was, died of the disease; several others my junior survived with severe, and possibly permanent, damage to their respiratory systems, joints, and mental clarity. I imagined getting infected, not knowing it, and infecting my family—the briefest lapse in vigilance giving way to the death of everyone close to me, leaving me the sole survivor, my body ruined by illness and my mind by guilt, shame, and loneliness.

In *Fallout 76*, you can have any kind of body you want. Players create a character at the game's outset by adjusting a fantastically detailed set of parameters; it's possible to turn yourself into a bizarre freak with just a few taps of the joystick. In single-player games, I usually invent a character unlike me, often a woman, and costume them fancifully, for kicks. But in *76*, I spent an hour re-creating my real face from a set of selfies. My wife, who had initially found this process entertaining enough to observe, eventually had to leave the room. "It's too close," she said. "I can't look at it." I dressed myself in the kind of clothes I might wear in real life: pink jeans, orange sneakers, a baseball cap from a local high school, and a letterman jacket advertising a brand of soda. If you encounter me in the game, you will see the real me: middle-aged father of adult children, trying to recapture his lost youth.

Fallout 76 is merely the latest in a long-running and beloved series. Its single-player forebears are praised for their strong writing, amusing voice acting, complex branching narratives, and memorable non-player characters. The consensus favorite is probably 2010's *Fallout: New Vegas*, which takes place in the ruins of Nevada in 2281 and features some of the franchise's funniest, weirdest, and most beloved characters, including the sinister amnesiac Dr. Mobius, the Elvis-impersonating gang leader the King, and the disfigured cultist Joshua Graham, a.k.a. the Burned Man. *Fallout*'s characters tend toward obsession, megalomania, and internal moral conflict, and their narratives are overloaded with dark irony. *Fallout*'s timeline—all the games share lore and history—diverged from our own sometime soon after the Second World War. Its aesthetic is retrofuturist and is heavily influenced by nineteen-fifties culture and style; its cracked and twisted highways are littered with tail-finned behemoths, and Bakelite radios play oldies in abandoned houses.

And though many of the games' most iconic elements are military in nature—like the power armor, a craftable and customizable mechanical exoskeleton designed for combat, which I despise and never use—their most important recurring theme is that of home: having once had it, losing it, rebuilding it.

"Every door and window in that house was recycled," Uncle Joe writes, of the home he built, with his own hands, on Green Creek in the summer and fall of 1976. A neighbor had an old shed he wanted to be rid of; he told Joe to salvage whatever of it he liked. He taught himself masonry:

> From April to November I worked my butt off to get in before the snow started falling. By then, I had faced the interior chimney with some beautiful salvaged brick, installed a wood stove for heat, and found a near perfect Home Comfort wood cookstove for the kitchen. . . . I felt like I had built a mansion. There is nothing like the secure feeling of being heated by a fire fueled by wood you cut and split, sleeping in a warm bed covered by a roof you just built, and hearing the cold autumn rain patter against the windows.

I saw this house for myself in 1979, when I visited Green Creek with my mother and grandparents. The road there was barely a road at all; it ran through creeks, not over them, and my teeth chattered as the car rumbled in the ruts. I was nine years old. In a photo I have, the house stands perched on cinder blocks, as straight as the trees around it. My memories of it are as vivid as any I have.

Though his adventures and achievements loomed large in my childhood, I saw my uncle only occasionally. So I was surprised to find I'd rated a mention in *The Making of a Field Hippie*, as usurper of his status as the family black sheep, a change that, during my college years, offered him a "temporary sense of relief" from the judgment of our professionally minded clan. "Then," Joe writes, "John had to screw it up for me by getting published, a huge paycheck, and eventually a tenured position at an Ivy League college," knocking him back to his former status. He's kidding—and also, like most people, mistaken about the lucrativeness of a writing career—but I truly was taken aback by the notion that my success had somehow exceeded his. I wore out the record he made with his West Virginia bluegrass cohort, Booger Hole Revival, and it unquestionably influenced my own musical endeavors. But, more significantly, my uncle *built a house. Alone.*

What took my uncle half the year in actual West Virginia took me only a few hours in the game. I salvaged lumber from fallen trees, metal and glass from the husks of old buildings and from roving robots I'd destroyed. I went on quests to learn how to build workshop tools, and bought plans for my own cookstove with money I'd earned selling weapons, armor, and drugs.

I'd chafed at the settlement-building mechanic in *Fallout 4*, the previous game—I wanted to have adventures, not make dollhouses!— but now I savored it, and derived deep satisfaction from the results. I loved my dollhouse; it immediately felt like home. I began fervently to search the wilderness for more plans, more collectibles. I acquired a display case for magazines and figurines I'd found, and earned in-game currency to upgrade the furniture and wall decor. Sometimes I'd walk into the house—the door thunking audibly shut behind me—and, in the real world, in my real body, I would endure a wave of intense emotion.

Also in the real world, we went to my in-laws for Rosh Hashanah. There had been some debate about whether we could take the risk: college students had returned to our town, and cases had spiked. If these new infections turned into a real outbreak, our chance of carrying COVID across the state would increase dramatically. This kind of depressing logic puzzle had become a commonplace in American life, once it was clear that our former president's cowardice and narcissism had locked us into an indefinite stalemate with the virus. In the early days, we were content to hold ourselves apart from our loved ones until the pandemic was over. It felt noble, almost romantic, for a couple of months. Now, of course, a year later, we dutifully indulge in exhausting probability exercises before eventually giving up, taking a deep, masked breath, and making the trip. This particular one was peaceful and uneventful, and no one got sick.

But on the second night of the holiday, I dreamt of home. Not the house in upstate New York where we actually lived, but my rustic bungalow perched on a hillside just west of Harpers Ferry, West Virginia. This was actually my fourth residence in the game. I'd first laid out a sleeping bag and a campfire just up the road from the Wayward. Later, once I'd gathered enough firewood and scrap metal, I built a cabin on the eastern shore of the Ohio River, just across the road from a ghoul-infested cemetery. Eventually I amassed enough supplies to move to a remote hilltop south of Seneca Rocks, and finally achieved my present tricked-out settlement, in close proximity to a small pond and a harvestable junk pile, and a short walk to the Berkeley Springs train station, where I trade loot with a sarcastic, vaguely threatening robot.

In the dream, I stepped carefully along the path I'd made through the mud out of scrap lumber, around the low white fence, over the carrot patch I'd planted, until I reached the structure's southeast corner. The joint where the clapboards met was irregular, the result of the wood's warp and my artisanal ineptitude. I reached out and stroked the weathered and peeling white paint with my thumb; flakes dislodged and rained down on the weedy ground. A breeze picked up, the trees sighed and whispered, and cool fall air filled my lungs.

The sensation of home was overwhelming—a feeling of comfort, dominion, mastery, and rightness that I've never felt about a real house before. The closest I'd come was the sprawling farmhouse I'd bought with my first wife, which I had tried and failed to maintain with skills acquired through books and the Internet. My sense of failure there had been compounded by the enormous sums of money I paid to other men, merely to return parts of the place—the roof, the well, the siding—back to functional condition. I gave the house up in the divorce, over the mild disapproval of my attorney, with a sense of profound relief.

Now, through my efforts in the virtual world, I had managed to create a home that, though imperfect, could be maintained without assistance from anyone, despite the malevolence and unpredictability of the environment. Could this be real? Could my in-game homesteading have transferred, somehow, to my actual life? I stood there, feeling the breeze on my cheek, hearing the moans of distant monsters, the hum of my generators, the genial clanking of my Collectron scavenging robot, and arrived at the disappointing conclusion that I was dreaming—that the game could exert its influence only in my imagination, and never in the ruined world I was about to wake to.

Fallout 76 was a mess upon release. It was plagued by technical problems, combat imbalances, and, more significantly, griefers—players who entertained themselves by destroying your house, shooting you dead, and stealing your stuff. What's worse, the game had no NPCs. The only humans alive were you and the other players; the only quests the game offered were given by robots, or derived from the diaries and voice recordings of the long-dead. Early adopters of the game complained of loneliness and boredom, and reviews were abysmal. Bethesda, the publisher who currently owns the franchise, responded with a pacifist mode and bounty system, and eventually a great deal more content, including, at long last, a smattering of NPCs organized into factions that players can align themselves with for special rewards, including rare weapons, armor, building materials, and silly outfits. (Today it's not unusual to fight a battle alongside, say, a cartoon mole, a businesswoman, a cow with two heads, a nurse, and an astronaut.)

76 is my favorite Fallout game. It's still crashy, imprecise, chaotic. Weapons or armor fail to work as expected; promised buffs and enhancements fail. Players can be seen floating nude in midair over a battlefield an hour after they've left the server. Sometimes buildings suddenly vanish, and sometimes they reappear where you're standing, trapping you underneath. NPCs converse with their backs to you, repeat themselves, and clip through walls and floors. And yet I love every flaw; my fondness for the game's perpetual brokenness is proportionate to my despair at the brokenness of the real world. Sometimes, when I fast travel back to my house, it isn't there yet—I have to wait for it to load into place, wall by wall, window by window.

It's a glitch, but it moves me every time—undisaster unfolding, my home in a state of undecay.

Do you remember houses? Other people's, I mean—the way they looked and smelled, how cushy their sofas were, the mysterious contents of their medicine cabinets? Do you remember inviting other people over to your house—people you knew, but just a little? That's something we used to do, in the before times. ("The before times" is something we used to say as a joke, in a priestly monotone, back at the beginning of the pandemic. We are not kidding when we say it now.)

Since I started playing *76*, I've made a point of doing as much visiting as possible. Each time I log on, I'm assigned to a random server with different players; visiting their settlements to trade supplies and marvel at their creations is one of the game's greatest pleasures. Some people have tried to make their houses resemble, as closely as possible, real houses from the real world, but most are as fantastical as the game's building elements allow. Early in my time in Appalachia, I stumbled into a public event, the game's second annual Fasnacht Day. I'd only been visiting its host village, Helvetia, to pick up some of the firewood I knew was stored behind a restaurant on the edge of town. Instead, I found preposterous chaos: a dozen players wearing colorful clothes and masks, gleefully parading through the streets to Oompah band music, annihilating waves of enormous mutated toads, bees, and wolves. A high-level player took notice of me and invited me to his house a short walk up the creek, a four-story neo-Victorian decorated with fairy lights and giant taxidermy apes. He let me take as much water as I liked from his purifier and gifted me a paper sack of rare guns and outfits. He was from Ohio and he wished his wife weren't at work, so he could introduce us. "She's, like, level three hundred. She's a badass."

The closest real-life analogue to holiday events in *76* is Halloween: costumed strangers thronging the streets, collecting loot. Thanks to COVID-19, we didn't have Halloween in the real world last year. But it's always Halloween in *Fallout*, and always has been, in every game. The bombs dropped on October 23, so Halloween decor is everywhere, forever.

Before this, I'd never played an online game. It took me months to work up the courage. I figured I'd be doing a lot of talking to other players, so I bought a gaming headset with integrated microphone. As it turns out, most players prefer to keep their mics muted, and communicate via a menu of gestures—"emotes"—accessible through their controller or keyboard. The sound of another player's voice can be jarring.

One day, not long ago, I fell in with a player who had left his mic open, perhaps unwittingly, while he talked to his real-world partner about their shared illness.

"I still feel like shit."

"Me too."

"You shouldn't go to work."

"I have to."

We were picking through the ruins of a ski resort. I was searching for a quest item—a holotape that would allow me to log into a computer miles away. He was lumbering around in his power armor, picking up scattered ski poles, presumably for the aluminum they contained.

"He's just going to send you home," his partner said, coughing.

"He won't even notice."

"It's obvious."

"He'll notice if I don't show up, that's for sure."

Unlike most of the American workforce, I am a member of a privileged class that hasn't needed to choose between their health and job. The private university where I teach closed early and quickly moved online; I haven't seen a student in person in more than a year. As it happens, the work I do—discussing short stories with small groups of young people—lends itself fairly well to teleconferencing. We can hear one another's voices and see one another's faces. We pass notes in the chat and share links to books.

What I most miss about my real-world workplace is the laughter. In a properly managed online meeting, with everyone on mute until called upon, every joke is met with crushing silence. But it's not even the laughter in my own classes I miss so much; it's the sound of other teachers and students, heard from the hall, reacting to one another's corporeality.

Between periods, we used to spill out into the corridors, threaded ourselves through crowds, eddied around each other like water over rocks. We waited in line for coffee and sandwiches, found vacant corners to check our phones. Being alive and present shaped our world.

In a 2011 study, a team of Notre Dame psychologists determined that moving from one room to another prompts us to forget, a phenomenon popularly known as the doorway effect. Performing actions in a space creates what they call an "event model," a temporary body of knowledge that contextualizes further actions there. Leaving that space means leaving its event model behind, clearing the mind for new activities in new spaces. Before the pandemic, my walks from the parking lot to the building to my office to the classroom to the café kept my mind refreshed, despite a tightly packed schedule of obligations. Now, my entire professional life is conducted through the same rectangle, in the same room. I go hours and hours without leaving it, until my event model is as crustily layered as a telephone pole outside a nightclub. It's the same rectangle and room I use to be entertained, to talk to family, to write fiction, and to play *Fallout 76*.

Surprisingly, the Notre Dame study was conducted not in physical spaces but virtual ones, in a rudimentary video game. The doorway effect works the same way whether the body is in motion or not. If I could hold my classes in *76*, I would probably feel a lot better. (Some frustrated workers have actually done something like this, holding business meetings around a campfire inside the cowboy-simulation game *Red Dead Online*.)

Or maybe not. There was something I didn't want to admit to myself: I was beginning to grow dissatisfied with the game, and my sojourn there would soon come to a ragged, unsatisfying end, much like Joe's time in the real West Virginia. "I became consumed," he writes, in the memoir's final pages, "by the dark feeling that some big change was happening":

> I began to sour on the band, and I made known my intentions to
> leave; these fine friends of mine probably happy to separate from

such an ever grumpy-growing fellow. Suddenly my happy little brightly lit home looked shabby and woefully isolated. . . . The only promise I could assume was a long lonesome existence, living as a pathetic old bachelor at the end of a dirt road.

In one of the main plotlines in *Fallout 76*, the player must vaccinate the game's NPC settlers against the "scorched plague," to prevent them from turning into hoarse, emaciated, gun-toting monsters. I had finished that quest, and around the time the real vaccines began to arrive outside the game, I realized I'd pretty much finished everything else too. So much of my love for *76* had derived from its many tiered goals: if you want to get this weapon, you have to fight this monster, so you had better get this armor, which means you need these plans, which you buy inside this bunker. You also need these crafting materials, which you can only get in nuke zones—zones you can only endure if you have this other armor, which is available only after completing this series of missions. Set against the backdrop of my adopted home, I found this grind immensely absorbing; it brought me all over the map, and helped me to unlock every last location, every perk and plan and ability in the game. It had been, in effect, my job for months—my real job, the job where I marched around doing stuff, as opposed to the imaginary job that I actually made money from, and that I did inside the same virtual space day in and day out.

In an email, I told my uncle about the game. Despite his DIY, off-the-grid roots, he is savvy about technology and the Internet. (I follow with interest his epic thread on a woodworking forum about his ongoing project, a fifties-style camping trailer.) I sent him a link to a couple of YouTube videos of in-game footage, one set in Charleston, the capital city I remember visiting with him, and one in Morgantown, home to West Virginia University and a charming elevated commuter train.

"We've always marveled that the capitol dome was gold-plated, in one of the poorest states in the country," Joe wrote back, suitably impressed. "The video was great. Having lived there I recognized several of those scenes and rode the monorail. Some of the apocalyptic roads looked a little too familiar." He concluded, "Well, if you run into a guy with a facial twitch, wearing a tie-dyed tighty-whitey as a doo rag, and carrying a five-string banjo with four strings, make sure you don't drink the lemonade he offers."

He can't have realized how perfectly he was describing a plausible *Fallout* NPC. I was reminded of Biv, an alcoholic robot in *76*, who occupies a former tattoo parlor in the shadow of the monorail. For decades, he has been carrying out the orders of a fraternity brother who, when the bombs fell, had been trying to create the ultimate party punch. If you complete Biv's quest, you end up with a few bottles of that drink, Nukashine, which causes you to black out and reappear in a random spot on the map.

As for Joe, he reappeared outside the map, in Wisconsin, where he lives today in another house he built himself. He and his wife rent part of it out, along with a small detached cottage, on AirBnB. He's retired from teaching, the vocation he eventually came to draw money and satisfaction from, but he still plays the fiddle.

In *76*, there will be more stories, more new NPCs and locations, in the years to come, and I'll doubtless return to the game to enjoy them. But for now, I'm trying to come to terms with the unavoidable fact that someday, *Fallout 76* will be gone. Preservation of single-player, offline video games is already a difficult problem; the systems they run on are forever advancing and changing, and many once-beloved games are now lost or unplayable. But online games—games like *76* that require active development and maintenance to run—are invariably doomed. A time will come when the *76* team will disband and the servers will be shut down; its players and their outlandish characters will disperse, and the game's world will disappear forever. *Fallout 76* will be, like the West Virginia of its setting, nuked.

The real world, of course, is still here; it never really went away. It may even soon be returned to us in something resembling its previous form. But the coronavirus has shown us how fragile our institutions are, how near we are to oblivion. Some of us are already there, were there even before the virus arrived. We've elected a new leader, presumably because we liked his optimism, but I fear that optimism is not an adequate tool for keeping the team together and the servers on. As I write this, the real West Virginia is playing a surprising role in our national drama; its Democratic senator may be the only thing standing between us and the election reform, economic justice, and health policy we need to survive the next decade.

Or maybe the die has already been cast, and we're hurtling ever closer to the grim vision the *Fallout* games predict, recalcitrant senator notwithstanding. In that case, the preppers, gun nuts, and libertarians will have been right, and our teleconferences will be little more than a vague memory, a passing triviality receding behind us on that all-too-familiar apocalyptic road. If you live in that world, centuries from now, you may be reading this, *Fallout*-style, in the glowing green text of a miraculously intact CRT screen. Hello from America, land of dead NPCs! Good luck with this ruined ground. We used to live here.

We're More Ghosts Than People

HANIF ABDURRAQIB

I don't find myself investing much in the kingdom of heaven. It has always been this way for me, even as a child. I prayed often, sometimes the requisite five times a day in my Muslim household. But I did it out of a sense of duty to my living, not what might exist after my living.

I can't control my own arrival to whatever the promised land may or may not be, because I don't have the rubric in front of me. I have sometimes been a good person who does bad things, and sometimes I've been a bad person who does good things. Forgive my reliance on binaries, but the way the afterlife is most often discussed is by way of a scale. I grew up with Muslims who insisted that every bit of food left on their plate after a meal would be weighed against them on the day of judgment. I considered this: arriving in front of the robed choir, a few grains of rice tipping the scale toward an irreconcilable level of bad, banishing me to some fiery underworld.

A new development for me in early 2019, spinning through *Red Dead Redemption* for the first time, was becoming obsessed with the idea of heaven for someone who wasn't real. Someone I had maybe come to love, but who only existed in a fictional realm. It was a private thought. Discussing love and sanctification like this seems foolish, probably a by-product of my many newfound chambers of loneliness. I want not only a kinship—even with someone not real—but I also want to save them, and save myself in doing so. And still, the obsession was singular, ever-present.

\ 211

Not only is this foolish, it also tilts toward what some might consider sacrilege. But if you will allow me to soften the message, what I am saying is that I'm not invested in my own entry into heaven, but I do find myself required to believe in its existence nonetheless. If enough people you have loved transition to a place beyond the living, you might grow to hope that place is heaven-*like*, in the way heaven has been formed in our imaginations. I want everyone I have buried to be in a place of abundance, a place beyond their pain. For me, being consumed by silence—and an obliviousness to whatever has become of you—is one definition of peace. I'm fine with that for myself, but not for my beloveds. Not for you, person I do not know and will likely never meet. I want an abundant dominion for you.

The first time Arthur Morgan goes into a coughing fit in *Red Dead Redemption 2*, the TV screen trembles and floods with a sharp red-orange. Your controller matches the screen's trembling and flashes some color I can't recall. This happens in what is essentially the game's final act, before its epilogue. There's still enough of it to be played through as Arthur. By this point in the game, you've grown close to him. Your gang begins to dwindle, beloved comrades are murdered, or they've run off in search of more prosperous terrain. You've survived with Arthur, who is beholden to his instincts that he can make what he has work for him until something better comes along.

His coughing fit sends him leaning up against a wall in the town of Saint Denis, and then stumbling into a doctor's office. The verdict is tuberculosis. The doctor grimly wishes Arthur well, in the way in which doctors wish people well when they know there isn't much time left.

Red Dead Redemption 2 takes place in 1899, at the turn of a century when law and order is raining down on America, and the days of the outlaw are coming to an end. These are more the game's words than my own—words that are shown as a preface to the opening. Arthur runs with a gang he's been with since he was a teenager. Its leader, Dutch, is a dreamer, often waxing rhapsodic about Tahiti or Australia or someplace not in America where the gang could live out their days and flourish without a care in the world. This, of course, requires money. As Arthur, you go through much of the game with the gang in pursuit of the ever-elusive One Last Score. Robbing trains for paltry bits of coin, taking down a stagecoach here or there. The idea, though, is that it isn't ever enough. Even if Arthur amasses individual wealth and pours it all into the gang's camp fund by the thousands, it isn't enough for the new world of Dutch's imagination.

The world of *Red Dead Redemption 2* is expansive and immersive. While riding along the landscapes, you might be greeted by a person moaning in pain, pleading for medicine after being bitten by a snake, or a person begging for a ride home. Occasionally, you might be submitted to more nefarious characters: the person faking injury who pulls out a gun to rob you as you get close, or a KKK meeting happening deep in the trees. How each of these encounters is handled impacts Arthur's honor throughout the game. There is a meter for this. It is quantifiable and certain, calculated and easy to see, like so many of our supposed good or bad deeds in our real lives perhaps should be but aren't.

In my first playthrough, I decided early on that Arthur was a good person who sometimes had to do bad things to survive, but even before he was stricken with his illness, I was committed to raising his honor as high as I could. I'd sometimes ride around searching for good deeds to take on, anyone calling out for help. I'd kill if I absolutely had to, but I didn't loot the bodies of those I killed, and I never drew my weapon on anyone out of a bloodthirsty recklessness. Only what I needed to do to survive, and nothing more. I figured there was something at the end of all this. Some way that Arthur might be rewarded for his goodness.

I am sorry to tell you now that you can't save him. You won't be able to, no matter how hard you throw yourself against the door of the closed doctor's offices at night while torches flicker above doors and virtual townspeople look at you with concern.

All of the video games I grew up loving had a fix for death. Nothing was permanent. At least not for you, the main character of the story.

The first time I played *Red Dead Redemption 2*, I barely remember being affected by the reality of Arthur's diagnosis. "It's fine," I thought to myself. "Something will come along and this will be fixed." When Arthur's friend—an Indigenous chief named Rains Fall of the Wapiti tribe—learns of Arthur's illness and gives him a blend of herbs, you think this might be what heals him, brings him back to health. But it's only temporary. Within a few in-game weeks, Arthur is once again coughing, collapsing on the street of another town.

I know it is foolish to talk about grief in this way. To discuss coming to terms with loss through a character I would lose every time I was taken away from the game, to run some errand or to return some email. My first time playing, the world was a different one than it would be when I played it a second time, which is of course true of any pursuit overtaken through the course of linear time. But what I mean, specifically, is that during my first run the world had not yet been shaken by a pandemic. In my experience grief hums at an inconsistent frequency; I know it well enough to know that grief is never entirely done with me. And so—even in a world unaffected by COVID—it didn't take much for me to mourn Arthur's slow fading into the inevitable.

I coped in phases: first, I kept up on my path of trying to do as many good deeds as possible, thinking that if I tilted Arthur's honor meter far enough in a "good" direction, it might save his life. Sure, the internet insisted that this was not possible, but what did they know? I might be on the verge of discovery! Yes, I will give you a ride to a town two towns away from where I need to be! Yes, you can rob me, person who perhaps needs my goods and wealth more than I do! And, Lord knows, more than Dutch does! Everyone can have all of my earthly possessions, my earthly time, whatever else can be spared!

When that didn't work, I gave in and just accelerated the process of ending the game. I sped through main story missions, with Arthur getting visibly weaker. Bartenders and passersby comment on his sickly visage. Members of his gang express sympathy, or mockery, depending on who they are. He fights to stay alive, and then he doesn't.

When it was all over, I found myself laughing, alone on my couch. Despite myself, I'd once again fallen for the first trick I was ever taught: that on the other end of some vague and broad attempts at goodness, there might be something that saves me, that saves anyone I love.

Arthur gets sick in the process of attempting to collect a debt from a man who doesn't have the money. This happens in the game's first act. The man is not well, as is made clear by the man's wife, who runs out of their modest log house after you, as Arthur, have grabbed the man, threatened him, and hit him a few times. During one such time, he coughs into your face. You might think nothing of it at the time, even as Arthur wipes blood from the man's cough away from his mouth after becoming resigned to the fact that there would be no money to collect. One act later, when it is revealed that the man has died, Arthur goes back to the man's widow and demands the money the man owed. That's the way it goes, of course. If the dead don't pay, the living must.

The building where I worked as a debt collector in the 2000s looked like it could have been a portal to anywhere. Like anything could have been inside of it. This is how all the debt collection buildings looked in Columbus, Ohio. Large, gray, nondescript slabs. Brick sometimes, if you were lucky. All of them on the outskirts of the city, nudging up against a suburb's borders but never in the suburb. Places where good people went to do bad work because they had to survive.

I needed a job. I had, by that point, accumulated a small criminal record, with a larger one to come. I had to find a place where I could build some form of legitimacy, and no one else would hire me. Debt collection companies would take anyone. There was a boom in the industry. This was right after the early-2000s recession but before the more robust late-2000s recession. Broadly, this meant that there were more people in dire straits than there had been before. Misery as a gateway to opportunity; you might even call it the American Dream.

The base pay was bad, by design: as long as the base pay was bad, collectors would strive to make commissions on the money they had to collect. In a cavernous room lined with tightly arranged gray cubicles, people put headsets on and dialed numbers for hours at a time. At some of the more upscale collection agencies, there were computers that autodialed the numbers for you. My pals who worked at those described a sense of blissful detachment. They were not scrolling through a person's information for long enough to make a person real. At my agency, we had to dial manually, finding the phone number at the bottom of a long file outlining a person's financial delinquency, scrolling past notes left by collectors who called before you got to a person. Notes about a call's hostility, or a person's anguish. There is something about the seeking of the number and dialing that made the work more intimate, for better or worse. Unmasking the hostage, so to speak. Occasionally, above the medium decibels of consistent chatter, you would hear someone shout, some display of aggression toward whatever person was on the line with them, threatening them, spitting out the word *debtor* like a curse. When they'd hang up the phone, they'd take pride in the fear they briefly injected into the life of a stranger.

I'd like to say, today, that I was bad at this job because it misaligned with my moral compass. It did, of course, but really I was bad at it because I was nonconfrontational. Because I didn't particularly like talking on the phone. Because when I would hear people—defiantly or weakly—insist to me that they didn't have anything, I felt like it was my duty to believe them. It was my duty to understand them because I, too, did not have anything. On my breaks, I would look at my prepaid cell phone and see messages from bill collectors, calling me to collect what I did not have, and what I was not making at this job. And still, I called. I called widows, sometimes mere weeks—according to them—after a burial. I called elders who spoke to me sweetly about what they could not do. Some who told me that my voice reminded them of a grandson, or a nephew. I called people who were sick. I called people who spoke to me while machines beeped slowly in the background.

Every day, I'd have to find some way to shake the guilt off after I clocked out, until I finally ran out of ways, clocked out, and never went back.

I don't know how to define honest work in a dishonest place. This isn't a noble thing, but back in those days, I didn't ever mind stealing if it also meant that I could eat a decent enough meal, or find enough cash for a bus ride somewhere. I have struggled to explain this to anyone who hasn't made a bed out of the concrete, below the sky in a quiet place. I was bad at stealing, and I was bad at lying, which is why I always got caught. But I didn't mind it nearly as much as I minded working at the collection agency, or at the door-to-door knife sales company, or at the front desk of the crooked insurance office that performed shady business I simply cannot discuss here but that anyone who has worked in such a place might understand. Call it selfish, but the thought was always that if I'm going to lie anyway, I don't wanna do it on someone else's clock. I don't wanna do it in a way that detaches a human element from it. I don't want to dull the sin. Sure, I'll walk into a grocery store and walk out with some shit I ain't have the money to pay for and wouldn't have paid for even if I did have the cash. The entity of the grocery store will be all right, probably, and I get to survive a little bit longer. It always felt different when there was a name, a voice, a person on the other end of a line. A person looking at me through a screen door. Do only what you have to in order to survive, and take nothing more.

It has always been easier for me to convince myself that the sins I've been immersed in and the average time I might have left to make up for them simply don't align. I'm a better person now than I have been in the past, though I've also dislodged myself from binaries of good and bad. If there is a place of judgment where I must stand and plead my case for a glorious and abundant afterlife, I hope that whoever hears me out is interested in nuances, but who's to say? I don't think about it, until I do. Until I get sick and wonder if I am sick with something beyond routine, or until I swerve out of the way of a car on the highway and feel the sweat begin to bead on my forehead. It's all a question of how close I feel like I am to the end.

I have no interest in playing God, but I do like low-stakes control of an outcome, which is why Arthur's predicament sort of suited me, in a way. Even without a player's interference in doing deeds to maneuver the honor meter in one direction or the other, Arthur is most commonly portrayed throughout the game as a conflicted but mostly decent man, trying to make sense of a world that doesn't want him around anymore. In game-controlled missions, he helps people of a lesser station in life than he is. He has a code that he operates by. He maintains a consistent level of curiosity about his surroundings and the people in them. He sees all of the people in the camp as equals, and wants to get to know them. Charles and Lenny and Sadie—all people who have, in some way, been cast off by the harsh realities of the era—find closeness and comfort in Arthur.

A therapist asked me once if I thought of myself as redeemable, and I'm almost certain I laughed it off, or detoured toward another answer that sounded satisfying but actually said nothing. I believe in redemption in the same way that I believe in heaven: I feel required to. Not only because of my personal politics, but also because of my social interests, and my investment in others beyond myself, and also—yes—because I do imagine that somewhere along the uneven path of my life, I've tried to be better more often than I have been worse. I suppose I'm cynical about all of it, though. The world, as it stands, is obsessed with punishment, particularly for the most marginalized. Punishment for living in the margins, or an intersection of the margins. I don't know if my personal beliefs in redemption can undo that massive ghost, hovering over so many of our lives, baked into our impulses, even when we know better. Even when we, ourselves, have been on the losing end of that impulse.

It is easy to attempt to redeem Arthur in a world that isn't real. To play a mission where Arthur kills, rides away over a trail of dead bodies, and then goes and helps the camp with chores. Picks some flowers along a hillside. Helps a family build a house. In a world where no one is reminding you of the wreckage you've taken part in, it's easy to compartmentalize your damage and chase after that which is strictly beautiful, or cleansing. Climbing your way toward the upper room by any means necessary, on the wings of anyone who will have you.

My most recent time playing through *Red Dead Redemption 2*, the world—the real one—had already ended, in some way. My pal Franny has a poem about the end of the world where she says that the world has already ended well before we arrived, and will end again many times through our lives, and I think I believe in that too. That each time there is a massive rupture in some corners of collective living, the world has ended and started over again. Each time I feel pushed beyond a place of past comforts to a point where I realize I can no longer return, a world has ended and started over again. Like most things, it is easier for me to consider the apocalypse as a series of small movements instead of a single event.

This time, the world felt, to me, like it was in a holding pattern after its ending and attempting to begin again. The world was a car, stalling after not running for a long winter. There were those who decided that the pandemic was over and they'd go back outside, only to be rushed back inside by the inevitable spreading of the virus. Amid the grief, and amid the rage, there was something fascinating to me about being suspended in the somewhat-stillness of the world I'd built for myself, which felt like as good a time as any to replay *Red Dead Redemption 2*, and take a less emotionally frantic approach. All I ever want is to know my exits before I enter, and I took some delight in knowing what was coming for Arthur before firing up the game again, almost two years after I'd eagerly taken to it with oblivious wonder for the first time.

This time, I have yet to finish the playthrough. I might not ever finish it in the traditional sense—finishing the story missions to work through the game's narrative arc. What I do love about the *Red Dead Redemption 2* story as it plays out in the game is that it starts out bad, gets worse, but then has a quick uptick of goodness before it descends again into bleakness. And it's not just Arthur's illness. The gang dwindles. Some die, some drink themselves into misery, some simply leave.

I've found myself enjoying the game's small pleasures, looking to slow down the realities that I know are looming around the corner. If large parts of my real, actual life are in somewhat of a holding pattern, I can force Arthur into that with me. I've stalled right before the game starts to turn completely downhill. Things are starting to get bad, but not so bad that my already somewhat fragile state might decline with the circumstances within Arthur's orbit.

It helps, of course, that there is a lot to do in the game that has nothing to do with the main story, and has nothing to do with the good deeds I became obsessed with pushing upon Arthur my first spin through. I fill my satchel with berries and plants that I never consume or craft anything with. I walk into the saloons and play card games for hours, winning or losing cents at a time. I drink and stumble around dirt roads with no aim.

And I seek out sunsets. This is my favorite part. The mountains along the virtual world's western landscape are the best for this. I climb up one, set up camp, and watch as the sun goes down. I allow Arthur to fold into these daily routines, which strip hours away from my own real-life daily routines. And this is, I think, how I will leave it. This is what the game will be for me now. I can untangle myself from the desire to save Arthur if I stop considering the inevitable.

In my own orbits, in the center of trying to wrestle with my own goodness or badness was another option: complete stillness. I was most stagnant in my youth when I was trying to prevent myself from pursuing my lesser angels. My self-control is only a little better now, and so I do welcome the idling world, no matter how it comes and no matter how it might end up going. I find a type of salvation in holding patterns. Not one heaven, but many small, disparate ones. I sit on my couch for an hour without moving, and make a man sit at the edge of a cliff without moving, both of us watching a fake sky drown in color, both of us not yet sure when we're going to die or how much time we have left. There are probably better ways to attempt the playing of God, but there are certainly far worse.

SOURCES

"I Struggled a Long Time with Surviving"

Ralstin-Lewis, D. Marie. "The Continuing Struggle against Genocide: Indigenous Women's Reproductive Rights." *Wicazo Sa Review* 20, no. 1 (Spring 2005): 71–95.

Naughty Dog. *The Last of Us*. Sony Computer Entertainment. Sony PlayStation 3. 2013.

"This Kind of Animal"

"The Feature That Almost Sank Disco Elysium." *Game Spot Audio Logs*, January 12, 2020, 17:20. https://www.youtube.com/watch?v=9X0-W5erEXw&t=253s.

ZA/UM. *Disco Elysium*. ZA/UM and Humble Bumble. 2019.

"Thinking like the Knight"

Fox, Toby. *Undertale*. Toby Fox, 2015.

Gibson, Ari, and William Pennen. *Hollow Knight*. Team Cherry. 2017.

Milner, David. "The Making of Hollow Knight." *Game Informer*, October 15, 2018. https://www.gameinformer.com/2018/10/16/the-making-of-hollow-knight.

"Mule Milk"

Dr. Mac. "Removing Wolf Teeth." *Farmer's Weekly*, March 7, 2013. https://www.farmersweekly.co.za/animals/horses/removing-wolf -teeth/.

Ducarme, Frédéric, and Denis Couvet. "What Does 'Nature' Mean?" *Palgrave Communications* 6, no. 14 (2020). https://www.nature.com /articles/s41599-020-0390-y.

"Kentucky's Equine Industry has $3 Billion Economic Impact." University of Kentucky Equine Programs, September 2013. http:// equine.ca.uky.edu/news-story/kentuckys-equine-industry-has-3 -billion-economic-impact.

Lesser, Casey. "These 18th-Century Painings of Interracial Mexican Families Are Based on a Lie." *Artsy*, June 27, 2018. https://www.artsy .net/article/artsy-editorial-18th-century-paintings-interracial-mexican -families-based-lie.

Masters, Madeline. "Did Humans Create Mules?" *Pets on mom.me*. https://animals.mom.com/did-humans-create-mules-3306.html.

"Neonatal Isoerythrolysis: When Mare's Milk Can Kill." *Horsetalk .co.nz*, June 3, 2015. https://www.horsetalk.co.nz/2015/06/03/neonatal -isoerythrolysis-mares-milk-kill/.

"The Quest to Revive Extinct Aurochs to Restore Ancient Lands." *The Conversation*, October 6, 2017. https://theconversation.com/the-quest -to-revive-extinct-aurochs-to-restore-ancient-lands-84649.

Rodriguez, Monica. "Why Can't Mules Breed?" *Tech Interactive*, June 20, 2007. https://genetics.thetech.org/ask/ask225.

Square. *Final Fantasy VI*. Square. Super Nintendo Entertainment System, 1994.

"What Is a Mule? 13 Things You Didn't Know." https://spana.org/blog /what-is-a-mule-13-things-you-didnt-know.

"Staying with the Trouble"

Lerner, Steven. *Stray*. Annapurna Interactive. Playstation 4 or later, 2022.

Benton, Chuck, Al Lowe, and Mark Crowe. *Leisure Suit Larry in the Land of the Lounge Lizards*. Sierra On-Line. 1987.

Haraway, Donna. *Staying with the Trouble: Making Kin in the Chthulucene*. Durham, NC: Duke University Press, 2016.

"Narnia Made of Pixels"

Cronenberg, David, dir. *eXistenZ*. Los Angeles: Miramax Films, 1999.

Kasdan, Jake, dir. *Jumanji: Welcome to the Jungle*. Culver City: Sony Pictures, 2018.

Knight, Steven, dir. *Serenity*. Beverly Hills: Aviron Pictures, 2019.

Levy, Shawn, dir. *Free Guy*. Burbank: Berlanti Produtions, 2021.

Lisberger, Steven, dir. *TRON*. Los Angeles: Walt Disney Productions and Lisberger-Kushner Productions, 1982.

Neveldine, Mark, and Brian Taylor, dir. *Gamer*. Santa Monica: Lionsgate Films, 2010.

Spielberg, Steven, dir. *Ready Player One*. Burbank: Warner Bros Pictures, 2018.

"Cathartic Warfare"

"Call of Duty: A Short History." March 17, 2017. http://microsites .ign.com/call-of-duty-a-short-history/index.html.

Fanon, Frantz. *Black Skin, White Masks: The Experiences of a Black Man in a White World*. Translated by Charles Lam Markmann. New York: Grove Press, 1967.

Stern, Jesse. *Call of Duty 4: Modern Warfare*. Activision. PlayStation 3. 2007.

Stern, Jesse. *Call of Duty: Modern Warfare 2*. Activision. PlayStation 3 or later. 2009.

"The Cocoon"

Beachum, Kelsey. *Outer Wilds*. Masi Oka. PlayStation 4. 2019.

Jorudan. *Alien vs. Predator*. Activision. Super Nintendo Entertainment System, 1993.

Matthews, Dylan. "This Guy Thinks Killing Video Game Characters Is Immoral." *Vox*, April 23, 2014. https://www.vox.com/2014/4/23/5643418/this-guy-thinks-killing-video-game-characters-is-immoral.

Ruggill, Judd Ethan, and Ken S. McAllister. "Computer Game Archiving and the Serious Work of Silliness." *Animation Journal* 19 (2011): 67–77.

"In the Shadow of the Wolf"

Alter, Alexandra. "'We've Already Survived an Apocalypse': Indigenous Writers Are Changing Sci-Fi." *New York Times*, August 14, 2020. https://www.nytimes.com/2020/08/14/books/indigenous-native-american-sci-fi-horror.html.

BioWare. *Dragon Age: Inquisition*. Electronic Arts. 2015.

de Gobineau, Arthur. *An Essay on the Inequality of the Human Races*. Translated by Adrian Collins. New York: G. P. Putnam's Sons, 1915.

Downham, Claire. "Vikings Were Never the Pure-Bred Master Race White Supremacists Like to Portray." *The Conversation*, September 28, 2017. https://theconversation.com/vikings-were-never-the-pure-bred-master-race-white-supremacists-like-to-portray-84455.

Grayson, Nathan. "How Twitch Took Down Buffalo Shooter's Stream in Under Two Minutes." *Washington Post*, May 20, 2022. https://www.washingtonpost.com/video-games/2022/05/20/twitch-buffalo-shooter-facebook-nypd-interview/.

Hartman, Saidiya. *Scenes of Subjection: Terror, Slavery, and Self-Making in Nineteenth-Century America*. New York: Oxford University Press, 1997.

Jackson, Peter, dir. *The Lord of the Rings: The Fellowship of the Ring*. New Line Cinema, 2001.

Kirkpatrick, David D. "Massacre Suspect Traveled the World but Lived on the Internet." *New York Times*, March 15, 2019. https://www.nytimes.com/2019/03/15/world/asia/new-zealand-shooting-brenton-tarrant.html.

McCoy, Daniel. "Elves." *Norse Mythology for Smart People*. https://norse-mythology.org/gods-and-creatures/elves/.

Ubisoft Montreal. *Assassin's Creed Valhalla*. Ubisoft. 2020.

"White Supremacists Adopt New Slogan: 'You Will Not Replace Us.'" Anti-Defamation League, June 9, 2017. https://www.adl.org/resources/blog/white-supremacists-adopt-new-slogan-you-will-not-replace-us.

Wood, Graeme. "His Kampf." *The Atlantic*, June 2017. https://www.theatlantic.com/magazine/archive/2017/06/his-kampf/524505/.

"Clash Rules Everything around Me"

Bai, Matt. "Master of His Virtual Domain." *New York Times*, December 21, 2013. https://www.nytimes.com/2013/12/22/technology/master-of-his-virtual-domain.html.

Edwards, Jim. "Arabs from the Middle East Are Paying Staggering Sums inside Clash of Clans." *Business Insider*, October 21, 2015. https://www.businessinsider.com/saudi-player-spends-1-million-in-clash-of-clans-2015-10.

Rigney, Ryan. "These Guys' $5K Spending Sprees Keep Your Games Free to Play." *Wired*, November 1, 2012. https://www.wired.com/2012 /11/meet-the-whales/.

Supercell. *Clash of Clans*. Supercell. 2012.

"The Great Indoorsmen"

Nintendo, *Super Mario Bros*. Nintendo Entertainment System. 1985.

Rockstar Studios. *Red Dead Redemption 2*. Rockstar Games. 2018.

"I Was a Teenage Transgender Supersoldier"

Bungie. *Halo: Combat Evolved*. Microsoft Game Studios. Microsoft Xbox. 2001.

Bungie. *Halo 2*. Microsoft Game Studios. 2004.

Bungie. *Halo 3*. Microsoft Game Studios. 2007.

Fall, Isabel. "Helicopter Story." *Clarkesworld*, January 1, 2020.

Felker-Martin, Gretchen. "What's the Harm in Reading?" *The Outline*, January 24, 2020. https://theoutline.com/post/8600/isabel-fall-attack -helicopter-moralism.

Flint, Emma. "Why Do Games Still Struggle with Trans Inclusion?" *Wired*, December 2, 2021. https://www.wired.com/story/trans-enby -representation-video-games/.

Holiwell, S. R. "A Maze of Murderscapes: Metroid II." *Game Developer*, January 30, 2015. https://www.gamedeveloper.com/audio/a-maze-of -murderscapes-metroid-ii.

Jones, Zinnia. "Born Dead: Learning How to Live after Depersonaliza-tion." *Gender Analysis*, April 30, 2018. https://genderanalysis.net/2018 /04/born-dead-learning-how-to-live-after-depersonalization/.

Kain, Erik. "'Halo 4' Is a Beautiful, Tragic Love Story." *Forbes*, November 9, 2012. https://www.forbes.com/sites/erikkain/2012/11/09/halo-4-is-a-beautiful-tragic-love-story/.

Palumbo, Alessio. "343i Acknowledges Halo 5 Storytelling Mistake, Will Double Down on Master Chief Focus." *WCCFTech*, April 25, 2017. https://wccftech.com/343i-halo-5-mistake-master-chief/.

Rogers, Tim. "halo 3 (****)." *Action Button*, January 2008. http://www.actionbutton.net/?p=312.

St. James, Emily. "How Twitter Can Ruin a Life." *Vox*, June 30, 2021. https://www.vox.com/the-highlight/22543858/isabel-fall-attack-helicopter.

343 Industries. *Halo 4*. Microsoft Studios. 2012.

"Ninjas and Foxes"

BioWare. *Jade Empire*. Microsoft Game Studios. 2005.

Team Ninja. *Ninja Gaiden Black*. Tecmo. 2005.

"No Traces"

Buse, Peter. "Nintendo and Telos: Will You Ever Reach the End?" *Cultural Critique* no. 34 (1996): 163–84. https://doi.org/10.2307/1354616.

Huizinga, Johan. *Homo Ludens: A Study of the Play-Element in Culture*. Boston: Beacon Press, 1938.

Kojima, Hideo. *Metal Gear Solid*. Konami. Playstation. 1987.

Poulton, Susan. "When Koko the Gorilla Chatted Online." *The Current*, Franklin Institute, June 21, 2018. https://www.fi.edu/blog/koko.

"Status Effect"

miHoYo. *Genshin Impact*. miHoYo. Android IOS or later. 2020.

"Ruined Ground"

Bethesda Softworks. *Fallout 76*. Bethesda Softworks. PlayStation 4. 2018.

Crowley, Nate. "People Are Using Red Dead Redemption 2 to Hold Conference Calls." *Rock Paper Shotgun*, May 19, 2020. https://www.rock papershotgun.com/how-to-conference-call-with-red-dead-redemption-2.

Mirenna, Joe. *The Making of a Field Hippie: A Memoir*. Belleville, WI: Still Point Publishing, 2020.

Radvansky, Gabriel A., Sabine A. Krawitez, and Andrea K. Tamplin. "Walking through Doorways Causes Forgetting: Further Explorations." *Quarterly Journal of Experimental Psychology* 64, no. 8 (2006): 1632–45. https://journals.sagepub.com/doi 10.1080/17470218.2011.571267.

"We're More Ghosts Than People"

Rockstar San Diego. *Red Dead Redemption*. Rockstar Games. 2010.

Rockstar Studios. *Red Dead Redemption 2*. Rockstar Games. 2018.

ABOUT THE CONTRIBUTORS

Hanif Abdurraqib is a writer from the East Side of Columbus, Ohio.

Nana Kwame Adjei-Brenyah is the author of *Chain-Gang All-Stars* and the *New York Times* best seller *Friday Black*. Originally from Spring Valley, New York, he graduated from SUNY Albany and went on to receive his MFA from Syracuse University. His work has appeared in or is forthcoming from numerous publications, including the *New York Times Book Review*, *Esquire*, *Literary Hub*, the *Paris Review*, *Guernica*, and *Longreads*. He was selected by Colson Whitehead as one of the National Book Foundation's "5 Under 35" honorees, is the winner of the PEN/Jean Stein Book Award, and a finalist for the National Book Critics Circle's John Leonard Award for Best First Book and the Aspen Words Literary Prize.

Charlie Jane Anders is the author of *Promises Stronger Than Darkness*, the third book in a young adult space opera trilogy. She cocreated Escapade, a trans superhero, for Marvel Comics, and is the science fiction book reviewer for the *Washington Post*. She's also the author of a book about writing, *Never Say You Can't Survive*, and an upcoming adult fantasy novel, *The Prodigal Mother*.

Octavia Bright is a writer and broadcaster from London. She cohosts *Literary Friction*, the literary podcast and NTS Radio show, as well as presenting programs for BBC Radio 4, including *Open Book*. She holds a PhD from University College London, and her writing has been published in the *White Review, Harper's Bazaar, ELLE*, and the *Sunday Times*, among others. Her book, *This Ragged Grace: A Memoir of Recovery and Renewal*, was published in June 2023.

Alexander Chee is most recently the author of the essay collection *How to Write an Autobiographical Novel*. A novelist and essayist, he teaches creative writing at Dartmouth College and lives in Vermont.

Max Delsohn's writing appears in *McSweeney's Quarterly Concern, Joyland, VICE, Triangle House*, and *The Rumpus*, among other places. They are an MFA candidate in fiction at Syracuse University.

Eleanor Henderson is the author of the memoir *Everything I Have Is Yours: A Marriage* and the novels *The Twelve-Mile Straight* and *Ten Thousand Saints*, which was adapted into a movie starring Ethan Hawke. With Anna Solomon she is the coeditor of *Labor Day: True Birth Stories by Today's Best Women Writers*. A professor of writing at Ithaca College, she lives with her family in Ithaca, New York.

Jamil Jan Kochai is the author of *The Haunting of Hajji Hotak and Other Stories*, a finalist for the 2022 National Book Award, and *99 Nights in Logar*, a finalist for the PEN/Hemingway Award for Debut Novel. His short stories have appeared in the *New Yorker, Ploughshares*, and *The Best American Short Stories*. He is a Hodder Fellow at Princeton University.

Ander Monson is the author of nine books, most recently *Predator: A Memoir, a Movie, an Obsession*. He just finished the most excellent *Subnautica* and is neck deep now in *Hollow Knight*.

MariNaomi is a video game veteran and award-winning cartoonist of nine books, including the graphic memoir *I Thought You Loved Me*. Their work has been featured in the *New Yorker*'s Daily Shouts, the *Washington Post, Los Angeles Times*, Smithsonian, Cartoon Art Museum, and Japanese American National Museum. They are the founder and keeper of the Cartoonists of Color, Queer Cartoonists, and Disabled Cartoonists Databases. MariNaomi.com.

Larissa Pham is an artist and writer in Brooklyn. Her essays and criticism have appeared in *The Nation*, the *New York Times Book Review*, *Bookforum*, and elsewhere. She is the author of *Fantasian*, a novella, and the essay collection *Pop Song*, a finalist for the National Book Critics Circle John Leonard Prize.

Stephen Sexton is the author of two books of poems: *If All the World and Love Were Young* (2019), winner of the Forward Prize for Best First Collection, and *Cheryl's Destinies* (2021). In 2020, he was awarded the E. M. Forster Award from the American Academy of Arts and Letters and the Rooney Prize for Irish Literature.

nat steele is a musician, socialist, organizer, writer, and sometimes gamer. She posts on social media at @stylo9000 and cohost.org/stylo and makes music at stylo-v.bandcamp.com.

Tony Tulathimutte is the author of *Private Citizens* and *Rejection*. A recipient of the Whiting and O. Henry Awards, he teaches an independent writing class, CRIT, in Brooklyn.

Vanessa Angélica Villarreal was born in the Rio Grande Valley to formerly undocumented Mexican immigrants. She is the author of the poetry collection *Beast Meridian*, recipient of a 2019 Whiting Award, a Kate Tufts Discovery Award nomination, and winner of the John A. Robertson Award for Best First Book of Poetry from the Texas Institute of Letters. Her work has appeared in the *New York Times*, *New York Magazine*'s *The Cut*, *Harper's Bazaar*, *Oxford American*, the *Paris Review*, *Poetry* magazine, and elsewhere. She is a recipient of a 2021 National Endowment for the Arts Poetry Fellowship, and fellowships from CantoMundo and Jack Jones Literary Arts. She is a doctoral candidate in English literature and creative writing at the University of

Southern California in Los Angeles, where she is working on a poetry and an essay collection while raising her son in Los Angeles. Find her on Twitter @Vanessid.

Elissa Washuta is a member of the Cowlitz Indian Tribe and the author of *White Magic, Starvation Mode,* and *My Body Is a Book of Rules.* With Theresa Warburton, she coedited the anthology *Shapes of Native Nonfiction: Collected Essays by Contemporary Writers.* Washuta is an associate professor at the Ohio State University, where she teaches in the MFA Program in Creative Writing.

Keith S. Wilson is a game designer, an Affrilachian Poet, and a Cave Canem fellow. His book, *Fieldnotes on Ordinary Love,* was recognized by the *New York Times* as a best new book of poetry; his nonfiction has won an Indiana Review Nonfiction Prize and the Redivider Blurred Line Prize, and has been anthologized in the award-winning collection *Appalachian Reckoning: A Region Responds to "Hillbilly Elegy."* Wilson's work in game design includes Once Upon a Tail, a storytelling card game designed for Lurie Children's Hospital of Chicago in collaboration with the Field Museum of Chicago, and alternate reality games for the University of Chicago.

ABOUT THE EDITORS

J. Robert Lennon is the author of three story collections and ten novels, including *Broken River*, *Subdivision*, and the forthcoming *Hard Girls*. He lives in Ithaca, New York, and teaches writing at Cornell University.

Carmen Maria Machado is the author of the best-selling memoir *In the Dream House* and the award-winning short story collection *Her Body and Other Parties*. Her essays, fiction, and criticism have appeared in the *New Yorker*, the *New York Times*, *Granta*, *Vogue*, *This American Life*, *Harper's Bazaar*, *Tin House*, *Timothy McSweeney's Quarterly Concern*, *The Believer*, *Guernica*, *Best American Science Fiction & Fantasy*, *Best American Nonrequired Reading*, and elsewhere.

Avatars created by Ben Rittman.

The text of *Critical Hits* is set in Adobe Garamond Pro.
Book design by Rachel Holscher.
Composition by Bookmobile Design & Digital
Publisher Services, Minneapolis, Minnesota.
Manufactured by Sheridan Saline on acid-free,
100 percent postconsumer wastepaper.